SPODE & COPELAND MARKS

SPODE &
COPELAND
MARKS

AND OTHER RELEVANT INTELLIGENCE

Robert Copeland

SECOND EDITION

including ten new appendices
and previously unrecorded marks

STUDIO
VISTA

This book is dedicated without permission but with plentiful thanks to the thousands of workers at the Spode factory who have contributed to the production and marketing of exceedingly fine ceramics.

Studio Vista

an imprint of
Cassell
Wellington House, 125 Strand
London WC2R 0BB

First published 1993
Second edition, revised and enlarged, published 1997

British Library Cataloguing in Publication Data
A catalogue record for this book is available from the British Library

ISBN 0-289-80172-9

Phototypesetting by Wood Mitchell and Co Ltd, Stoke-on-Trent

Printed in Great Britain by
Bath Press.

Contents

Acknowledgments

It would be appropriate, in this second and enlarged edition, not only to repeat the full page of acknowledgements from the first edition but to add several more. However, despite the publishers' generosity in allowing additional pages for still more appendices, there is space only to mention my gratitude to those persons who have helped me to add information to this book.

Firstly, any second edition must record the author's thanks to his editor, and here I recognise the enthusiasm and support of Barry Holmes.

Secondly, my deep gratitude goes to Peter Roden, and my renewed thanks to Paul Holdway and Bill Coles for many suggestions.

Thirdly, special acknowledgement is due to those many collectors who have raised queries and so drawn my attention to interesting items and marks.

My renewed thanks to you all.

Foreword by the late Arnold R. Mountford

Considering the hundreds of factories which operated at various times throughout the length and breadth of the Staffordshire Potteries during the past three centuries, it is rare indeed to discover a manufacturer sufficiently interested in the age-old craft to collect wares made by his firm; and rarer still for a potter to write comprehensive books relating to his forebears in particular and the local staple industry in general with such a degree of dedicated research and scholarship. In this regard Robert Copeland must now join that select group of ceramic historians, actively connected in one way or another with Stoke-on-Trent factories, such as Marc Louis Solon, George E. Stringer, Colonel Josiah Wedgwood, Percy W. L. Adams and of more recent date, Reginald G. Haggar.

With origins as far back as the last quarter of the 18th century one could assume that Josiah Spode and his successors would have used, in common with other potters, a fair number of backstamps to identify their products over the years, but it comes as something of a shock to be informed that the number of marks over that period was in excess of 300. Now that these have been systematically catalogued, mistakes in dating Spode, Copeland & Garrett and W. T. Copeland & Sons should in future be obviated. The author also includes relevant Patent Office registration marks and factory pattern-numbers with dates of recording, all clearly listed and without doubt of immense importance in any investigation of this leading Stoke-on-Trent manufactory. He also includes some particularly useful notes on the 1890 McKinley Tariff Act, together with an essay on pottery trade sizes which will be of interest to all students of ceramics, not solely those concerned with Spode and Copeland, as will the essay on bone china, stone china, earthenware and parian.

As a work of reference *Spode & Copeland Marks and other relevant intelligence* fills a huge gap in the available information on one of the world's leading manufacturers. It offers a wealth of fascinating new information, easy to follow and supported by over 250 illustrations some of which depict rare or unusual specimens shown for the first time. There is little doubt that all Spode aficionados will be delighted and grateful for this latest offering from Robert Copeland but it should be stressed that there is also much valuable material in it for the student, collector, dealer and curator alike and the work deserves to be made available to an even wider public for it really is an indispensable book of inestimable value.

1991   Arnold R. Mountford CBE MA

Author's preface to the second edition

The success of the first edition has shown the need for more copies of this book, and the publisher's willingness to re-publish it has given me the opportunity of adding more useful information as appendices.

Although the catalogue of marks was the main reason for the book, it also contains much additional relevant intelligence of interest to museum curators, collectors and students of ceramics, retailers and antique dealers, and owners of Spode and Copeland wares.

It is a book of reference which is also useful to those with a general interest in ceramics. The essays on different bodies, trade sizes, The McKinley Tariff Act, scale of rarity and authenticity, hints on photographing pottery and the table of the purchasing power of the pound will be of value to very many people.

Much of the new material is the result of research and general study since 1991, and of special value is the recent research of Peter Roden into the early history of Spode I.

The re-designed Museum at Spode now enables visitors to have ready access to the main Collection, while the famous Blue Room and the reserve Collection in the Art Gallery may be visited by special request. Mrs.Stella McIntyre is the Curator, while still in 1997 I am pleased to continue as part-time Historical Consultant.

Here I express my sincere thanks to my recent collaborators, especially Peter Roden, Stella McIntyre and Pam Woolliscroft, as well as those acknowledged earlier, particularly Paul Wood for granting me continued access to all the Spode Collection.

January 1997

A brief outline of the history of Spode and Copeland

JOSIAH SPODE I

To see his father buried in a pauper's grave must have held out the prospect of a grim future for six-year-old Josiah Spode. It seems that there were two options open to any boy or girl in the Potteries in the 1730s – go down the pit or go into pots. Spode chose pots. At this time the pottery industry was taking shape rapidly: 1740 to 1800 was the most innovative period in its history.

Working in a local pottery by the age of seven, life was very hard; beginning work at six in the morning and not leaving until six in the evening, and sometimes at the mercy of a cruel man who treated his young helper very badly. Times were tough in those days in most industries and the pottery industry was no exception. Spode was sixteen before fortune smiled on him. In 1749, he was apprenticed for five years to Thomas Whieldon, the most enterprising and successful potter in the district; Whieldon recorded in his notebook on 9th April "Hired Siah Spode to give him from this time to Martelmas next 2/3 or 2/6 if he deserves it". Whieldon taught him well, and on leaving in 1754, Spode worked for Turner and Banks at their pottery in Stoke-upon-Trent. He married in that year, and his first child, Josiah, was born on 8 May 1755. Spode left Banks in 1761 to rent the factory lately occupied by Baddeley and Fletcher which he managed sufficiently profitably to enable him to return to Stoke as proprietor of the Banks manufactory. It is now believed this was in 1764 (although for very many years the date of the founding of his business has been thought to have been in 1770). He completed the purchase of the freehold in 1776.

In 1778 Spode, realising that London was the principal centre of taste and trade, despatched his son thence to open a retail establishment at No. 29 Fore Street, Cripplegate. In 1784, William Copeland, aged 19, began to work for Spode in London and was soon travelling for him; it seems that he also dealt in tea, carrying samples and stocks in the same trap in which he was carrying Spode's samples. In this way Copeland not only promoted his master's business, but also built up some capital for himself. Spode's trade in London prospered and he moved to larger premises at No. 45 Fore Street. In 1796, probably as a result of the success of his blue printed wares and in readiness for an expected increase in trade due to the introduction of his father's new 'Stoke China', Spode II acquired an extensive warehouse and showrooms at No. 5 Portugal Street, with domestic dwelling house attached and facing Lincoln's Inn Fields.

The site is now occupied by the Royal College of Surgeons.

EARLY PRODUCTIONS

Details are lacking about the products made in the very early years of Spode's occupancy of the Stoke manufactory. Shards from excavated ditches in the area close to Church (once High) Street suggest that he made green-glazed earthenware, black basalt, white stoneware and blue-painted pearlware, including shell-edged pieces. In 1984, during the re-laying of a ground floor, shards of blue-painted 'House and Fence' type, unfired and un-glazed, were excavated. These might be of Spode's or Banks' output. Few examples have survived because nearly all of Spode's productions were functional and in the course of daily use suffered damage and destruction. Those pieces which are thought to date from the late 1770s and early 1780s are very well potted and nicely decorated. From that period he added red stoneware, caneware, various jasper-type bodies and drabware. These, too, were simply designed and well made to appeal to the practical minds of the middle classes.

The popularity of creamware in the 1780s and 1790s will not have gone unnoticed by Spode and it is reasonable to suppose that he manufactured it, decorating it either with hand painted blue or polychrome patterns. This popularity was due to it being ideal for use in the neo-classical homes which were being constructed; the sophisticated shapes and decorations pioneered by Wedgwood blended very well with the interiors of Robert Adam for the Palladian-style buildings. The fashionable furniture, too, was now made of mahogany, rosewood or satinwood to the designs of Chippendale, Hepplewhite and Sheraton. Added to this, there was a growing interest in Classical Greek and Roman antiquities, and all these facts led to the partial eclipse of the previously dominant oriental values with the result that there was a gradual decline during the 1780s in the sales of imported Chinese porcelain, especially of the blue and white wares. The Honourable East India Company, who enjoyed a monopoly in this trade, steadily reduced their imports to nothing by 1798. Owners of such

1779 Spode I installs a coal-fired steam pumping engine to raise water to drive an overshot water wheel for powering grinding pans and throwing wheels.

1784 Spode I masters the art and technique of transfer-printing in blue under the glaze on earthenware. William Copeland, 19, goes to work for Spode II in London.

Stand printed in Cyanine blue. Two Figures I pattern. c. 1784. Mark 1a.

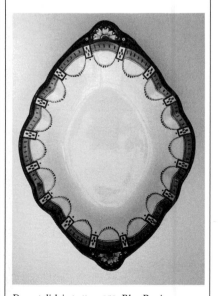

Dessert dish in pattern 159, Blue Powis.

Model of a Newcomen pumping engine illustrating the type of steam engine installed by Spode in 1779.

1784 *The Commutation Act passed, reducing the duty on tea from 119% to 12½%, so encouraging more tea drinking.*

1785 Spode II moves to larger premises at No. 46 Fore Street.

1787 Spode II finally pays off the mortgage on the Stoke manufactory.

1789 Spode II takes still larger premises next door, at No. 45 Fore St. By now, Copeland is travelling for Spode and also dealing in tea on his own account.

1790 Spode rents an extra warehouse in Moor Lane, a few yards away.
Spode II, with other potters, forms the Fenton Park Colliery Company in Lane Delph, and leases for 14 years.

1792 Spode I pays £200 mortgage for the Tittensor-Talke Turnpike Road (now the A34 trunk road).

1795 *The Newcastle branch of the Trent and Mersey Canal is built to pass alongside Spode's manufactory.*

Chinese porcelain plate c. 1785, with Spode copy (above), Mandarin pattern.

services who needed replacements or additions turned to English manufacturers to copy the original as best they could. Caughley, in Shropshire, obliged first with up to about eight patterns copying Chinese landscapes which were printed from engraved copper plates onto artificial porcelain; by 1784 Spode had perfected the technique of transfer-printing in blue under-glaze on earthenware and led the field in this form of decoration from then on.

1784 is an important date in the history of English ceramics. The Commutation Act (24 Geo. III Cap. 38. An Act for repealing the several Duties on Tea) was passed by which the duty on imported tea was cut from 119% to 12½%, thereby rendering the smuggling and adulteration of tea no longer profitable; this resulted in an increased demand for duty-paid tea which, in turn, increased the demand for teaware from which to serve and drink it. Also, the duty on silver plate (sterling) was re-imposed, which would have persuaded customers to choose ceramic teapots and vessels instead of silver ones.

BLUE AND WHITE AND THE CHINESE INFLUENCE

These are some of the factors which faced the Spodes in 1784. They saw clearly the market need for items to match Chinese porcelain; English artists could not equal the intricately blue-painted landscapes at the price, but transfer-printing offered a solution. Much progress had been made in developing the process, but the credit is given to Spode I for perfecting it for underglaze blue decoration on earthenware. Blue decoration looks best on a white or pale grey body, rather than on creamware, so blue patterns were printed on 'pearlware', basically a creamware body but with a glaze stained to pale grey by the addition of a little cobalt.

Many Spode copies of Chinese porcelain designs are known and are displayed in the Blue Room at the Spode Factory in Stoke-on-Trent together with the Chinese originals. The Willow Pattern itself is derived, but not copied, from a Chinese landscape. The original had no bridge, nor fence in the foreground, and Spode called this early pattern Mandarin. Using this as a basis, he added the familiar features to create a pattern more in accord with the European ideal of a 'balanced composition'; the human interest helped to make it the best known pattern in the world. There were many other Chinese patterns which included a bridge in them, but normally it has only one or two persons on it, and names have been given to each based on those used familiarly at the Spode Works. The next most popular pattern are two similar ones – Temple, and Broseley – which are collectively called Two Temples I and II, but in reality the scene depicts a tall temple in the background with an imposing gatehouse in the foreground; between these two elaborate buildings is a large courtyard, but the Chinese artists did not make this clear because perspective did not enter into their scheme of representation.

It was this trade in replacements for Chinese porcelain services which influenced so many Spode designs. Wedgwood followed the Classical while Spode followed the oriental inspirations. Of course, Spode's choice of patterns was not entirely 'after the Chinese'; some were 'borrowed' from printed illustrations of Roman sites (Tower, Italian, Rome, Castle), of antique ruins (Caramanian), of Indian sporting scenes, and even of Greek mythology (Greek). Then there were floral designs, as Botanical, Floral, British Flowers; sheet patterns as Lyre, Daisy, Convolvulus and Sunflower; Aesops Fables and many other designs.

ENGLISH CHINA AND BONE CHINA

The essay on Bone China (see p. 127) explains the story of porcelain and the development of what is now called bone china, but some more details may be of interest. It seems sensible to give the credit to Spode I for producing the original bone china, a true porcelain with the addition of its own weight of calcined ox bone, and to Spode II for marketing it extremely well.

Spode I, in the manufactory in Stoke-upon-Trent, had the experience of a first-rate master potter, all the raw materials necessary and the skills of the modellers, mouldmakers, potters and firemen, with the high temperature kilns outside his office door. In short, every facility was to his hand.

Spode II, however, although instructed in the potting trade by his father, had been in the marketing field since 1778, concentrating on this most important side of the business. Only on his father's death in 1797 did the younger Spode remove permanently to Stoke. Of course, he could have instituted trials at once and been able to launch the new 'Stoke China' in 1800 – but did he?

In 1981, an invoice was found among documents at Tatton Park, in Cheshire; this was hand-written:

W. Tatton Esq

1796   To Josiah Spode

July 9   English China

18 Dishes in sizes

2 doz Soups

6 doz large Plates

2 doz less – &c..

184 items in total of this particular service cost £15 15s. 0d., an average price of 1s.8½d. each. On the third page of this invoice, dated in December of the same year, is a tableset of 'Queens Ware' consisting of 80 items at a total cost of £2 6s. 0d., an average price of just under 7d. each. The 'English China' is three times more costly than the Queensware. In another entry, 6 China plates cost 5s. 0d., while 24 Queensware large plates cost 5s. 0d. – a factor of four times. I

1796 *Champion's Patent for true porcelain expires.*

Spode I invoices W. Tatton with several services of 'English China', as well as some Queensware. The earliest known record of Spode selling porcelain dinnerware, 9th July, and December. Spode II acquires extensive premises in London at No. 5 Portugal Street, Lincoln's Inn Fields. This was needed to meet the increased trade and for handling the new English China.
William Copeland believed to be living at No. 45 Fore Street.

1797 William Taylor Copeland, son of William Copeland III, born 24th March, in London.
Josiah Spode I dies, 17th August, in Stoke.
Spode II leaves London and resides in Stoke.

Oval dish, length 31.5 cm, bone china, Spode pattern 488.

Dessert dish, Stoke China, pattern 282.

Part of the Tatton invoice, 1796.

1799 Josiah Spode II, Thomas Wolfe and others lease the Carloggas Moor china clay and china stone pits in Cornwall. Indenture dated 11th November binds William Shaw apprentice to Josiah Spode to learn the art of 'Handling & pressing of earthenware & *China* for . . . six years. . .'.

1800 Spode II producing his new bone china by this year.

The Bute shape teacup, 1800 or earlier, lasted in popularity at least until the mid-1830s. Named after the Earl of Bute, who suggested the shape to Josiah Wedgwood.

The Royal Flute shape teacup, c. 1800, is seldom seen and then with early blue printed patterns.

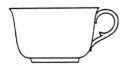

The Porringer shape teacup, c. 1810, is not commonly seen.

think this disposes of the suggestion that English China was a term for a better class of earthenware. [Today, Spode's least expensive bone china pattern dinner plate is just three times the price of a Blue Italian earthenware dinner plate – so the proportion is correct.]

The invoice has not a printed heading and there is no mention of a place of origin. No printed invoice earlier than 1812 has been found with the Stoke manufactory heading taking precedence over the London address, so at this early date it seems unlikely that the manufactory had a printed invoice, and as the destination was in Cheshire it is doubtful if the ware was shipped via London.

Another suggestion was that Spode was acting as a middleman for another porcelain manufacturer like Derby, whose wares could be likened to those described in the invoice. Twitchett quotes prices obtained by Christies at auction in 1785 for a wide range of Derby porcelains where the prices compare reasonably with some of the more expensive Spode sets listed on this invoice, but if Spode was a middleman he must have sold at a loss.

Now, one of the objectives of Spode was to be able to make china dinnerware as well as dessert and teawares, and to do so with less loss than the manufacturers of English artificial porcelain, and so be able to sell at lower prices than them. There are very few dinner plates in Christies' lists of Derby porcelain and no big dishes. Spode, however, commences the invoice with "18 Dishes in sizes". Surely this would mean at least 16 inch if not larger as well as smaller? My belief is that Spode the younger, in London, recognised a market need for good quality china dinnerware to fill the gap left by the virtual elimination of imported porcelains. This might have occurred to him in 1793 when the East India Company's sales proceeds for porcelain had dropped by 33%. Spode the elder set to work to find an English alternative, beginning with true porcelain and some hybrid porcelain mixtures. Two items are known which seem to represent this stage: both are marked beneath by hand. One is a garden pot inscribed No. 19, the other is a Low Scent Jar inscribed No. 14 and decorated with pattern number 671; chemical analysis of the latter item has shown that it contains only a trace of calcium phosphate – insufficient to consider it as a bone porcelain. [The decorations were almost certainly applied several years later.] There is also a bulb pot in a similar material which has an impressed SPODE mark in small upper case letters. These three objects are all pale grey in colour and have the appearance of porcelain of a hard paste variety.

By 1794, after varying the ingredients and their proportions, Spode found that a mixture eliminating glass-forming substances yielded a practical porcelain in which large plates and dishes could be made and fired straight enough to be saleable. However, when this stage was reached, he still needed time in which new models could be prepared and of more refined shapes than earthenware, especially as the contractions were different. By the time that Champion's Patent for true porcelain had expired in June 1796, Spode I, in Stoke-upon-Trent, was ready with his 'English China'. The move by Spode II in London to very much larger premises in that same year seems to have been in preparation for this new product as much as it was to cater for the general expansion of business in blue transfer-printed and other earthenwares. It is a pity that no porcelain remains at Tatton Park which relates to the invoice or to this early period of Spode's manufacture, but my conclusion is that Spode I was producing a satisfactory dinnerware in a porcelain of some sort by 1796. By 1799, a body with about 50% of calcined ox bone added to a true porcelain was in production.

POTTER AND ENGLISH PORCELAIN MANUFACTURER TO HIS ROYAL HIGHNESS THE PRINCE OF WALES

This was the appointment conferred on Spode II by the Prince of Wales after his tour of the Stoke manufactory and showroom on September 12th 1806. So began the supply of fine bone china and other ceramic products to members of the British Royal Family. In those days there were no journals and glossy magazines carrying illustrated advertisements and the finest recommendation was – and still is – the personal approval and admiration of a satisfied customer. The Royal Warrant of Appointment is an accolade of the highest recommendation. There is no doubt that Spode cherished it and both he and his successors have aimed at maintaining the high standards of design, workmanship and finished goods which continue to justify the holding of the Royal Warrant of Appointment as China Manufacturers to Her Majesty Queen Elizabeth II.

THE PATTERN BOOKS

The most valuable records surviving on the Spode Works today are the pattern record books and about 25000 engraved copper plates. Plain prints produced under-glaze were not recorded unless some extra decoration required an enamel firing: the pattern would then be entered in the pattern book. When were these pattern books begun? Spode II contracted with Henry Daniel to set up a decorating establishment on the Spode Works for the on-glaze painting and gilding of Spode's wares – whether they be of one body material or another. Spode's under-glaze plain prints and plain, undecorated wares were not part of the deal.

Daniel built up a team of highly skilled artists which, in 1821, numbered 73 males and 119 females, 192 people employed solely on decorating china, stone china and earthenware. To keep a register of patterns was essential, and it was Daniel who started by asking some of his artists, who he had taken over from Spode, to remember what had been done before. Very many had been forgotten so the record, which starts at number 133, has many gaps before number 256, and about 200 more up to pattern number 5350. In 1988 Sothebys offered a number of pattern book sheets which they advertised as being from the Davenport factory; several observant collectors raised doubts about this and it was shown that they were from Daniel's working copy which he used in his

Spode installed a 10 HP Watt rotative beam engine in 1802.

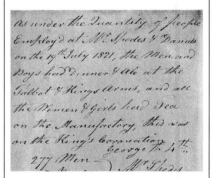

Memorandum written in the recipe book of Thomas Grocott.

Josiah Spode II signs a deed of partnership with William Copeland and William Spode, 1805.

Suite of teaware, c. 1806, pattern 1112, incorporating the badge of the Prince of Wales.

1802 A 10 HP Boulton & Watt rotative steam engine installed at the Spode manufactory to supplement the earlier engine.

1805 Spode II passes over the London business to a new partnership between his eldest son, William, 29, and William Copeland, 40, each holding two shares. Henry Daniel has, by now, become Spode's decorating contractor and remains until 1822.

1806 The Prince of Wales and the Duke of Clarence visit the Spode manufactory on 12th September, following which Spode was appointed 'Potter and English Porcelain Manufacturer to H.R.H. the Prince of Wales'.

1810 A 36 HP Boulton & Watt rotative steam beam engine replaces the 10 HP one installed eight years earlier.

1811 *The Prince of Wales sworn in as Regent, 5th February.*
William Spode retires, and that partnership dissolved, 31st December.

1812 New partnership between Spode II with one share and William Copeland with three shares. London stock valued at £32,534. This at London wholesale price less 20%.

Pierced border creamware plate. Pattern 245 in a very old pattern book.

decorating establishment at Spode. Several pages gave additional information to that which is recorded in the Spode Museum Trust's copies which evidently were the best, or master's, set.

Then, in 1989, another pattern book in private ownership came to my attention: there are several pattern numbers in this book which are identical with the same pattern numbers in the 'Spode' pattern books, and the quality and layout of this discovered book are in every way consistent with the sort of record which one associates with Spode and comparable with the known Spode pattern records. I am of the opinion that this other book predates the Daniel books; one pattern on earthenware of which a dinner set was offered for sale a few years ago and of which I own a plate, is recorded in this early book as number 574, although this number in the Daniel originated books does not correspond with the decoration; the explanation seems to be that the details were forgotten when the Daniel book was started, and that, as no matchings were ordered, there was no reason to record it in later years. The patterns which *do* correspond exactly seem to provide circumstantial evidence that this recently discovered pattern book was the Spode record before the contract with Daniel. These early records do not specify either the body or shape name of any pattern, so it is only when an actual example is seen that further details can be added. Landscapes, for example, were painted freehand on the ware, but usually were not painted in the record book, but merely noted as 'landscapes'. Many, in fact, would have been named views, but this cannot be judged from the record, which sets down only the groundlaid and gilded ornamentation. Pattern number 557, for example, shows only a broad gilded band at the edge of a Bute cup with a fine line inside, and the written word 'landscapes'. Collectors know that these are finely engraved 'bat' prints, usually of landscapes in black, but prints in blue, red, brown, green and gold are known with the same pattern number.

Many examples of Spode's ware carry no pattern number. Why not? Indeed, there are many examples which are not even marked with his name. The design may have been made as a special commission for a private customer, in which case it would only be repeated when a sample was supplied.

Alternatively, a set of ware would have been sold complete as a dinner, dessert or tea set, so the name of the manufacturer and the pattern number only needed to be written on the most important pieces. After all, Spode had to pay for this to be done, but when it was done it was very legible. Now that many of these sets have been broken up and dispersed by antique dealers, the authentication of unmarked pieces can sometimes present a problem.

The secret of many great leaders is the ability to select first-rate brains and skills in those they employ. Spode II certainly exhibited that quality when he chose Henry Daniel, who, besides designing and executing thousands of superb patterns, was the first to use platinum lustre in an English pattern. The recipe was probably that discovered by John Hancock while in Daniel's employ. He was among the earliest to adopt the new form of gilding, using an amalgam of 'brown gold' (pure gold precipitated from a solution of gold chloride by ferrous sulphate) with mercury, ground in turpentine and applied with a 'pencil', that is a brush. The brilliance of the gold imparts a magnificence to Spode's wares which sets them apart from those of most of his competitors. In the Imari patterns the quality of the gilding is seen at its best, interpreting rather than copying the imported designs originating in Arita.

Some collectors of eighteenth century porcelain regard as vulgar the rich and permanent gilding of Spode, Davenport and others. Contemporary with the former were the delicate sounds of Haydn and Mozart, whilst with the latter was the more powerful music of Beethoven. Tastes were changing with the years and there is no doubt about the sumptuous effect of flickering candlelight on the brilliantly gilded china of Spode.

STONE CHINA

Spode II adopted the stone china body in about 1813, with the earliest pattern number 2053 known to have been produced first on this material being recorded in May 1814. I discuss this in the essay, but here it is emphasised that there is no evidence to support the belief that Spode acquired the rights to the Turner Patent in 1806 on the bankruptcy of the Turner brothers. I believe that he made stone china because a better material than pearlware, and pale grey in colour, was needed to match the more elaborately decorated designs of Chinese porcelain. His earliest body is often found to be translucent and has been stated to be technically porcellaneous. Although many examples are known of 'one off' copies of Chinese porcelain designs, most patterns have the outline transfer-printed with the colours being painted by hand on glaze. Once engravings were available, Spode could and did produce many different coloured versions on all ceramic bodies, often mixing the border of one design with the centre of another. Bowpot, Tumbledown Dick, and Chinese Flowers exemplify the former, while Mosaic border with Willis centre is typical of the latter. [The name Willis refers to the proprietor of the Thatched House Tavern in St. James's Street, London.]

FELSPAR PORCELAIN

In 1821 Spode bought a large quantity of feldspar from Thomas Ryan, who had pioneered the extraction of this stone from the Middletown Hill lead mine in Shropshire on the border with Wales. Spode's Felspar Porcelain is really a bone china with some of the Cornish stone replaced by feldspar, and it is most often seen as dinner and dessert services, particularly with armorial bearings on them.

1813/4 Spode adopts the Stone China body to enable more durable replacements to be made of Chinese Export Porcelain. The earliest known pattern number on stone china being 2053.

1813 Fenton Park Colliery lease renewed with Thomas Minton as one of eight new partners.

1816 Spode in partnership with Thomas Wolfe and others in the Cornwall Clay and Stone Company. Cobalt from Wheal Sparnon used for transfer-printing in blue.

1817 Visit of H.M. Queen Charlotte to Spode's London showroom, 3rd July. *The Times* reported that Her Majesty ordered some of the "newly invented china, called stone china, by Mr. Spode . . ." but, so far, there is no evidence that the order was delivered before her death in 1818, nor details of the pattern that was ordered.

1819 William Copeland granted armorial bearings, and enters into the Lordship of the Manor of Wyck, Surrey.

1820 On his accession, Spode re-appointed to be Potter to H.M. King George IV.

1821 Spode introduces Felspar Porcelain, a variety of bone china, using feldspar from the Middletown Hill Mine to replace some of the Cornish stone.

1822 The formula of stone china is altered, and the name changed to New Stone, the pattern numbers starting about 3435.
The London business is styled Spode & Copeland on invoices.

London shape teacup, c. 1813. After the Bute shape, the London shape was the next most used cup throughout the Staffordshire industry, continuing in use, off and on, until the 1960s, and even today for Blue Italian.

The London warehouse of Spode & Copeland, once the Theatre Royal, in Portugal Street, Lincoln's Inn Fields.

New Dresden shape cup, c. 1817.

New Dresden embossed cup, c. 1817. This features in patterns up to c. 1824.

Pearlware plate, printed outline in Tumbledown Dick pattern and hand coloured. Pattern 3023, Marks 2a and 22. See page 138.

Cream coloured earthenware plate printed outline Chinese Flowers pattern in red and coloured to match a Chinese porcelain plate.

Invoice to His Majesty the King from Spode and Copeland, 1822, for a set of three vases. £55.10s would be about £1850 now – still a bargain!

SPODE'S LATER EARTHENWARES

Spode's earthenwares, like his bone china, show an enormous variety of styles and diversity of objects. Many patterns display brilliant on-glaze colourings often touched with gilding to produce a magical effect of richness and warmth. Even with no gilding the quality of his creamware and pearlware was of the highest standard.

The early patterns were hand painted, with the less expensive earthenwares being printed underglaze in blue. Why blue? Because it was the most attractive colour which could be achieved at glost temperatures in those days; also, it had become so familiar on Chinese porcelain, it looks wonderful on oak furniture, and it enhances the appearance of any food placed upon it. The other colours which were available for use underglaze were manganese purple (rather dull), black, and ochre; none of these became popular! Underglaze chrome green was not in use before about 1822-5, and the earliest date for the use of underglaze pink is probably 1832, when it was made of about 40 parts tin oxide to 1 part of chromium oxide with whiting and flint-glass. Spode's underglaze colours have been the clearest and brightest in the industry since their introduction to the present day.

A new pattern book was begun in 1822 using B as a prefix to the numbers, and these patterns were all decorated underglaze. The introduction of this series of numbers coincides with the cessation of the contract with Henry Daniel.

Freehand painted patterns must have appealed to certain overseas markets because very few examples have been seen in the United Kingdom. Many are bold designs in two or three colours applied with firm brush strokes and have earned them the name of 'peasant style'.

The aristocrat of earthenware was the badged service made to a special commission. An armorial device or regimental badge printed underglaze on earthenware enabled a large motif to be used as the central decoration on dinnerware. In bone china, this would not be practical because the decoration would be over-glaze and would suffer considerable wear and damage in use. Regiments and institutions often had their dinnerware of earthenware with a more elaborate dessert service of porcelain or bone china, when only silver knives and forks were used and then only for cutting or peeling fruit.

USEFUL WARES

Most collections concentrate on tablewares or ornaments which are attractive, but Spode was not only Potter to the Royal Family but to Everyman. In the days before heat resistant glass, tin-enamel, aluminium, plastics and other substances, glazed earthenware and porcelain were the most hygienic materials. Many functional items were very beautiful, too. Chamber candlesticks could be very attractive, and desk sets could be magnificent with sumptuous colour and richly gilded ornamentation. Spode made wares for all sorts and conditions of men and women: pot-pourri or scent jars, incense burners, spittoons, vieuilleuses or pap-warmers, invalid feeding pots and pap boats, syrup jars for pharmacies, bidets, chamber pots, ladies' slippers, or bedpans, and bourdaloues, leg baths, labels for dairies to mark the price of cheese or butter, and many other items. In the kitchen: pestles and mortars, bread crocks, egg separators (for poached eggs), lemon strainers, jelly moulds, and dairy ware for every need.

The dining room might have need of cheese containers, so Spode offered, besides the usual round stand, a deep covered 'Stilton cheese pan' to retain the freshness of the cheese, and a 'cheese cradle' to hold a big farmhouse cheese on its edge. When hosts had their own conservatories they might have grown pineapples for which Spode made a special stand on which the fruit could sit with its segments laid on the wide rim.

Decanter and bottle coasters were made. In the salon the pianoforte might stand on a thick pottery cup, printed to look like marble, so that the castor would not make dents in the floor. We tend to take modern sanitation for granted, but up to 1918 many large houses lacked piped water to every part, so Spode and Copeland supplied the basic necessities for both Royal and humbler seats; for example, there is entered in the Palace Ledger for 5th April 1831 "China supplied for his Majesty. . ." which consists of toilet wares destined for Windsor Castle. The enormous variety of objects made on the Spode factory is truly a mirror of social customs.

SUMMARY OF THE SPODE PERIOD UP TO 1833

Two of the foundation stones of the British ceramic industry were laid by Josiah Spode I – underglaze transfer-printing in blue on earthenware, and the development of bone china. His son, Josiah II, built an imposing business on these foundations in the service of an appreciative public for whom he and his successors have aimed at maintaining the high standards of fine quality and the pioneering spirit of the Spodes.

In this quest, Spode I was the first potter to install a steam powered grinding mill in 1779. Spode II led a team of contemporary potters to form a company to mine coal at Fenton Park Colliery in 1790, and another to mine china clay, in 1799; he supported the improvement of the turnpike road from Tittensor to Talke (now A34) and encouraged the cutting of the Newcastle Canal in 1795.

Spode II formed a company of potters to mine china clay at Carloggas in 1799. Their concern for their workers was very apparent and probably stemmed from a determination to avoid for them the appalling conditions and privations that Josiah I had suffered when he was a small boy. It was not every employer who had started life in such humble ways who took that view, however, and this makes the Spodes stand out as humanitarian manufacturers. He built cottages for some of his workpeople and paid their wages in cash, not in 'truck' as very many employers did; truck is the payment of wages in goods, kind or vouchers instead of money.

1824 William Taylor Copeland admitted to the partnership, with one share being given to him by his father. He is also admitted as a member of the Worshipful Company of Goldsmiths, and he joins the Livery on 20th January.

1826 William Copeland dies, 20th January.
Josiah Spode II and William Taylor Copeland enter into partnership in the London business to run for seven years, each having two shares. W. T. Copeland marries Sarah Yates, 29th April, the daughter of John Yates, china manufacturer of Shelton.

1827 Spode II dies, 16th July. Spode III comes out of retirement to oversee the factory which is run on a day-to-day basis by William Outrim.

1828-9 W. T. Copeland serves as Sheriff of London & Middlesex. He joins the Court of Assistants of the Goldsmiths' Company, 24th October.

1828-32 W. T. Copeland is elected Liberal M.P. for the County of Coleraine.

1828 William Fowler Mountford Copeland, son of WTC, born 28th November.

1829 Copeland is elected Alderman for Bishopsgate Ward in the Corporation of the City of London.
Josiah Spode III dies, 6th October. The factory is administered by the executors of Spode's will.
Many Turner moulds bought by Copeland, December.

1832 Copeland continues as M.P. for Coleraine.

Stilton cheese pan, Blue Italian pattern, c. 1825. One of the many unusual items made to meet specific market needs. Mark 33.

Swag embossed on Bute shape, c. 1813. The Flower embossed design on Bute shape was also introduced in 1813.

Flower embossed on London shape, 1821.

French embossed, or Floral Wreath, 1822.

The Etruscan shape cup. The tall cup was first recorded in 1823, the low cup in 1824; probably both date from 1823. They remained in use until c. 1832, to reappear in the late 1800s.

THE COPELAND CONNECTION

The association between the Spodes and the Copelands began in 1784, when William Copeland III (born 1765) was employed by Spode II in his London establishment. Now, it is thought that Copeland, besides travelling for Spode, also sold tea on his own account, and in this way built up sufficient capital to enable him to become an equal partner with William Spode in the London business in 1805. William Spode was Spode II's elder son and remained in London until December 1811 when he retired, leaving the management in the hands of Copeland. From 1812-1823 Copeland held three quarters of the shares to Spode II's one quarter. William Taylor Copeland (born 1797) joined the firm in 1824 with a quarter share given to him by his father, on whose death in 1826 a new agreement for seven years as equal partners was made between Spode II and W. T. Copeland.

Although Spode II died in 1827, the agreement was continued by his executors until March 1st 1833 when Copeland bought the Spode share and took Thomas Garrett as a partner to administer the Stoke business, while he remained in London.

THE COPELAND & GARRETT PARTNERSHIP 1833-1847

Following the death of Josiah Spode II on July 16th 1827, his son, Josiah, kept an eye on the Stoke manufactory until his own death on October 6th 1829; he had retired from the business in 1802 after his arm was amputated due to a gear-wheel severing it during the installation of a Watt beam engine. From 1829 until the termination of the Spode and Copeland agreement of 1826 the Works were administered by the executors of the Spodes' wills, Hugh Henshall Williamson and Thomas Fenton. Both were relatives but neither were potters and took little interest in the day to day running of the business which they left in the hands of William Outrim. The London business, although nominally the responsibility of the executors, continued to be run by William Taylor Copeland who probably also determined the policy of the whole concern. In view of the variety of new shapes introduced between 1827 and 1833 it may be assumed that Copeland, working in London and aware of the changing tastes of fashionable society, exercised considerable influence in the business. On March 1st 1833, when the agreement ended, he bought the manufactory, the remaining shares in the London premises and much property in Stoke. Thus he secured the life of the business until the present day, 133 years of it held by members of the Copeland family, all of whom have continued the tradition and high standards set by their predecessors.

WILLIAM TAYLOR COPELAND

It was a coincidence that William Taylor Copeland was born on the day next to the birthday of Josiah Spode I and in the same year that he died. Copeland's grandfather had been a yeoman farmer at Hollybush Farm, near the Longton Hall manufactory in Staffordshire. His son, William Copeland (born 1765), moved to London in about 1784, becoming a partner with Spode II and William Spode in 1805 in the London concern. When William Copeland died on January 20th 1826, he left more than £86,000, so giving his son the financial means to purchase the Spode interests seven years later.

On 29th April 1826, W. T. Copeland married Sarah, daughter of John Yates, a china manufacturer of Shelton, near Stoke-upon-Trent in North Staffordshire.

Born in London, he was to spend the rest of his life there, becoming one of its most respected citizens. In 1828-29 he served as Sheriff of London and Middlesex, and during that year he was elected Alderman for the Ward of Bishopsgate. In 1835, at the age of only 38 he was elected Lord Mayor of London. He remains the third youngest Lord Mayor of London and although during his mayoralty it was reported that he was to be created a baronet, this did not happen.

In 1824, he was admitted a member of the Worshipful Company of Goldsmiths, and in the same year was elected to the Livery; he was elected to the Court of Assistants in 1828, becoming Prime Warden in 1837. He served a second term as warden, becoming Prime Warden again in 1851.

In 1831, he became Liberal Member of Parliament for Coleraine, a seat he held until 1837, when he stood as Conservative candidate for Stoke-upon-Trent and for which, with John Davenport, another highly successful and respected potter, he was successfully returned; he kept the seat until he was defeated in 1852. He regained the seat in 1857 and continued to represent Stoke-upon-Trent until 1865. Copeland does not appear to have taken an active part in political debates in the House of Commons, but "he was a useful committee member and guardian of the interests of the Borough of Stoke-upon-Trent". In 1837, he served on the Select Committee on Fourdriniers' Patent, in which the applicants were claiming reimbursement of the loss of royalties due to considerable infringement of the protection which should have been observed by users of their paper-making machinery, including the Government printing offices. Copeland testified as a pottery manufacturer to the improved quality of 'pottery tissue' used in transfer-printing which was made on Fourdriniers' machines.

Though he did not live in North Staffordshire, he did take an active interest in local affairs, subscribing to the building of the Wesleyan Sabbath School, as a Vice-President of the North Staffordshire Infirmary, supporting the annual Pottery Races, and in many other ventures. In 1837, he was appointed a Director of the London and Birmingham Railway Company, and a few years later was closely involved, with his fellow M.P. J. L. Ricardo, in the formation of the North Staffordshire Railway Company. Together they performed the ceremony of cutting the first sod on 23rd September 1846; Ricardo became Chairman of the Company and Copeland remaining a Director until 1852.

Perhaps most importantly, Copeland was keenly interested in the formation of Schools of Design, both in London and in Stoke. At the end of 1836, Parliament sanctioned £1,500 to establish a School of Design in London for the arts connected with manufacturers. A council was formed consisting of artists and representatives of the manufacturers. Among the former were such eminent names as Sir Francis Chantrey, Calcott, Eastlake, and Cockerell, while Copeland represented the pottery industry. In 1847, the Potteries Schools of Design were opened. ". . . under the superintendence of Mr. Murdoch, Artist from London" for boys and girls over the age of 12. The list of subscribers contains the names of many well-known pottery manufacturers including that of Copeland who gave a personal subscription of 10 guineas. The firm of Copeland & Garrett gave a similar amount.

Copeland seems to have been an amiable person with many friends and few enemies. He was a keen racing man with a fair-sized stable of thoroughbred horses, including the famous horse 'King Cole'. There were many tributes on his death, on 12th April 1868. *The Hornet* said that "He combined and exemplified in his own person the manufacturer, the merchant and the gentleman."

1833 Copeland acquires the Spode factory, the Spode shares in the London business, and much property besides, 1st March.
Thomas Garrett is taken into partnership, and the firm becomes Copeland & Garrett. First pattern number 5192.

1835 W. T. Copeland becomes Lord Mayor of London (aged 38 years, the third youngest). He is elected the first President of St. Mark's Hospital.
Edward Capper Copeland, son of WTC, born, 28th November.
The Hudson's Bay Company accept C. & G's tender to supply china and earthenware, 17th December.

1836 First delivery of goods to the Hudson's Bay Company.

1837 Copeland elected Conservative M.P. for Stoke-upon-Trent. He sits on the Parliamentary Select Committee on Fourdriniers' Patent. He retains the seat until 1852.
He is appointed a director of the London & Birmingham Railway Company.
Alfred James Copeland, son of WTC, born, 6th April.
Copeland is Prime Warden of the Goldsmiths' Company.
Thomas Garrett elected to the Livery of the Goldsmiths' Company.

1841 Richard Pirie Copeland, son of WTC, born, 27th September.

1842 Thomas Battam, art director, introduces the statuette of Apollo, in a porcellanous body, to the Duke of Sutherland.

1845 The new Statutory Porcelain, body used for figures and vases, displayed at the Manchester Exhibition of Art and Manufactures.

1846 The North Staffordshire Railway begun; W. T. Copeland a director.
Spencer Garrett patents special mortice tiles.

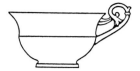

Bell shape cup, 1824-1825.

Antique shape cup, 1824-1831.

The Flower embossed design was applied also to Antique, Etruscan, Pembroke, Persian and Porringer shapes.

Gadroon shape teacup, 1824 and still in use.

Persian, or 4643, shape teacup, c. 1830, the first pattern recorded on this shape – later called Persian – being 4643.

Pembroke, plain, cup shape, 1827.

Pembroke, embossed, c. 1827. The cup has a scalloped edge. Later called Seve (Sèvres) shape.

THOMAS GARRETT

Garrett is an enigmatic figure, for little is known of his early life. He was born in 1784 or 1785, in Norwich, the son of Thomas Garrett, but nothing more is known of him until his marriage to Mercy Garnham at St. Mary's, Lambeth, on 31st January 1809. An article in the *Art Union,* November 1846, states that Garrett "had taken an active part in the management of the London house for many years". The first mention of him in connection with the firm is as a witness in January 1826 to William Copeland's will, where he is described as 'Clerk to Spode, Copeland and Son'. Other sources suggest that he was the prinicpal traveller and London correspondent for the firm.

On 1st March 1833, W. T. Copeland acquired the Spode share in the London business as well as the Stoke Works and much surrounding property, both residential and commercial. According to Llewellyn Jewitt, he took Garrett into partnership "shortly afterwards". On 3rd April in that year Garrett was accepted as a member of the Worshipful Company of Goldsmiths and took up the Freedom of the City of London by Redemption. In the Court minutes of the Goldsmiths' Company he is described as "Potter of Herne Hill" and as "Potter and Merchant of Portugal Street" in the Freedom Register. He was elected to the Livery on 24th November 1837.

There is no evidence that he put any money into the partnership, and it seems that he was invited to become a partner so that he could oversee the running of the Stoke Works by William Outrim, while Copeland, with his heavy Corporation responsibilities, remained in London and ran the Company from there. Garrett lived in Trent Vale, near Stoke-upon-Trent, but by 1836 he had built himself a house which Copeland was to use as his base for his electioneering in the following year. It was described by Ward in 1843: "Near Cliffe Ville is Cliffe Bank Lodge, a handsome villa, recently erected by Thomas Garrett Esq., resident partner of the firm of Copeland and Garrett".

Of his work at the manufactory, little is known, but some light is shed by his obituary in the *Art Journal:* "…upon him devolved in connection with the late Mr. Thomas Battam [the Art Director of the firm] the working of the artistic arrangements of the establishment in its earlier attempts to unite true Art with Manufacture". It seems that he did not prove entirely satisfactory for the partnership was dissolved on 30th June 1847, and he returned to London where he took up residence at Sidmouth Lodge, Ealing, Middlesex (now 31 Ealing Road) where he died on 2nd April 1865.

His son, Spencer Thomas Garrett, also played an active part in the work of the manufactory and in civic affairs, and continued to do so for some years after 1847. He played some part in the development of the Statuary Porcelain (Parian) body in 1845, and took out a patent in December 1846, Number 11,249, for 'Certain Improvements in Cements, Bricks, Tiles, Quarries, Slabs, and Artificial Stones' generally called Patent Mortice Tiles. It is known that he was still resident in Stoke in 1865, but he moved to Chester after his father's death until 1885, after which his whereabouts have not been traced.

THE PURCHASE OF THE SPODE WORKS BY W T COPELAND

A memorandum in the Spode-Copeland papers dated 1st March 1833 specifies the agreement of Copeland's purchase of certain freehold and copyhold "messuages potworks lands hereditaments and premises . . . in Stoke-upon-Trent. . . for . . . £13,986". For the stock, materials, tools, etc., he paid a further

£30,387 19s 5d. An indenture dated 2nd March 1833 stated that the land and appurtenances had been conveyed. This agreement was between the executors of the will of Josiah Spode III, Mary Spode (the widow of Josiah Spode III), and William Taylor Copeland. (Hugh Henshall Williamson, one of the executors, was brother to Mary Spode).

Agreement had been reached for the purchase of houses in Stoke-upon-Trent, but it was not until November 1833 that a letter from Copeland stated that he will have "the whole of the houses", and that he would pay for them on 2nd January 1834. According to the schedule they were valued at £12,824 0s 0d but Copeland offered £11,000, receiving all the rents from 1st March 1833 and such titles as the executors possessed. On behalf of Mr. Fenton and himself, Mr. Williamson accepted the offer.

To secure his trade as a manufacturer even further, more investments were made, especially in coal. Coal was a vital commodity for the pottery industry, the firing of the ware being entirely dependent upon it, and upon its quality. At the same time that he purchased the Spode Works and the London business, Copeland was astute enough to buy the Spode half share in the Fenton Park Colliery, one of the most important in the district. The price paid was £8,950. In April 1836, Copeland increased his interest in coal by purchasing Berry Hill Farm, which "is supposed to abound in coal" for 18,000 guineas. [In 1990, it is estimated that there are 3 million tons of coal under Berry Hill!].

THE FACTORY

Copeland was naturally eager to add to the size of the factory so that he could secure enough land for expansion. In 1834, he successfully negotiated the purchase of a plot of land measuring 7,955¾ square yards, from the executors of Josiah Spode III. In that year he bought two plots of glebe land totalling 14,801 square yards, from the Rector of Stoke, and in 1838 another 114 square yards of land from Spode III's executors.

It is not surprising, therefore, that the manufactory appears to have been the second largest in the district, rivalled only by that of Davenport.

Octagon shape cup, 1831.

Craigle shape, swirl fluted cup, 1832. This is the shape drawn for pattern 5146.

Melan shape cup, first recorded for pattern 5189, 1832.

Scale embossed on Melon shape, 1833.

Louis embossed shape, 1833. The first new shape after Copeland had bought the Spode business.

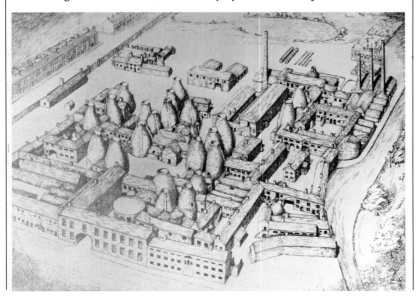

The Spode Factory, 1834. Drawing by Harold Holdway from a contemporary earthenware model.

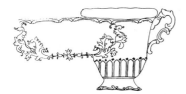

Wellington embossed shape, 1835.

Royal, or Plain, Wellington shape, 1835.

Lotus embossed on Wellington shape, 1835. The Lotus embossment appears also on plain Pembroke shape.

Lowther embossed shape, 1837.

Lowther, Plain, shape, 1837.

Victoria, Plain, shape, 1837.

Entry in the Fixing Book of 1841 for '1 sett of Chimney slabs' for the Queen.

A Chamber of Commerce was formed in 1836 for manufacturers, financed by funds being raised by a levy of 5 shillings per oven. According to these records Copeland and Garrett had 25 ovens, Davenport having 30; by comparison, Minton and Alcock had 20 each, Wedgwood and Sons 15, and Hilditch and Sons 3. The manufactory employed 800 workers in 1819, the number having dropped to 700 by 1833. By the time of the Children's Employment Commission in 1842, the numbers were 454 men, 249 women, and 77 children under 15 years old – a total of 780. From the same source it is learned that Davenport had 1400 employees, Adams 650, Ridgways 500, and Thomas Mayer 500. The average number of employees in a factory was 130. John Ward in 1843 quotes 800 as the number of employees on Copeland and Garrett's factory, as also does William Cartlidge, a clerk at the factory in his evidence in a court case in 1847.

The Factories Inquiry Commissioner in 1833 reported that the factory was "in the best order". Nine years later, Scriven reported in greater detail ". . . there is neither conformity, order or system of arrangement in any or either appartment, except in the dipping house, green house and one or two others . . .". He goes on to say that certain rooms are "hot and unhealthy. There are no means of ventilation . . ." On the other hand, "The premises are well drained and great order and regularity is observed by the work-people". The report also indicated that the employers treated the work-people well. They inaugurated a Savings Bank in 1834, and there was no truck system of payment, wages being paid only in cash.

The author of the *Penny Magazine* in an article of 1843 presents a less critical analysis: "The Works . . . appear more like a small town than a manufactory". "There is a labyrinth of passages and courts intersecting each other at all angles and bounded by buildings. The buildings are . . . not confusedly mingled but are divided into certain groups or compartments. . ."

By 1846 the factory had been extensively improved and enlarged. The part used for porcelain manufacture was 'new' and "the modellers' and engravers' departments are also modern", being built for the comfort and convenience of the work-people.

INDUSTRIAL DIFFICULTIES

These important fourteen years of the factory's history were not without some problems, however. There had been unrest in the pottery industry for several years and this came to a climax in the years 1833 to 1836, when there was a series

of strikes. In 1836 the trade union turned its attention to two abuses of labour (as it saw them) and determined to have them abolished.

'Good from oven' meant that the work-people received payment only for perfect items which emerged from the firing, even though several people may have handled them after they had left the maker; usually the seconds were sold, and seldom was the maker allowed to see the ware complained of. The union wanted payment to be 'good from hand'.

The second abuse was the system of annual hiring; this meant that an employee was bound to his employer for a whole year, and could not go to any other employer whether his master had work for him or not. The contract was renewable at Martinmas, November 11th. As early as October 1835 Copeland and Garrett brought a case before Leek magistrates against five gloss'd-oven men, who, having absented themselves from their employment on 25th and 26th September because their employers would not agree to an extravagant increase in prices from the next Martinmas, caused a loss of at least £300. They were imprisoned for one month.

By September 1836 the union had called a strike which lasted sixteen weeks, and involved fourteen manufactories, including Copeland and Garrett. In early December, a Mr. Glasse from the union was questioned as to the cause for turning-out at Copeland and Garrett's. This, he said, was "not against price, but against principle". Thus the union was using Copeland and Garrett, not because it felt that that employer was being unfair, but as a lever for its own cause. The strike came to an end on 27th January 1837 when the union ran out of money.

[At this time, there was no one Union of Pottery Workers, but rather each craft had its own union; thus there was a union of Firemen, one of Hollow-ware Pressers, one of Plate-makers, etc.. Sometimes they joined together in a common cause as in this case, hence the use of the small 'u' for union.]

Trouble struck the factory again a few years later because of the introduction of machinery. Various machines had been made in the early 1840s and introduced into some of the factories of the Potteries, but it was not until early in 1847 that Copeland and Garrett introduced a 'jolley' – for making cups (A 'jigger' is for making plates and saucers). This was known as the Scourge and had been developed by Anthony Scott of Southwick, near Sunderland. The Potters Examiner and Workmans Advocate denounced this, and the potters' union circulated all the pottery districts of the country with a petition. Within two weeks, Copeland and Garrett had halted the use of the machine, but apparently kept it locked in a room where it was regularly oiled and maintained in proper working order. During his election speeches of that year, Copeland was subjected to much heckling, being interrupted by the angry crowd shouting 'Jolley". Jolleys were not heard of again in the Potteries until six machines were installed at Thomas Cooper's jug works in Shelton in March 1863.

THE PRODUCTS

The 1830s and 1840s were important periods for the development of ceramic design. The severity of neo-classicism gave way to the flamboyance of revived Rococo, largely due to the influence of continental porcelain. For a factory to remain successful it had to be aware of and meet the needs of social taste.

As early as 1829, new shapes were introduced at the Spode Works, and this may be due to the greater influence which Copeland had after the death of Josiah Spode III. After 1833, when Copeland had still greater control, the styles became

Figure of a shepherd. Biscuit bone china. Height 14.3 cm. Impressed mark 101a.

A 'flatmaker' making a plate on a 'jigger', while the mould-runner holds a mould ready to replace on the jigger. A 'jolley' is the same as a jigger, but used for making hollow-ware and cups.

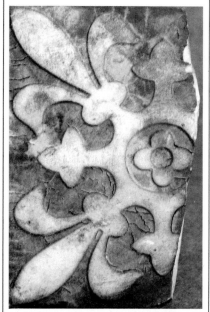

Broken encaustic tile of buff clay with blue infilling. Marked

COPELAND
&
GARRETT

Decorative slab mounted beneath a window in one of the Duke of Sutherland's residences. Floral scrolls united by a ducal coronet. c. 1860.

more elaborate. Likewise, the variety of products increased as new uses for porcelain were discovered, and as demand at home and abroad increased.

Tiles were being made by 1836, and an early form of encaustic tile of buff clay with a blue engobe was made during the period.

By 1840, Etruscan style vases, introduced by Wedgwood in the late 1700s but abandoned for many years, were being made again, this time adopted for domestic use as toilet services, etc.

Porcelain slabs – some of immense size, door furniture, panels for furniture, flower-pots, and Cadogan teapots were produced in large quantities as well as tablewares in the greatest variety.

Tea services showed a "vast superiority ... over the forms of cups and saucers which were in use some years ago". Some were of high decorative quality, embossed with heavy gilding, but others were of simple form, "unaided by extraneous ornamentation". The traditional Bute and London shapes of teacups, so popular during the Spode period, were continued after 1833 but held a less prominent place than hitherto. They were steadily superseded by Pembroke, Melon, Lowther, Wellington, and others of varying degrees of moulded fluting and embossment.

Dessert wares received a great deal of attention, attracting the art of the flower painter as well as that of the landscape artist. Perhaps it was the dessert service above all others which demonstrated a man's wealth and position; richly gilded, with all the decoration individually applied by hand, it was the *pièce de résistance* of the dinner, coupled, of course, with the exotic fruit which had been grown in the host's own hot-houses.

Although tablewares were the principal products, toilet wares constituted a large and important volume of business in those days before domestic piped water supply. Deliveries continued to be made to Buckingham Palace and Windsor Castle during the reign of Her Majesty Queen Victoria from 1838 onwards.

Porcelain slabs for fireplaces were an important product, indeed, Copeland and Garrett and, later, Copelands were the leading manufacturer of large slabs, sometimes making table-tops measuring 48 x 24 inches, a wondrous feat of potting when one realises that they had to undergo at least three firings but usually five. In the 1830s, Trentham Hall, near Stoke-upon-Trent, was being rebuilt by Sir Charles Barry for the Duke of Sutherland, and here porcelain slabs were to be found "in every fireplace", where their decoration harmonised with the general character of the room. In the bedrooms "washstands, panels of the toilet tables, curtain holders, bell-pulls, door furniture etc., were all of decorated porcelain, manufactured by Messrs. Copeland and Garrett expressly for the Duke of Sutherland".

Patronage came from further afield than the local aristocracy. In 1841, a set of

fireplace slabs were supplied "for the Queen", with hand-painted landscapes. In 1846 it was reported that Messrs. Copeland and Garrett "have had the honour of executing several sets (of porcelain panels etc.) for Her Majesty. Those just completed for the drawing and dining rooms of Osborne House are of very great beauty . . . The door furniture, bell levers, &c., are also in porcelain to suit". It was no doubt in respect for this patronage that the factory named colours after its patrons: Sutherland Green, Trentham Buff, and Albert Brown occur regularly in the pattern books of this period.

Although porcelain (both bone china and felspar porcelain) attracted the greatest attention at this time, earthenwares were made in much larger quantities. At least six earthenware bodies were produced between 1833 and 1847: Spode's New Stone, New Japan Stone, Royal Opal, New Blanche, Royal Alba, and New Fayence.

1833 seems to have been a watershed for design in the pottery industry in general and on the Spode Works in particular. The change in design is noticeable not only in the more elaborately modelled shapes but also in the applied decoration. While some of Spode's patterns continued to be produced, most of the transfer-printed designs were in radically new styles, more often in colours other than blue and with much more white space than was usual in Spode's day.

Finger plate, key drops, handle knob and rosette on the door to Queen Victoria's private rooms in Osborne House. 1846.

EXPANSION ABROAD

Earthenware was about one-third the price of china. Because of this there was great demand from home and abroad. In 1835, Copeland and Garrett were negotiating to supply the Hudson's Bay Company with earthenware, and in a letter dated 17th December that company replied "Your letter to Mr. Simpson of 28th Ult. quoting the prices at which you would supply the Hudson's Bay Co. with earthenware &c. has been submitted to the Governor and Committee, and I am directed to acquaint you that the same has been accepted". The significance of this is that Copeland and Garrett became the sole exporter of high quality earthenware to the Hudson's Bay Company, a position that was retained until 1872. The earliest known invoice, of May 1836, shows that wares to the value of £145 7s 4d were supplied to the Company for delivery in North America.

Goods were supplied to Persia, India and many other countries overseas, and by 1846 it was reported that "the kingdom, our Colonial dependencies and nearly all the Continental markets are extensively supplied from this establishment", and that Copeland and Garrett's products are "exported in crates by the thousand".

Factory standard of York shape teapot. Named after the Hudson's Bay Company's York factory. c. 1846. (A different shape of teapot was later called York.)

PARIAN, OR STATUARY PORCELAIN

It is evident that the Spodes and their successors rose to meet current market needs by producing goods which not only stimulated it into new life, but gave the industry a product which enabled it to supply the needs of the changing fashions of the different periods. Under Josiah Spode I it was the perfection of blue transfer-printed wares, while under Josiah II it was the commercial exploitation of porcelain with the successful marketing of bone china. Now, under Copeland and Garrett, came the development of a new porcellanous body – statuary porcelain, or Parian, as it became to be commonly known.

It seems that in the 1840s several firms were experimenting with porcelain bodies and each produced slightly different ones for the reproduction of statuettes and busts. Despite conflicting claims, it emerges that Copeland and

Teacup and saucer, pattern 5866, supplied to the Persian market and marked only with Mark 166.

Figure of Narcissus, 1846. Mark 165.

Figure of Innocence, 1888. Mark 202.

Garrett were the first to make and to market a porcelain which, in the words of John Gibson R.A., was "the next best to marble". Although credit for the introduction was claimed by three people, Thomas Battam the art director, Spencer Garrett, and John Mountford, all working for this firm, it appears that Mountford was the originator of the perfected formula and method of production. In a letter to the *Staffordshire Advertiser* in 1851 during an exchange of correspondence on the subject, Mountford claimed "in the latter part of the year 1845 I discovered after various experiments that material known…as 'statuary porcelain'; that I gave to Mr. S. Garrett the Receipt for its production . . .". In the same letter he states that Battam wrote the article in the *Art Union* of 1849 in which he claimed the invention.

The fact seems to be as follows. In 1842, Battam had the idea of producing such a material and had a statuette of Apollo made in a modified version of Spode's Stone China, eliminating the cobalt stain; this would have yielded a result very close to marble. The example was shown to the committee of the Art Union of London, who enlisted the judgement of John Gibson who offered his sculpture 'Narcissus' to be reduced and made in the material. The Art Union commissioned fifty copies to be made in stone china and offered as prizes in its lottery of 1846. In the meantime, John Mountford had joined Copeland and Garrett, having moved from Derby where he was a figure-maker. He worked on the problem of improving the material so that the natural qualities of the raw materials developed the specially sensuous sheen which is characteristic of the very best parian. His work culminated in several examples of statuettes and vases being displayed on the company's stand at the Exhibition of Manufacturers in Manchester in late 1845. The Art Union of London's promotion was very successful and was followed by a commission to reproduce copies of J. H. Foley's 'Innocence' for the lottery of 1847. Battam, then, had the original idea and 'introduced' the product (rather than 'invented' it), Spencer Garrett supervised the trials as they went through the different stages of production and firing, while the origination of the recipe (ingredients and the method) was the work of John Mountford. Many of the Art Unions chose parian subjects for their prizes from the late 1840s until the 1890s, but few new models were introduced after 1870, and the quality of pieces made after about 1900 lack the clarity and superb surface finish of earlier ones. Nevertheless, parian was a very important material, with all manner of decorative objects being made in it including lamps, vases, comports and centrepieces.

THE END OF THE PARTNERSHIP

The partnership between William Taylor Copeland and Thomas Garrett was dissolved on 30th June 1847. In a report of a court case involving some stolen wares it was stated *en passant* that the partnership had ceased on 1st July. This is confirmed by the draft of a letter written by Copeland: "This partnership of the above firm having ceased since 1st July 1847 . . ." In November 1847 the London showroom and warehouse in Portugal Street was sold, and the firm moved to 160 New Bond Street in order to be in the fashionable area of town. For the next twenty years W. T. Copeland was to manage the London business with the help of his son, Alfred, and the Stoke manufactory with the help of his son William Fowler Mountford Copeland.

COPELAND 1847-1970

"The most splendid assortment of China ever yet offered to the public in South Australia". This announcement in 1847 by the Adelaide importer William Foot was referring to a newly arrived consignment from the Spode factory of "the very best and most fashionable English ware". Variety and high quality have been consistent features of the Spode factory productions throughout its existence.

Always willing to accept a challenge, the factory has undertaken some remarkable assignments. In 1868, the roof of the Reading Room at the National Library in Paris was completed. It was formed of nine cupolas lined with ceramic tiles; made by Copelands to an engineering standard of accuracy which no other ceramic manufacturer was prepared to meet.

Another venture involving tiles was the large panel of bone china tiles, white with a thin layer of blue clay on the face and with white, domed, circular discs at the joints which surrounded the moulded coat of arms of the Imperial College of Technology, in Prince Consort Road, London. This was completed in 1957 to the design of Professor Robert Baker.

These challenges were consistent with the tradition of meeting the needs of clients and customers wherever possible. The firm had already shown its ability in making large slabs for table tops, plaques, fireplaces, &c., and continued to supply such items for several decades. Tablewares and ornaments of every imaginable sort were made to meet, and possibly to influence, the changing tastes of the times.

USEFUL WARES

Besides adapting designs which were introduced during the Spode period, hundreds of patterns and shapes were designed for everyday use which owed nothing to the earlier influences. Many of these patterns were formal and rather dull. The earthenwares were often printed in grey, brown, or other sombre colours like flow-blue; the subjects ranged from formalised floral sprays, like Kangra pattern, to multi-view patterns like Duncan Scenes, Ruins and Ionian.

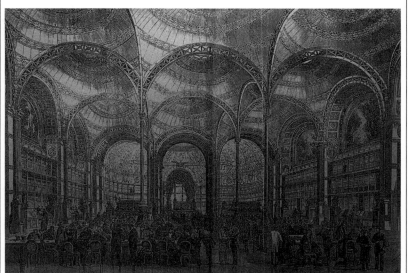

1847 Copeland & Garrett partnership dissolved, 30th June. Firm now known as W. T. Copeland. Last pattern number about 7600.
Installation of Fourdrinier's patent steam printing press.
London premises at Portugal Street sold, and showroom transferred to 160 New Bond Street, November.
Attempt to introduce machinery for plate-making – 'the Scourge', but this was thwarted.

Meissen shape, 1843, the forerunner of the shape later called Florence.

Acanthus embossed shape, 1840.

Berlin, Plain, shape, 1843.

Berlin embossed shape.

Most of the cup shapes have been traced from the pattern books. Many appear three dimensional as the insides were decorated.

The Reading Room of the Bibliotèque Nationale, Paris, showing the uniquely tiled cupolas.

Seasons pattern, c. 1842. Mark 163.

Plate from a dinner service supplied in 1867 to Charles Dickens.

One of the 60 dessert plates made for use at the top table during the City Banquet, June 1863. Pattern D7909. Mark 235.

All twelve of the Dancing Houris, c. 1933. Mark 259.

Several patterns, first introduced in the years 1833-47, continued in popularity such as Seasons, Byron Views, Wellington. These tablewares are not so attractive as the earlier Spode ones and this may explain why there are so few examples seen in collections or offered for sale. Huge quantities were shipped to Northern America, however, to the Hudson's Bay Company, who sold it to both white settlers and Indians. Excavations on historic sites have revealed shards of over 112 different patterns from the Spode factory. In general, blue and white was much less popular than hitherto, although Blue Italian and Blue Tower seem to have maintained their position with the Willow Pattern among the world's favourites.

A substantial trade was conducted in catering wares for railway companies, hotels, clubs and tea rooms, shipping lines, hospitals and institutions, as well as a dominant share of the market for military messes. Specimens of these wares are very difficult to find, but archival records show that clients included the P & O Steam Navigation Co., the Royal Mail Steamship Co., White Star Line, Cunard, the Royal Navy, the royal yacht from 1849 to the present time, Christ's Hospital and hundreds of other institutions and regiments.

Towards the end of the nineteenth century renewed interest was shown in blue and white patterns of Chinese style. The result was the re-issue of the Willow Pattern, Mandarin, Broseley and a newly engraved version of Bridge pattern which was called New Bridge (not Queen Charlotte as is sometimes believed) and issued on the New Stone body, which was not marked as such.

Other stoneware bodies were made, especially in grey with dark blue slipped grounds, a buff-coloured stoneware with a pale blue matt surface, and a brown body with a drab green slipped ground; all these were ornamented with sprigged motifs, and, apart from traditional hunting, drinking and classical subjects, these wares were often used for commemorative items.

China dinnerware, too, seems to have been less colourful and attractive than in earlier days. Patterns with simple coloured bands and gold beads with no decoration in the centre do not present an appealing display in a collection, so, apart from armorial services like those supplied to members of the Royal families and other notables, like Charles Dickens in 1867, china dinnerwares are seldom seen.

Nevertheless, it was this trade in everyday table and toilet wares which represented the bulk of the Spode factory's output, and five sixths of this was earthenware. The elegant dessert and tea services and ornaments which are so much admired accounted for only a small fraction of the total volume, but it was the cream and provided employment for large numbers of artists, gilders and burnishers.

DECORATIVE WARES

The development of the statuary porcelain, or parian, body was the most important contribution made by Copelands to the ceramic repertoire in the nineteenth century. It enabled remarkably beautiful objects of sculpture to come within the grasp of the aesthetically minded middle classes. Statues and portrait busts of abstract notions, like Love and Maidenhood, Innocence and Narcissus, were as popular as the copies of classical sculptures and studies of contemporary personalities. Mary Thorneycroft was commissioned by Her Majesty Queen Victoria to sculpt busts and statuettes of her children, and in 1847 W. T. Copeland paid her a fee of £200 for the right to reproduce half-size copies of the four statuettes; these were of Victoria (the Princess Royal), Edward (the Prince of Wales), Princess Alice, and Prince Alfred, each representing one of the four seasons, all listed as 'in preparation' in the 1848 price list. Many objects other than those depicting people and animals were produced; lamps for use with oil, and later fitted for electric light, were designed, often adapting a statuette to hold the lamp or for it to be supported by an obliging tree!

The International Exhibitions afforded the opportunity to potters to display their wares of outstanding merit to a much wider public than could be reached normally. The contemporary illustrations of some of these displays seem overcrowded with ornamental vases of complicated design, but when the individual pieces are seen, one may admire the consummate beauty of the painting and gilding, and often the chasing of the gold bands, etc.. At no time has the skill of the ceramic artist reached a higher level of intricacy. These pieces were the makers of reputations: "Two firms only – the two which produce the greatest amount and the finest porcelain – come forward to sustain the reputation of England in the Competition, Messrs. Minton and Co. and Messrs. Copeland and Sons, both of Stoke-on-Trent". So runs the report in the *Illustrated London News* of the ceramic section of the Paris Exhibition of 1867. The vase, in bone china, was the item which was regarded as proof of the high quality of the English flower painting. C. F. Hürten was the principal flower painter at Copelands (and, indeed, in the whole industry) with George Eyre as the manager of the art department at the time. Magnificent examples of the productions of Copelands were displayed at the 1851 and 1862 International Exhibitions in London, and the firm won medals for its displays in Paris, Sydney and New York, and would have won one in Dublin in 1853 if Alfred Copeland had not been a juror.

It is in the dessert and teawares that most collectors have the best chance to appreciate and admire the exquisite creations of the many talented artists and gilders who worked on the Spode factory during the Copeland period. The practice of allowing artists to sign some of their work began in the 1860s, but manuscript books of earlier date in the Spode archive collection sometimes record the names of the artist or gilder responsible for a particular pattern or object. These books are called the Fixing Books and record the costs of decorating the different objects; there are several occasions when slabs were made for H. M. the Queen and H. R. H. Prince Albert; one slab, supplied in July 1849 measured 48 x 20 inches, and was painted by Daniel Lucas with a landscape subject.

The firm was expert in the design and manufacture of specially commissioned dessert services like that supplied in 1857 to the design of Mr. W. H. Goss, (it is not known who ordered this service, but it may have been by Her Majesty as a gift to the Emperor Napoleon during the period when better relations with France were

1850 Copeland appointed local Commissioner for the 'Great Exhibition of the Works of Industry of all Nations'. William Fowler Mountford Copeland elected to the Livery of the Goldsmiths' Company, 19th April.

1851 The Crystal Palace International Exhibition. Copeland awarded personal medal, but conflict over the award of the Council Medal.
W. T. Copeland Prime Warden of the Goldsmiths' Company for the second time.

1852 Charles Dickens tours the Spode Works, and writes 'A Plated Article', an account of his visit, which he publishes in his magazine *Household Words*.
Copeland purchases a consignment of Derby moulds from Samuel Boyle of Fenton and also some from Derby.

1853 Firm exhibits at International Exhibitions in Dublin and in New York.

1855 Firm exhibits at Exposition Internationale in Paris. Wins gold medal.

1857 Copeland first pottery manufacturer to install the newly patented filter press of Needham & Kite, and is appointed agent for the Potteries.
Copeland re-elected M.P. for Stoke-upon-Trent.

Dessert plate, Jewel shape, with view of Pisa, painted by Daniel Lucas, Jnr, 1857.

1861 W. T. Copeland is President of the Royal Hospital of Bridewell & Bethlem.

1862 Firm exhibits at the International Exhibition in London. Alfred James Copeland elected to the Livery of the Goldsmiths' Company, 26th March.

1865 Thomas Garrett dies in London, 2nd April.
Richard Pirie Copeland elected to the Livery of the Goldsmiths' Company, 20th December.

1866 W. T. Copeland appointed China and Glass Manufacturer to H.R.H. the Prince of Wales.

1867 Copeland's four sons, William, Alfred, Edward, and Richard taken into partnership, and the firm now W. T. Copeland & Sons.
Firm exhibits at the second Exposition Internationale, Paris.

1868 Alderman William Taylor Copeland dies, 12th April, at Russell Farm, Watford.
R. P. Copeland marries Emily Henrietta Wood, of the Wood family of potters, 9th December.
The Biblioteque Nationale in Paris is opened.

1870 William Fowler Mountford Copeland, senior partner, elected to the Court of Assistants of the Goldsmiths' Company.
System of impressing datemarks begun. See page 92.

1872 William Fowler Mountford Copeland II, son of RPC, born 13th February.

1875 Edward Capper Copeland dies, 25th May.

1878 W. F. M. Copeland I, Prime Warden of the Goldsmiths' Company.

1881 London Showroom moved to 12 Charterhouse Street, August.
Alfred James Copeland retires and leaves partnership.

1884 Richard Ronald John Copeland, son of RPC, born 9th February.

1889 Alfred Gresham Copeland, son of RPC, born 12th June.

1895 W. F. M. Copeland I retires, leaving RPC the sole proprietor of the firm.

1897 Visit of H.R.H. the Princess Alexandra, Princess of Wales, to the Spode Works, 6th January.

1898 Lease of 12 Charterhouse Street renewed for 14½ years.

being sought); a selection of pieces were loaned from H.I.M. the Shah of Iran and exhibited at the Spode Bicentenary Exhibition at the Royal Academy in 1970. Another service, made to the order of H.R.H. the Prince of Wales in 1863 to celebrate his wedding, was of the Shield Pierced shape with panels of roses and oranges with blossom painted by Hürten; the superb tall comports were surrounded at their bases with parian figures, whilst the finest was the centre-piece, which was dominated by the seated female figures of Asia, Africa, Europe and America, representing the four quarters of the globe. This service was completed in 1866, and was displayed for public exhibition when it drew the most ecstatic review in the *Art Journal*. Shortly afterwards, Alderman W. T. Copeland was rewarded with the Royal Warrant of Appointment to his Royal Highness, an honour which was renewed by the Prince when he became King Edward VII in 1901, but now in the name of Richard Pirie Copeland trading as W. T. Copeland and Sons.

The artists in the earlier years seem to have undertaken the gilding of their own work, but later they specialised to an increasing degree, even being restricted to one subject – as long as the orders continued to flow in – such as flowers, or fish, or landscapes, or birds, enabling them to become expert at their specialised subject. Hürten was a veritable paragon among painters of flowers, fruit and foliage, being as competent in the minute detail needed in the panels of a dessert plate as in the bold treatment on huge plaques and lily pans. Daniel Lucas, Junior, seldom signed his landscapes, yet he exhibited a characteristic style which is identifiable on both the pieces he painted and in the pattern books where he recorded his designs.

Scores of artists have worked at Copelands, but perhaps one of the most versatile was Arthur Perry, who was equally competent at every subject except the human figure; his skills were fully developed by the early 1900s.

The front entrance of the Spode Works on High Street (now Church Street), decorated for the visit in 1897 of the Princess of Wales. This building was demolished c. 1929 for road widening, but the two large stones and the iron gates were replaced further back in the position they occupy today.

THE TWENTIETH CENTURY

Praise for the artists and gilders of yesterday should not overshadow the excellent work done today. Unfortunately, patronage of these skills is seldom demonstrated these days, but when it is Spode have artists and gilders equal to the task. In 1948, for example, three dessert services were commissioned by Lady Freyburg, wife of the Governor of New Zealand, in readiness for the planned tour by Their Majesties King George VI and Queen Elizabeth. Each of these services was painted with subjects typical of the country: birds, flowers and ferns. The design and painting of the first two could be derived from illustrated books, but there were no books on New Zealand ferns, so Roy Trigg spent weeks in the Fern House in the Royal Botanic Gardens at Kew, perspiring freely, while he painted the many different sorts of fern from life. On his return, he adapted these drawings to form a very fine series of two ferns on each plate and dish, which must surely have drawn the admiration of Her Majesty the Queen and Prince Philip when they undertook the visit some years later. (Incidentally, the dessert dishes had been pressed by me earlier in that year!).

Bill Hall copied with remarkable accuracy a fine painting of 'The Tower of Comares' (thought to have been painted by Daniel Lucas, Junior, and exhibited at the 1851 Exhibition); this was the centre of the farewell bowl presented to Art Director Harold Holdway on his retirement in 1978. Then there are the original seascapes painted by Denis Emery for the various limited editions: the American Maritime series, the English Maritime series, the Armada series, and the Explorer series. Each one of these original scenes is a work of art, and this means that the lithographic transfers which are produced from them are also of the highest quality.

Behind the scenes in any 'potbank' are scores of craftsmen and women of all ages who make the wares on which such artists may lavish their skills. Some are talented artists and sculptors who are special to the industry, the engravers and modellers, while others are sliphousemen, mouldmakers, potters and their assistants such as fettlers and scallopers, printers and transferrers, kiln placers and firemen, dippers, paintresses, slide-off transferrers, warehousemen and packers. When Sydney Smith first joined Copelands in September 1900, he saw Charlie Pearson, the big hollow-ware presser, throw a soup tureen into the scrap box. He asked "What did you do that for?". "There's something wrong with it and nothing goes out of here unless it's right". This precept is still the objective and, like in days gone by, it is still only by vigilance that it can be achieved.

1900 Visit of the Duke and Duchess of York to the Spode Works, 27th July.

1901 Copelands appointed Manufacturers of China to H.M. King Edward VII, 19th December.

1902 Richard Ronald John Copeland joins the firm.

1903 Alfred Gresham Copeland joins the firm.

1908 W. F. M. Copeland I dies, 11th April.

1910 Copelands appointed Purveyors of China to H.M. King George V, 10th December.

1913 R. P. Copeland dies, 13th March, at Kibblestone Hall, Stone. Ronald and Gresham Copeland assume control of the firm.
Visit of King George V and Queen Mary to the Spode Works, 22nd April.

1918 Richard Spencer Charles Copeland, son of RRJC, born, 18th December.

1919 R. R. J. Copeland elected to the Livery of the Goldsmiths' Company, 17th December.

1920 John Gresham Copeland, son of AGC, born, 16th December.

1921 A. G. Copeland elected to the Livery of the Goldsmiths', 11th May.
A. J. Copeland dies, 5th September.

1923 Electrification of the factory using Bellis & Morcom marine engine to drive own alternator, and removal of Watt beam engine.
Appointment of Sydney E. Thompson as Sole Agent for the United States and setting up of Copeland & Thompson Inc., New York, and Copeland & Duncan Ltd., Toronto, Canada.

1925 Thomas Robert Copeland, son of AGC, born 27th June.

c1928 London Showroom at 14-18 High Holborn.

1929 Frontage of Spode factory demolished for road widening. Row of shops built.

1931 Visit of H.R.H. the Duke of Kent, 1st July. A. E. Hewitt joins the Company.

1932 Company incorporated as W. T. Copeland & Sons Ltd. Jackson & Gosling – Grosvenor China – purchased when Arthur Edward (Ted) Hewitt appointed a director of Copelands.

Visit of King George V and Queen Mary, with Ronald and Gresham Copeland, April 22nd 1913.

Thomas Hassall appointed Art Director. Ronald Copeland elected Chairman. A. C. Copeland and Ted Hewitt joint Managing Directors.

1934 Installation of Gibbons' Rotalec Kilns, for firing on-glaze decorations, installed.

1936 Replacement of bottle kilns by Davis gas-fired tunnel kiln for firing glost earthenware. New printing shop and dipping house, with drying 'mangle' and 'hardening-on' kiln, erected.

1937 Ronald Copeland elected to the Court of the Goldsmiths' Company.

1938 Copelands appointed Purveyors of China to H.M. Queen Mary, 1st March.

1939 *War declared, 4th September.*

1940 London Showroom bombed.

1941 Visit of T.M. King George VI and Queen Elizabeth to Spode Works, 14th Feb. Patent for Utility Teapot.

1946 Electrically-fired glost tunnel kiln, the 'Meadow', for bone china installed. Ronald Copeland Prime Warden of the Goldsmiths' Company.

1948 Spencer Copeland elected to the Livery of the Goldsmiths.

1952 Extensive additions for earthenware clay production; biscuit tunnel kilns, gas-fired, 'Black' and 'Canal' kilns. Also biscuit warehouse and printing shop. Built partly over the site of the Newcastle Canal.

1954 Murray-Curvex off-set printing machine installed as prototype and further developed with Guy Murray. New decorating and design block built.

1955 Development of epoxy resins and plastics for use in mould-making. London Showroom opened, 66 Grosvenor Street.

1957 Shelley 'Top Hat' kiln installed for china glost firing.

1958 Exhibit at Brussels International Exposition and awarded Diplome d'Honneur.
Closure of Grinding Mill at Spode Works.
Ronald Copeland dies, 22nd August.

1960 Granted the Duke of Edinburgh's Award for Elegant design for Apollo, the undecorated Royal College shape in fine bone china.
Gas-fired, open flame, tunnel kiln, the 'Jubilee', installed for firing bone china biscuit. Last firing of bottle oven on Spode.

Whereas the products of the Spode factory dominated English ceramics for the better part of the nineteenth century, competing only with Mintons, and perhaps with Worcester in ornamental wares in the latter quarter, it was joined by several other firms of repute during the twentieth century. Today, however, many people consider that Spode has regained its predominant position of prestige, having only yielded in size to firms seeking even larger markets. The market for Spode remains that of people with a taste for the beautiful and well-produced pot. Throughout its history the Spode factory has aimed to satisfy the ceramic needs of such people with wares ranging in price from blue prints on earthenware to magnificent patterns on bone china in glorious colours and richly ornamented. Once again in the 1980s and '90s, individual clients may order services with their own personal crest, coat of arms or monogram.

When few pottery companies can or wish to manufacture wares of traditional design, it has been mainly left to Spode to fill this need.

Chinese patterns, ever since the start of the business, have been a very strong influence upon Spode's productions and still may be seen in some of today's wares. But the granting of the Duke of Edinburgh's Award for Elegant Design in 1960 for Apollo – the Royal College shape in fine bone china – demonstrates that Spode can lead the way even in modern design.

The production, in 1964, in a statuary porcelain of a limited number of studies of the ballet dancers Antoinette Sibley and Anthony Dowell, after the sculptures of Enzo Plazzotta, showed that the potters of today may stand proudly beside their forbears in the Halls of Craftsmanship.

Dinner plate and soup cup and saucer in the Royal College shape, 1960.

The wares made to commemorate events of national rejoicing will compare favourably with the gorgeous productions of the past. Ornateness, like age, does not necessarily impart worth to an object. Many humble objects, like the fruit bowl in Blue Italian, or the sandwich plate in Byron pattern which were made in thousands in the 1930s to help to keep the factory busy in that recession, are treasured possessions of families all over the world. It is a strange attribute of much pottery and glass, that it can become an object of great emotional attachment. Long may it remain so. The value of much pottery is in its sentimental associations.

The Art Nouveau style never found an important place at Spode at the turn of the century, but Art Deco patterns were designed for the current taste, and the pattern books show that Copelands were in the vanguard of designing in this style. The market, however, seemed not to accept many of their productions, preferring the more traditional designs; nevertheless, examples do appear from time to time to demonstrate what was available then. Two patterns which were introduced in 1938 and continue to be extremely popular are Christmas Tree and Queen's Bird. Both were designed by Harold Holdway, the former having become established as a tradition in the United States where it is brought into use on Thanksgiving Day and remains the everyday tableware until Twelfth Night. Also in the 1930s, the sculptured figures of Eric Olsen were admirable and were produced in two new earthenwares – Onyx, a soft grey colour, and Velamour, the ivory earthenware with a vellum textured glaze. The latter was revived after 1945 and proved very popular.

It is a fact that Spode contributed greatly to the war effort by exporting large quantities of ware to North America to earn valuable currency for the payment of munitions in the fight for freedom.

During those years of wartime, no decorated pottery was permitted to be sold in the United Kingdom except seconds and 'export rejects', so the main tableware was 'Utility' which, in the case of Spode, was made of exactly the same high quality materials and to the same high standard as was expected from a leading manufacturer; as a result it was eagerly sought after. As soon as there was a slight relaxation of the restrictions, the same items were made available in Flemish Green, and later in English Lavender in a more modern shape; both of these were enjoyed in thousands of British homes until their withdrawal in 1963.

1962 Robert Copeland elected to the Livery of the Goldsmiths.

1964 The Company acquired by Wedgwoods, who rescind after three months.

1966 Company joins the Carborundum Group of Companies, 1st July.

1967 Alfred Gresham Copeland dies, 21st February.

1969 Extensive enlargements of production facilities, including fully equipped sliphouse, advanced making machines, and gas-fired glost tunnel kiln, the 'Apollo', for both earthenware and china. Acquisition of North American agencies of George Thompson.

1970 Celebration of the Bicentenary of the founding of firm by Spode. Name of Company changed to Spode Limited. H.R.H. Princess Anne attends celebration banquet in Goldsmiths' Hall, and Exhibition of specially commissioned ware. H.R.H. Princess Margaret attends the Exhibition in the Royal Academy and visits the Spode Works.

1971 Spode Limited appointed Manufacturer of China to H.M. Queen Elizabeth II.

1976 Company merges with Worcester Royal Porcelain Company in the formation of Royal Worcester Spode Limited. Carborundum hold 45% of the shares.

1977 Royal Worcester Spode mount a display at the Silver Jubilee Exhibition in Hyde Park, London. Showroom opened in St. George's Street, London.

1979 Installation of 'Gemini' moving hood kiln for glost firing.

1983 Exhibition to mark the 250th anniversary of the birth of Spode in 1733, held in Stoke-on-Trent Museum, entitled 'Spode-Copeland 1733-1983 Potters to the Royal Family since 1806'.
The 'Canal' earthenware biscuit kiln replaced with 'Voyager' moving hood kiln with three plinths. Royal Worcester Ltd. purchased by Crystalate plc.

1984 Royal Worcester Ltd. purchased by the London Rubber Company.
The 'Black' tunnel kiln replaced with 'Columbia' moving hood kiln with three plinths.

The Blue Room in the Spode Works. A display of blue transfer-printed ware laid out on antique oak furniture.

1986 The Spode Society established.

1987 Spode collection registered as a Charity as the Spode Museum Trust. Gas-fired central heating with individual units replaces steam heating. Reidhammer kiln installed for firing earthenware biscuit.

1988 Royal Worcester Limited purchased by Derby International.

1989 The two firms separated, and given own Boards of Directors. Retail division still operates jointly. Holding Company is the Porcelain and Fine China Companies Limited, a Division of Derby International, a private company.

1990 Spode organise own Trade Show at factory. Main frame computer installed at Spode. Bone china biscuit being fired in Reidhammer kiln, and earthenware fired in 'Jubilee' kiln. Boiler house converted for two ram presses and spongers benches.

SUMMARY

William Taylor Copeland was a worthy successor to the Spodes. Like them he was an innovator, introducing a steam printing press in 1847, and the Needham & Kite filter press to the industry in 1857; like them he supported moves to improve transportation, especially the railways. He was M.P. for Stoke-upon-Trent and took an active part in the relief of the physically and mentally ill, as well as using his influence in supporting the setting up of Design Schools. His sons, William Fowler Mountford, Edward, Alfred and Richard Pirie were made partners in 1867, although the youngest, Richard Pirie, was the resident partner and ran the firm until his death in 1913. His sons, Ronald and Gresham, then took over the business at a crucial point in its history, but encouraged, no doubt, by the visit of King George V and Queen Mary, they struggled to maintain the high standards of product and employment.

In 1932, the partnership became a limited liability company with the title W. T. Copeland and Sons Limited and A. E. (Ted) Hewitt joined the board of directors with the art director Thomas Hassall.

By 1955, the sons of the directors had joined the board: Spencer, son of Ronald, Gordon, son of Ted Hewitt, John and Robert, sons of Gresham, and in 1956, on the retirement of the senior directors, William Newton was chosen as Chairman with Spencer Copeland as Managing Director.

Throughout the period after 1944, the gradual replacement of old buildings took place along with the installation of tunnel kilns for firing biscuit, glost and decorated ware. The last bottle oven to be fired was in 1960. Spode is the longest established pottery firm still on the site on which it was founded, and these improvements have not been easy to achieve. By 1984, the twin tunnel ovens installed in 1952 to fire earthenware biscuit were replaced by intermittent kilns, and much more up-to-date equipment is being introduced to keep abreast of contemporary technology, but only so long as the quality is kept to a very high standard. In 1954

Low scent jar, pale grey porcelain, pattern 671.

Meat dish (Storming of Guidad Rodrigo) and dessert dish (Skirmish near Busaco) from the Wellington service, illustrating scenes from battles in which Arthur Wellesley, Duke of Wellington, participated. Marks 105 and 148.

one new process was pioneered with Copelands by Dr. Guy Murray – the Murray-Curvex offset printing machine, and in the early 1960s, Spencer Copeland developed the use of epoxy-resins for mouldmaking.

In 1966 the Company joined the Carborundum Group of Companies and celebrated its Bicentenary in 1970 with exhibitions in the Royal Academy and in Goldsmiths' Hall, London, where a banquet was held at which H.R.H. Princess Anne was the guest of honour; there was also a visit to the Spode Works by H.R.H. Princess Margaret. In 1970 the name of the Company was changed to Spode Limited to honour the founder and to avoid confusion in the markets caused by the use of both names, Spode and Copeland.

In 1976 the Worcester Royal Porcelain Company and Spode were merged as Royal Worcester Spode Limited, originally owned jointly with Carborundum but later owned by Royal Worcester Limited.

In 1983 Royal Worcester Limited was bought by Crystalate Ltd and, after the acquisition, the Welwyn Electrics Division was kept and the remainder sold to the London Rubber Company in 1984. As part of the deal it was a condition that the Spode collection of ceramics, engravings, documents and moulds by Turner and Derby should be formed into a Charitable Trust, and this took place in 1987. In 1988 Royal Worcester Spode was bought by Derby International. In 1989 the two companies were given back their respective identities with their own boards of directors under the new name. The Porcelain and Fine China Companies Ltd.

Early dessert dish. Willow I Pattern, pearlware, c.1795. Mark 2a.

Garden pot, English China, c. 1796-1800, decorated at a later date, causing imperfections in the surface.

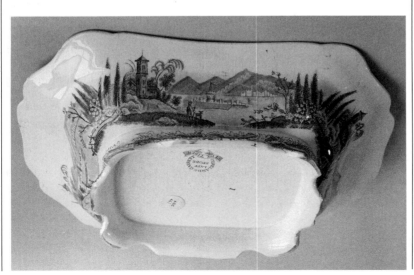

Byron Views pattern, the base of the covered vegetable dish showing the well known mark The Tiber, 161.

The catalogue of marks

INTRODUCTION

Marks may be of many types depending on the purpose for which they were made. They are often called 'backstamps'. I refer in this section to marks of identity and not to those marks caused during the placing and firing of ware.

The PURPOSES of marking are to:

A   Identify the manufacturer, that is, the owner or proprietor of the concern

B   Identify the worker responsible, both for ensuring payment if the work is satisfactory and for corrective measures if the work was unsatisfactory

C   Identify the design, shape or pattern, by name, number or size

D   Identify any exclusive right to a patent or registered design

E   Identify the name of a retailer, wholesaler or importer, &c.

F   Identify the type of body material, eg. Fine Bone China, Stone China.

G   Indicate the date when the clay object was made (by impressing a marker) or the decoration was applied (by a coded letter, number or symbol)

H   Identify experimental ware –
    – when a new body or glaze is being tried, so that the 'trials' will not be lost among the regular ware
    – when a new pattern is produced for testing by offering it to agents and customers. Spode applied 'X' numbers to such designs. A regular pattern number was allocated only when the pattern went into production

I   Show that an object has been made especially to commemorate some event. This mark may take the form of an inscription, and might include the number of the particular piece in the limited edition

J   Identify the country of origin

K   Show that an object has been rejected as being of 'best' quality, but is still good enough to be sold as 'seconds'.

L   Enable cover and base of an object to be re-united after separation during firing and warehousing. See Mark 19.

The WAYS of marking are:

1   Incising, or scratching, the clay with a tool

2   Impressing a marking instrument into the clay while it is still soft

3   Applying a pad of clay, possibly of a different colour, which might have been formed in a mould, like a 'sprig' (q.v.), or which in turn may be marked by methods 1 or 2 above.

4   Moulding. A name or number may be marked in the mould and so be reproduced on each item shaped in that mould. This method is often used for identification of an item either by number or name, or the size of an object. It is, of course, only used for pressed, cast or jollied items.

5 Painting a colour onto the clayware when dry
6 Painting a colour onto the biscuit ware with brush or crayon. Crayon marks are usually made to identify trial pieces; the crayon is made of a material that will withstand the fire. Marks applied by brush are usually decorator's marks, including transfer-printing team marks, or pattern numbers
7 Transfer-printing a coloured mark onto the biscuit ware
8 Transfer-printing a coloured mark onto the glost ware
9 Applying a pre-printed mark by transfer to the ware, either onto the biscuit or glost surface. In the early days of lithographic transfers the surface needed to be 'sized', that is, painted with a substance to enable the transfer to adhere. Since the 1960s water slide-off transfers may be applied directly to the ware
10 Painting a mark in colour or gold onto the glost surface of an object

"I have looked up all the reference books and cannot find this mark at all". This is a frequent statement in letters and conversations with me at the Spode Museum. Looking at the catalogue of Spode Factory marks and backstamps, it is not surprising. It should not be expected that a general encyclopaedia of marks should include every mark of every manufactory. In the case of Spode, there are about three hundred marks; some just name the manufacturer, some name the pattern or body type, while others incorporate the name of a dealer. The mark for Blue Italian is the one which causes most trouble – perhaps because there is so much of it about!

In the Spode period from *c*1770 to 1833 not every piece was marked. This was for two reasons: the painter or gilder needed to be paid for applying each mark and pattern number, and, more importantly, it was seldom necessary to mark every piece anyway because most pieces were part of a *set* of tableware. Such a set was sold as a complete unit, just like a motor car is sold as a unit; the manufacturer's name appears only about eight times on a car, so it was with a set of tableware. Nowadays, when most sets have been divided up, there are many pieces which do not carry the name or pattern number.

Where a pattern was transfer-printed, the mark was often engraved on the copper plate and printed at the same time as the pattern, so Spode printed wares are more often marked, but not always. Sometimes a printed mark includes the name of the body material, like NEW FAYENCE. If the pattern is printed on a different body, like a drab brown one, the transferrer might apply the mark, wrongly, onto the back and so, unwittingly, mislead collectors and dealers.

After March 1833, nearly every piece was marked, apart from some covers.

This was because the name COPELAND & GARRETT was too long, three times as long as SPODE, and the cost of painting it would not only have cost three times as much but also occupied the artists and gilders wastefully. All but a very few rare examples are printed either under or on the glaze; apart from those applied at the clay stage, of course.

There does not seem to have been any particular policy of mark design on the Spode Works until 1970, when all marks were designed to a standard format by a professional graphic designer, John Sutherland-Hawes. Previous to this, it seems that artists, designers, engravers and modellers were given a fairly free hand in designing the marks; more so after 1833, as this book shows.

Importers and retailers in the nineteenth and first half of the twentieth centuries often paid extra to have their name, and sometimes their address, printed on the ware.

Whiter has shown that Spode probably came to the present works in 1764, but no early wares of his can be dated until about 1784, so the 'traditional' date of 1770 for the start of the Spode period is kept.

The layout of this catalogue of marks is divided into six main sections with sub-divisions.

I Spode period *c*1770 to March 1833
    1 – 20 Clay wares with impressed marks
    21 – 30 Painted marks
    31 –   Transfer-printed marks

II Copeland & Garrett March 1833 to June 1847
    101 – 120 Clay, impressed and embossed, pad type, marks
    121 – 125 Painted marks – so far, only one is known
    130 Transfer-printed version of mark 121
    131 – Transfer-printed marks

III W T Copeland & Successors July 1847 to January 1970
    201 – 230 Clay, impressed, embossed, moulded, inscribed
    231 – Transfer-printed

IV Retailers' marks which incorporate the Copeland name up to 1970
    301 – Transfer-printed. Most obtained from the Engravers' record book

V Marks incorporating the pattern or design name up to 1970
    401 – Transfer-printed and slide-off transfer

VI Spode Limited 1970 onwards
    501 – Transfer-printed and slide-off transfer

This system of numbering takes account of the numbers listed by Leonard Whiter in *Spode,* but diverges somewhat in order to include additional marks. It was devised in 1978, and the relevant numbers were used in my *Spode's Willow Pattern & other designs after the Chinese,* and reference is made to them in the chapter on Spode in *Staffordshire Porcelain.*

Reference has also been made to these RC numbers by Drakard and Holdway in their excellent *Spode Printed Ware,* by Spencer Copeland in his guide to the Copeland collection at Trellissick, Cornwall (1989), and in the catalogue published by the City of Stoke-on-Trent Museum to the exhibition *Spode – Copeland 1733 – 1983 Potters to the Royal Family since 1806.* Inevitably, several previously unknown marks have appeared since the system was devised, and this has led to the inclusion of a,b,c suffixes, and in one case, 130, in numbering 'backwards' – that is starting a new sub-section at nought instead of one. Where some other authors have allotted a number to a mark, this is quoted.

Footnote.
GG Geoffrey Godden's Encyclopaedia of British Pottery and Porcelain Marks', numbers 3648 & 3648a cover marks RC 1-4 and 31-34 (printed). LRW Leonard Whiter 'Spode'.

Display of all known Spode factory marks

Spode period 1770-1833

Impressed marks

SPODE
1a

SPODE
b

SPODE
c

SPODE
d

SPODE
2a

SPODE
b

Spode
3

Spode
a

SPODE
4

SPODE
5a

b

StokeChina
6

SPODES NEW STONE
7a

SPODES NEW·STONE
b

N.S
8

Spode
9

Spode and Copeland
10

SPODE & COPELAND, LONDON.
11

O
15

S
16

❀
17

✝

F
18

527
19a

16
b

Painted marks

SPODE
21

SPODE
22

Spode
23

Spode
a

Spode
24

Spode
a

SPODE.
Stone China.
25

Spode & Copeland
26

Transfer-printed marks

Spode
31

SPODE
32

SPODE
33

SPODE
a

SPODE
34

SPODE
35

SPODE
36

SPODE
37

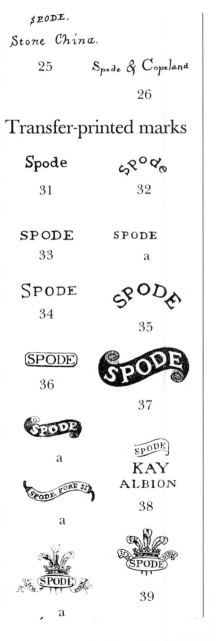

SPODE
a

SPODE·FORE ST
a

SPODE
KAY
ALBION
38

SPODE
a

SPODE
39

40

41

Pattern 1224. Mark 39a.

a

42

Spode & Copeland
LONDON

43

Pattern 3520. Mark 40c.

b

47

48

49

Imperial

a

c

50a

b

Pattern 4920. Mark 42.

51a

b

B. N°

61

63

64

This BLUE-WARE is printed
from the CALX of British COBALT
produced from Wheal Sparnon Mine
in the County of Cornwall.
August 1816.

65

This BLUE WARE is printed
from the CALX of British COBALT
produced from Sparnon Mine
in the County of Cornwall.
August 1816.

a

**DOOREAHS LEADING
OUT DOGS.**

66

67

Copeland & Garrett period 1833-1847

Impressed marks

COPELAND
& GARRETT

101

COPELAND &
GARRETT
8

a

102

7

a

103

104

105

106

107

F

109

108

110

Embossed marks

111

Painted marks

C & G
4952

121

Transfer-printed marks

C & G

130

Marks incorporating LATE SPODE

131

132

133

134

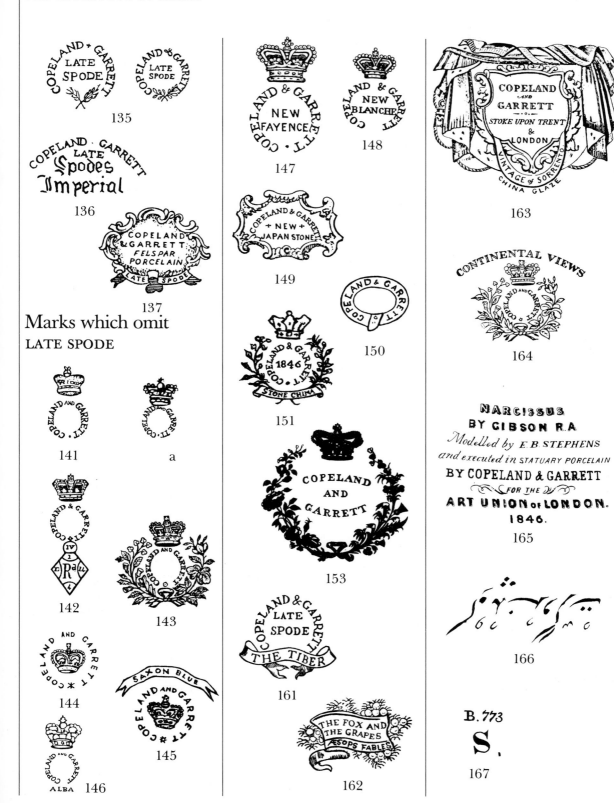

135

136

137

Marks which omit
LATE SPODE

141

a

142

143

144

145

146

147

148

149

150

151

153

161

162

163

164

NARCISSUS
BY GIBSON R.A.
Modelled by E.B. STEPHENS
and executed in STATUARY PORCELAIN
BY COPELAND & GARRETT
FOR THE
ART UNION of LONDON.
1846.

165

166

B. 773
S.

167

168

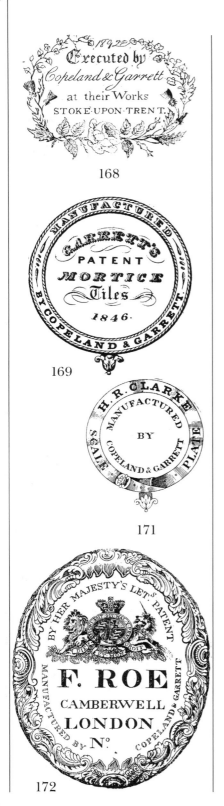

169

171

172

173

Copeland period 1847-1970

Impressed marks

201

COPELAND

202

COPELAND

a

Spode Imp!

203

COPELAND
B

204

COPELAND
I

205

COPELAND
Y

206

207

COPELAND
WHITE
BODY

208

IRONSTONE
COPELAND

209

COPELAND
COLLEGE
IRONSTONE

a

COPELAND
*Spode
Imp!*
Rd Nº 90067

211

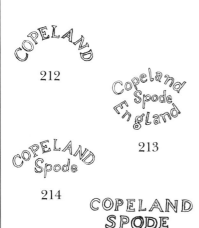

COPELAND
212

Copeland
Spode
England
213

Copeland
Spode
214

COPELAND
SPODE
a

215

216

Copeland
Spode
Imperial
217

Copeland
Spode
Imperial
a

218

220

COPELAND
FRESCO
219

221

COPELAND
IRONSTONE
222

COPELAND
THE
WATFORD
223

Embossed mark

COPELAND
30
227

Transfer-printed marks

Copeland
231

Copeland
Late Spode.
232

COPELAND
233

Copeland
Late Spode
a

COPELAND'S
234

COPELAND'S
PORCELAIN STATUARY
a

COPELAND
235

COPELAND
236

237

238

COPELAND'S
234b

COPELAND
239

COPELAND'S CHINA
240

COPELAND'S CHINA
ENGLAND
241

SPODE
COPELAND'S CHINA
ENGLAND
242

COPELAND
LATE SPODE
160 New Bond Street
LONDON.
243

COPELAND
LATE SPODE
243a

W. T. COPELAND & SONS
160 New Bond St.
LONDON
MAKERS
244

MANUFACTURED BY
W. T. COPELAND & SONS.
—LONDON—
MANUFACTORY STOKE-UPON-TRENT
245

W. T. COPELAND & SONS.
STOKE-UPON-TRENT.
246

247

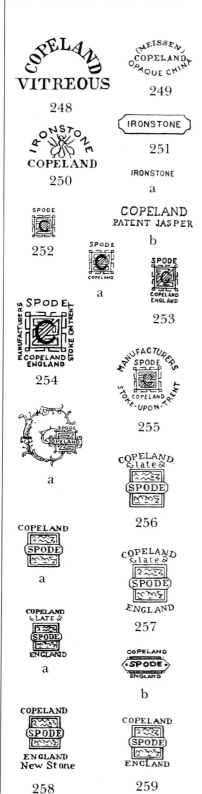

COPELAND VITREOUS
248

(MEISSEN) COPELAND OPAQUE CHINA
249

IRONSTONE COPELAND
250

IRONSTONE
251

IRONSTONE
a

SPODE
252

COPELAND PATENT JASPER
b

SPODE COPELAND
a

SPODE COPELAND ENGLAND
253

MANUFACTURERS SPODE COPELAND ENGLAND STOKE ON TRENT
254

MANUFACTURERS SPODE COPELAND STOKE·UPON·TRENT
255

SPODE COPELAND
a

COPELAND late SPODE
256

COPELAND SPODE
a

COPELAND late SPODE ENGLAND
257

COPELAND LATE SPODE ENGLAND
a

COPELAND SPODE ENGLAND New Stone
258

COPELAND SPODE ENGLAND
259

COPELAND late SPODE ENGLAND
b

COPELAND SPODE ENGLAND
259

COPELAND SPODE ENGLAND
259a

COPELAND SPODE GREAT BRITAIN
b

X COPELAND SPODE ENGLAND Fine Stone
260

Copelands Jewelled Porcelain
261

W.T.COPELAND & SONS STOKE UPON TRENT
262

Spode Imp!
a

Spode Imp! Rᵈ Nº 90067
263

COPELAND LATE SPODE TRADE MARK R'd 1600846 ENGLAND
266

COPELAND LATE SPODE
265

COPELAND'S LEADLESS GLAZE ENGLAND
a

W.T.COPELAND & SONS STOKE·ON·TRENT LEADLESS GLAZE
b

W.T.COPELAND & SONS STOKE·ON·TRENT ENGLAND
267

TRADE SPODE COPELAND ENGLAND MARK
268

کریلند لندن
270

COPYRIGHT RESERVED COPELAND
269

COPYRIGHT RESERVED
a

BY APPOINTMENT W.T.COPELAND & SONS STOKE-ON-TRENT.
a

BY APPOINTMENT
271

BY ROYAL WARRANT W.T.COPELAND & SONS STOKE·ON·TRENT.
b

COPELANDS BONE CHINA ENGLAND
272

SPODE COPELAND CHINA ENGLAND
274

SPODE BONE CHINA ENGLAND
275

Spode BONE CHINA ENGLAND
276

Spode BONE CHINA ENGLAND
a

Spode Imp! ENGLAND
277

Spode's Imp! COPELAND ENGLAND Rᵈ Nº 667194
a

SPODE COPELAND ENGLAND
278

COPELANDS LEADLESS GLAZE ENGLAND SPODE COPELAND'S CHINA ENGLAND
279

SPODE'S Royal Jade ENGLAND
280

Spode's Velamour ENGLAND
282

SPODE COPELAND ONYX ENGLAND
281

Spode's
"Royal Jasmine"
England

283

COPELANDS
EARTHENWARE
Rᵈ Nᵒ 159276
ENGLAND

284

285

Spode
Copeland

286

Spode
Copeland
England

287

GᵛⁱR
COPELAND
1945

288

Spode

289

Spode
Impᵈ

a

Spode
Flemish Green
England
B

290

Spode
FORTUNA
England.

291

SPODE'S
English Lavender
ENGLAND
B

292

Spode
ENGLAND
Alenite
FLAME-PROOF
OVENWARE
B

293

SPODE Meadow Sweet
ENGLAND

294

295

Spode
FINE STONE
ENGLAND

296

Retailers' marks which incorporate the Copeland name

304

305

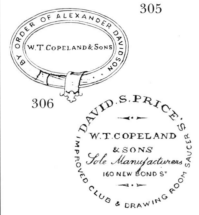

306

DAVID S. PRICE'S
IMPROVED CLUB & DRAWING ROOM SAUCER
W.T. COPELAND
& SONS
Sole Manufacturers
160 NEW BOND Sᵗ

307

MANUFACTURED
SOLELY FOR
J.M. SHAW & Cᵒ
NEW YORK
W.T. COPELAND & SONS
TRADE MARK REGISTERED 1876

308

ALERT

309

310

311

DAVIS COLLAMORE & Cᵒ
B'WAY COR 21ᵗˢ S
NEW YORK

COPELAND

315

COPELAND
DER OF
EL

316

GILMAN COLLAMORE & Cᵒ
COPELAND
UNION SQUARE NEW YORK

320

MANUFACTURED
BY
W.T. COPELAND & SONS
FOR
RICHARD BRIGGS.
BOSTON.

321

JOHN MORTLOCK OXFORD STREET
LONDON

322

W.T. COPELAND
& SONS
ESTABLISHED
1770.
131 BROADWAY NEW YORK
DAVIS COLLAMORE & Cᵒ

324

GILMAN COLLAMORE & Cᵒ
W.T. COPELAND
& SONS
ESTABLISHED
1770
UNION SQUARE NEW YORK

323

Wᵐ.MORE'S
DANIELL
LONDON
COPELAND'S CHINA

327

SPODE
COPELAND
MANUFACTURED
FOR
T. GOODE & Cᵒ
LONDON

326

OVINGTON BROTHERS
COPELAND'S CHINA
BROOKLYN

328

COPELAND'S CHINA
TRADE MARK
O C
WELTIBOURNE GROVE
LONDON W
ENGLAND

334

F. CROOK
COPELAND
LATE
SPODE
NOTCOMBE S.HOUSE
BELGRAVE S.W.
LONDON

335

CHEESMAN
CHINA & GLASS
WAREHOUSE
NORTH ST BRIGHTON
COPELAND

336

W.T. COPELAND & SONS
STAFFORDSHIRE
J. McD. & S
Importers

338

Borough of Stoke upon Trent.
Fredᵏ Geen,
MAYOR.
J. B. ASHWELL, TOWN CLERK.
W.T. COPELAND & SONS
STOKE-UPON-TRENT

339

341
T.G.OODE & Cᵒ
LONDON
COPELAND'S CHINA
ENGLAND

342
PRESENTED BY
T.GOODE & Cᵒ
LONDON
W.T.COPELAND & SONS
STOKE ON TRENT

355
COPELAND
ENGLAND
A.T.WILEY & Cᵒ Lᵗᵈ
MONTREAL.

356
"Spode's Regal"
COPELAND
ENGLAND
A.T.WILEY & Cᵒ Lᵗᵈ
MONTREAL.

376
HEAL & SON Lᵗᵈ
SILVER & JADE
SPODE
COPELAND

377
W.T COPELAND & SONS Lᵗᵈ
MANUFACTURERS
OF
Grosvenor China
ENGLAND

345
COPELAND
SPODE'S
TROPHIES
JAMES GREEN & NEPHEW
LONDON

346
SAVOY
HOTEL
COPELAND'S
ENGLAND
R.Nᵒ 512428

367
ALGONQUIN · CLUB
MANUFACTURERS
SPODE
COPELAND
STOKE · UPON · TRENT
A. FRENCH. & Cᵒ.

349
1492 - 1892
"COLUMBUS"
Made in England.
by
W.T.Copeland & Sons
Stoke upon Trent
for
BURLEY & Cᵒ
CHICAGO
Rᵈ Nᵒ 196703

368
SPECIALLY DESIGNED
BY LIONEL EDWARDS.
MANUFACTURED BY
W.T. COPELAND & SONS.
ENGLAND.
SOLELY FOR SOANE & SMITH Lᵗᵈ
OXFORD ST, LONDON, W.I.
Rᵈ Nᵒ. 691240.
No 7
"HOMEWARD"
BY
LIONEL EDWARDS

380
COPELAND - SPODE
SBL
STRENGTH & RELIABILITY

350
CHAˢ M. VAN HEUSEN
IMPORTER
NEW YORK
COPELAND'S CHINA
ENGLAND

351
"BURN'S PATTERN"
MANUFACTURED
FOR
LIVINGSTONE'S CHINA
- OBAN -
BY. W.T.COPELAND & SONS
LATE SPODE

352
MADE EXPRESSLY FOR
HOTEL ST REGIS
Copeland China
IMPORTED BY
DAVIS COLLAMORE & Cᵒ Lᵗᵈ
5ᵗʰ AVE AND 37 ᵗ⁸ ST

353
SPODE
ENGLAND
COPELAND
MAISON TOY
6 RUE DE LA PAIX.10
PARIS

391
JUGGINS'S
MANUFACTURED
BUTTER
BY
W.T.COPELAND
STANDS

354
CHICAGO PITCHER
DESIGNED
BY
FRANK. E. BURLEY
EDITION DELUXE
BURLEY & Cᵒ
CHICAGO
Nᵒ
COPELAND
LATE
SPODE
ENGLAND

369
"SUTHERLAND"
SPODE
COPELAND CHINA
ENGLAND
R8940
TIFFANY & Cᵒ
NEW YORK

370
EXCLUSIVE
TO
HARRODS
KNIGHTSBRIDGE
LONDON S.W.I.

371
COPELAND
SPODE

392
COPELAND'S
DRIVER & SONS
SCALE MAKERS
MINORIES, LONDON

Copeland period pattern names

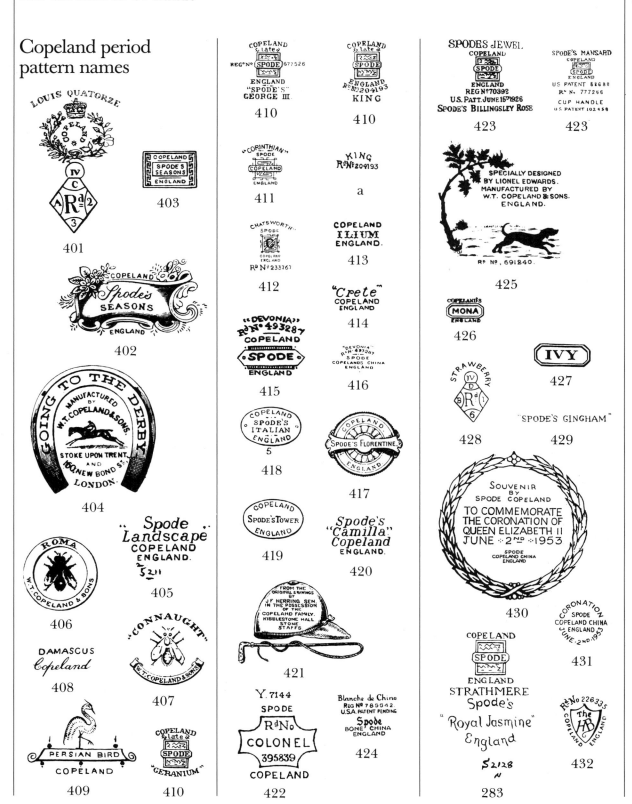

LOUIS QUATORZE

403

401

402

404

405

ROMA
W.T.COPELAND & SONS

406

DAMASCUS
Copeland

408

"CONNAUGHT"
W.T.COPELAND & SONS.

407

PERSIAN BIRD
COPELAND

409

COPELAND
late
SPODE
"GERANIUM"

410

COPELAND
late
REG Nº SPODE 677526
ENGLAND
"SPODE'S"
GEORGE III

410

"CORINTHIAN"
SPODE
COPELAND
ENGLAND

411

CHATSWORTH
SPODE
COPELAND
ENGLAND
Rª Nº 233767

412

"DEVONIA"
RdNº 493287
COPELAND
SPODE
ENGLAND

415

COPELAND
SPODE'S
ITALIAN
ENGLAND
5

418

COPELAND
SPODE'STOWER
ENGLAND

419

FROM THE
ORIGINAL DRAWINGS
BY
J.F HERRING SEN.
IN THE POSSESSION
OF THE
COPELAND FAMILY.
KIBBLESTONE HALL
STONE
STAFFS

421

Y. 7144
SPODE
RdNº
COLONEL
395839
COPELAND

422

COPELAND
late
SPODE
ENGLAND
Rº Nº 204193
KING

410

KING
Rº Nº 204193

a

COPELAND
ILIUM
ENGLAND.

413

"Crete"
COPELAND
ENGLAND

414

"DEVONIA"
Rª Nº 493287
SPODE
COPELANDS CHINA
ENGLAND

416

COPELAND
Spode's Florentine.
ENGLAND

417

Spode's
"Camilla"
Copeland
ENGLAND.

420

Blanche de Chine
REG Nº 785042.
U.S.A. PATENT PENDING
Spode
BONE CHINA
ENGLAND

424

SPODES JEWEL.
COPELAND
SPODE
ENGLAND
REG Nº70392
U.S. PATT. JUNE 15TH 1926
SPODE'S BILLINGSLEY ROSE

423

SPODE'S MANSARD
COPELAND
SPODE
ENGLAND
US PATENT 88688
Rº Nº 777286
CUP HANDLE
US PATENT 102458

423

SPECIALLY DESIGNED
BY LIONEL EDWARDS.
MANUFACTURED BY
W.T. COPELAND & SONS.
ENGLAND.
Rº Nº 691240.

425

COPELAND'S
MONA
ENGLAND

426

STRAWBERRY
IV
D
Rd
B 1
6

428

IVY

427

"SPODE'S GINGHAM"

429

SOUVENIR
BY
SPODE COPELAND
TO COMMEMORATE
THE CORONATION OF
QUEEN ELIZABETH II
JUNE 2ND 1953
SPODE
COPELAND CHINA
ENGLAND

430

CORONATION
SPODE
COPELAND CHINA
ENGLAND
JUNE 2ND 1953

431

COPELAND
SPODE
ENGLAND
STRATHMERE
Spode's
"Royal Jasmine"
England
52128
N

283

RdNo 226335
The HB
COPELAND
ENGLAND

432

Spode's
"Royal Jasmine"
England
Autumn
by
Ronald Copeland
RᴰNᵒ 798464

441

COPELAND
SPODE
ENGLAND

REQUEST
DESIGNED BY

J. Hassall.

442

Spode's
"Royal Jasmine"
England

"DIANA"
DESIGNED BY

Pinder Davis

443

"Cutie-Kitten"
SPODE
COPELAND
ENGLAND
S.3243

444

BARBECUE
SPODE
COPELAND
ENGLAND

445

Away in
a manger.
Designed by
J C Boulton
Hand Engraved by
J Longmore
SPODE
COPELAND
ENGLAND

446

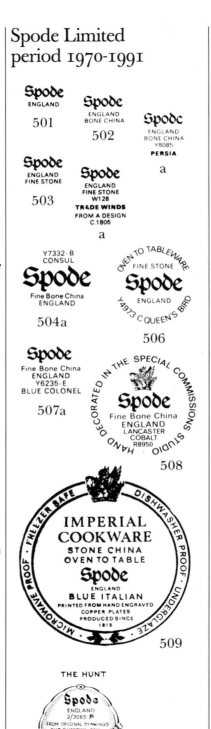

Spode Limited period 1970-1991

Spode
ENGLAND

501

Spode
ENGLAND
BONE CHINA

502

Spode
ENGLAND
BONE CHINA
Y8085
PERSIA

a

Spode
ENGLAND
FINE STONE

503

Spode
ENGLAND
FINE STONE
W128
TRADE WINDS
FROM A DESIGN
C.1805

a

Y7332-B
CONSUL
Spode
Fine Bone China
ENGLAND

504a

OVEN TO TABLEWARE
FINE STONE
Spode
ENGLAND
Y4973 C QUEEN'S BIRD

506

Spode
Fine Bone China
ENGLAND
Y6235-E
BLUE COLONEL

507a

HAND DECORATED IN THE SPECIAL COMMISSIONS STUDIO
Spode
Fine Bone China
ENGLAND
LANCASTER
COBALT
R8950

508

MICROWAVE PROOF · FREEZER SAFE · DISHWASHER PROOF · UNDERGLAZE
IMPERIAL
COOKWARE
STONE CHINA
OVEN TO TABLE
Spode
ENGLAND
BLUE ITALIAN
PRINTED FROM HAND ENGRAVED
COPPER PLATES
PRODUCED SINCE
1816

509

THE HUNT
Spode
ENGLAND
2/3265 F
FROM ORIGINAL DRAWINGS
BY J. F. HERRING. SEN.

"FIRST OVER"

510

PLAZZOTTA
by
Spode

511

THE SPODE MUSEUM TRUST
COLLECTION

512

Spode
ENGLAND

513

Spode
Fine Bone China
ENGLAND

514

The marks of Spode & Copeland

The sizes of marks as illustrated may not be exact; some have been reduced or altered in preparation.

Section I

SPODE PERIOD
1770 to 1833

Impressed marks.

1a   SPODE

An early mark (1785 to 1790) which has been seen on a small dish of *Two Figures* blue-printed pattern *(Whiter plate 3)* LRW 1a.

b   SPODE

Only seen on an early stoneware flask *(Whiter plate 140)* LRW 1b.

c   SPODE

An oval shell edge plate in pearlware exhibits this mark *(Whiter plate 104)* LRW 1c.

d   SPODE

Seen on several pieces painted in blue: the drainer *(Whiter plate 105)*, items of a creamware dessert set *(Copeland p15, Figs 8 & 9)*, and on very early versions of the blue-printed *Two Figures* pattern *(Copeland p69, Fig 95)*. An early creamware stand also has this mark *(Whiter plate 103)*. LRW 1d. No special significance can be attributed to the variations of Mark 1; they all appear on the very early wares of Spode.

2a   SPODE   b   SPODE

Always neat and varying in size. They usually occur on dry bodies, basalt, red stoneware, caneware and jasper, early printed pearlware and cream wares, and sometimes on bone china. About 1790 to 1802.
Mark 2a varies from 6 to 10mm long. LRW 2a. Mark 2b is larger, varying from 11 to 14mm and occasionally found with a slight curve. There is no serif to the S. LRW 2b.

3   Spode   a   Spode

1800-20. Found both with a slight curve, Mark 3, and in a straight line, Mark 3a. Mark 3a seems to be the more common. They occur on all wares. There is probably no significance in the curve on impressed marks as it might have occurred while the stamp was being pressed into the clay. LRW 3.

4   SPODE

1815-33. The latest of the impressed marks, it was used on all bodies up to the end of the Spode period. It may be distinguished from Mark 2 by the serifs on the S. It is frequently found with numbers below it: these are thought to be clay-workers' marks (q.v.). LRW 4.

5a   b

Mark 5a is rare, being found on very large items of pearlware. Two garden seats, one large salmon dish and foot baths are known. The white earthenware body of Spode became known on the factory as 'Crown', possibly derived from this mark. LRW 5a. Mark 5b, until September 1990 had been seen only on bone china and felspar porcelain. Now a sauce tureen stand of Copeland & Garrett's New Japan Stone (Mark 149), decorated with under-glaze pattern B625, one of the many versions of *Peacock* pattern, has appeared. It has been seen on Etruscan shape sugar box, pattern 3743 with gold bat print: on a fine bone china ice cream pail, pattern 4104 *(Whiter colour plate I)*, and on a bone china saucer with *Union Wreath* printed in blue. LRW 5b.

All items have been made by hollow-ware and big-ware pressers, and these marks *may* be the marks of two such pressers.

Mark 5a may date about 1815, while mark 5b is thought to be from 1826.

6   Stoke China

About 1796-1800. Every object seen so far with this impressed mark is dense, heavy, white and, when crazed, displays the type of crackle associated with bone china. The piece discussed by Leonard Whiter *(p139)* was submitted to analysis at the British Ceramic Research Association in 1980: this showed, from the content of calcium and phosphorous, to have an amount of bone between 20% and 40%.

Despite its opacity, it is bone china. Three objects decorated in pattern *282* have been noticed up to the present. Also a footed dessert comport painted with blue sprigs, and a vegetable dish base in pattern 319. LRW 6.

7a   b

SPODES   SPODES
NEW STONE   NEW·STONE

1822-1833. Adopted when a new formula for Stone China was introduced about 1821-2. See mark 48 for recipes. The

52

lowest pattern number found on New Stone is 3435 *(see Whiter p196)*. The mark is frequently found with Copeland & Garrett printed marks: this probably means that there was a large stock of 'whiteware' made before March 1833, and merely decorated after that date. It seems unlikely that its use was continued on clayware made after March 1833. LRW 7, GG 3652. The two forms are shown here, but they may only be because of the marker being twisted during the impressing action.

8   N.S.   N.S

Uncommon mark. Seen on a few pieces of New Stone, including an example of pattern *2061*. Being small, it was useful for marking the bases of eggcups. GG 3653.

9   *Spode*

A mark seen once, so far, on a white earthenware plate with a blue printed border pattern enamelled in colours, and with the armorial bearings of James Craggs, Secretary of State for War in 1717. This plate was a replacement for one in the Chinese Export porcelain service made about 1720. The pattern was *Windsor,* introduced in the Copeland period; it is recorded in the 8th Arms Book, pattern *2/3215,* in September 1889. The mark is probably part of mark 203.

10   *Spode and Copeland*

About 1824. This mark is moulded into the back of a portrait bust of the Duke of Wellington. It measures 5.1 cm long. The bust is of red stoneware, glazed and coloured to simulate bronze.

11   SPODE & COPELAND,
        LONDON.

About 1824. Impressed, with sharply defined edges, into the back of an unglazed earthenware label. The label is more likely to have been for use to mark the price of butter or cheese in an high street dairy than for use in the garden. Only one is known so far.

19a **527**   b **16**

19a Impressed numbers occur on the bases and covers of Old Oval shape teapots and covered sugar boxes. (LRW 8 & 9). They were to enable bases and

covers which were fitted together in clay to be re-united after firing to ensure correct fitting. See illustration and also note under Makers marks, page 88. Ref. Drakard & Holdway, p. 212.

19b This impressed number occurs either with or without a 'frame' on items of Felspar Porcelain, a plate of which in Chester pattern is printed in blue; this also has Mark 33 printed in green. The mark almost certainly refers to China Body No. 16, dated March 1831. The 'frame' is where the number has been pressed too deeply into the clay.

Marks 15-18 are taken from Drakard and Holdway's SPODE PRINTED WARE

15   O S

About 1803-12. These letters, either singly or together as shown, are found impressed into the foot ring of bone china teapots, sugar boxes and cream jugs, usually of the New Oval shape. Their significance is uncertain.

16

In the Recipe Book of Thos. Grocott, started by him Jany 1825, he records on Feby 9 1828
China Body No 10   with this mark.

2 times 70lb Sand Fret		7.66%
1 time 70lb Flint		3.83
3 times 94lb Felspar		15.44
4 times 111lb China Clay		24.31
2 times 60lb Black Clay		6.57
7 times 110lb Bone		42.17
1½oz Blue Calx	} for stain	
1½oz Manganese		

This is a variation of China Body No 8 which contained 3 times 70lb Sand Fret and no flint. The recipe for this frit was.

112lb Isle of		mixed well together
White Sand	}	and fired in Biscuit
9lb Pearl Ash		Oven, in Sagers thin
		wash'd with Flint,
		then to be took out
		of the Sagers and
		pound(ed).

This China Body No 8 may have been the original Felspar porcelain recipe of 1821.

17

From Dec 1829. This simple crucifix impressed mark was used on China Body No 13 as given in Thos. Grocott's book

18   F

Sept 1832. Grocott lists this as the mark for China Body No 17

360lbs Felspar	18.99%	
700lb Cornwall Clay	36.92%	
836lb Bone	44.09%	
27Dᵣˢ Blue Calx	}	Ground fine
27Dᵣˢ Calcined Manganese		for stain

This mark continued in use during the Copeland & Garrett period. See marks 109 & 137

Painted Marks

21 *Spode*   22 **SPODE**

23 *Spode*   a **Spode**

1799-1833. Different styles adopted by the various decorators, over nearly thirty five years. Usually applied (LRW10) in iron red; also known in purple, black, sepia brown, and very rarely in gold.

Red was the easiest colour to apply and was (LRW10a) usually available, on the decorators palette. It needed an 'easy' fire – at the same temperature as gold – about 720°C – so, being applied last thing when the decoration was completed it is sensible to use a colour which looks best when given a 'gold fire'. It also (LRW11) saved the cost of a gilded mark.

24   *Spode*

Frequently the pattern number was applied close to the mark – beside or below it – and both on the base close to the foot ring. Only occasionally – and then on dessert wares – is the mark found in a central position: this usually occurs on specially commissioned services which do not have a pattern number. (LRW12).

a   *Spode*

Marks 24 and 24a are not often seen, and then on later wares. Etruscan shape, pattern 3907.

Garden seat with the Crown Mark, 5a.

Leg bath in Lange Lijzen pattern. Although of large size, the Mark is 1d.

Mark 6a on a footbath in Blue Italian pattern.

Mark 1, in its various forms, is often impressed rather faintly, and may be difficult to discern. On plates with no foot ring, especially creamware, the mark may be impressed where the foot ring would be normally and is liable to have been rubbed with wear.

Mark 4 is often seen with a number impressed below. A list of some of these numbers is given on page 89. It is probable that the number was the maker's identity number.

The red stoneware portrait bust of the Duke of Wellington, on the reverse of which is the moulded Mark 10.

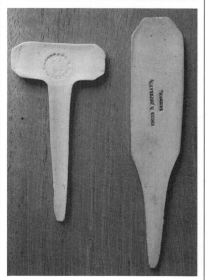

Two unglazed earthenware labels. That on the left was found in a garden rubbish heap, while that on the right was in the drawer of a desk once used by a shopkeeper. It seems more likely that they were for use in a dairy. Marks 102 and 11. The fronts are illustrated above.

Mark 203 is thought to be the origin of Mark 9, which does not have the COPELAND name. Rather than an attempt to defraud, it is likely that the stamp was applied at an angle.

Suite of teaware, Old Oval shape with Bute teacup and saucer, bone china, pattern 857, gilded, with red flowers.

Inside cover of teapot.

Close-up of the base of the teapot.

Spode soup plate, stone china, Mark 25. An exceedingly close copy of a Chinese export porcelain design. The border reproduces the bianca zopra bianca decoration of white enamel leaves on the pale grey of the stone china which matches the colour of the porcelain.

Inside cover of sugar box.

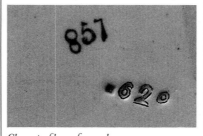

Close-up of base of sugar box.

Mark 19a. These impressed numbers (7 and 620) were to enable cover and base to be reunited after firing. The impressed square occurs only on the base of the object.

Coffee cup, Bute handle, pearlware. Seldom seen Daisy pattern with the rare Mark 37a. Transfer-printed in blue with the sheet pattern all over and a broad border inside. Best gold band around the top, inside and outside.

Thin transfer paper pulled from a very old and faint engraving. The subject is the rotunda, at Ranelagh Gardens in London, and it shows Mark 38a. This illustration is in reverse. See Drakard and Holdway for more details and illustrations, pp. 120-2.

Dessert plate, Rosette pierced shape. Bone china, exquisitely painted and richly gilded, it is marked in red with the hand painted Mark 26.

Painted marks are only found on wares which have been decorated over the glaze. Pattern numbers, however, were applied under the glaze when additional colour was added to a transfer printed outline, before glazing.

A selection of three bone china recipes (Whiter p174)

	1	2	3
Bone	35.5%	26%	50%
China clay	23.5%	15	19
Blue clay	11.7%	11	6
China stone	17.6%	37	19
Flint	11.7%	11	6

25 *SPODE.*
Stone China.

This mark painted in black has been noticed – on a soup plate made to match a Chinese porcelain soup plate: it is likely that any other similar pieces made to match also carry this mark. (See Whiter, Fig 297) (LRW14).

26 *Spode & Copeland*

Spode & Copeland was the style of the London business from 1813-1823 and 1826-1833. Although wares with this mark could have been decorated at the works in Stoke, it is also possible that some or all of them were made in Stoke but decorated in London. This notion might apply especially to the objects decorated with portraits of King George III, the Duke of Wellington, and Futteh Ali Shah. (Whiter Figs 173, 159) (LRW13).

Transfer-printed Marks

31   Spode

1800-1820. The straight mark frequently is found on pieces with Mark 9, and although common on earthenware is also found on bone china, especially in blue on blue printed patterns. It was usually printed in the same colour as the pattern because the Mark was engraved on the same copper plates. Printed in blue, 31a is 17.5mm long. (LRW15a).

32   *Spode*

The curved form of Mark 31 is found rarely, and then most often on cups. (LRW15b)

33   SPODE   a   SPODE

34   Spode

1810-1833. The most common printed mark for earthenware and bone china prints. Usually in blue, it occurs in other colours (see note on Mark 31). Green and brown marks begin to appear on wares of 1825 and after, while pink prints date from about 1832 (LRW16a) [GG3650] Mark 33a in the smaller size is engraved on a copper of Two-Temples II, variation Broseley, Mark 34 occurs on old copper engravings of Buddleia and Trophies – Nankin patterns, and may pre-date Mark 33.

35   *SPODE*

A rare mark, being a curved form of Mark 33. Seen on a small sauce tureen stand, printed in blue, decorated with Milkmaid pattern; also on a bowl (shard excavated on Spode factory), a complete bowl and a mug all in Milkmaid.

36   (SPODE)

1805-1815. A mark rarely seen except on the blue-printed patterns of Rome, Buffalo, and Filigree. Introduced about 1805 it remained in use possibly for ten years. Also seen on Convolvulus & Sunflower pattern. (LRW16b)

37

a

About 1805-1818. Rarely found mark on blue-printed wares. It has been seen on Italian, Daisy and Net patterns. (LRW 16c) [GG 3654]. An engraving of Rock pattern has a smaller version of it, Mark 37a, and an example of Buffalo is known with this smaller mark. Also a coffee can Royal Flute shape with Temple pattern on bone china, and a plate of Buddleia pattern but with a variation in the border.

38   SPODE   *Kay*
    KAY   ALBION HOUSE
    ALBION

About 1819. This mark is only known from an engraved copper plate of a chinoiserie pattern. Beneath the mark is engraved KAY ALBION – perhaps the name of the proprietor and that of his hotel. Also on the copper plate is Mark 47. The pattern relates to number 2862. A later version of pattern 2862 on New Stone has Kay ALBION HOUSE. See page 103 of the *Spode Review*.

a   

About 1780-95. Engraved on a copper plate with a representation of the Ranalagh Gardens, London, showing the exterior view of the Rotunda derived from *London and its Environs Described* (1766). Spode's London Warehouse and Shop was at No. 29 Fore Street, Cripplegate from 1778-85 when he moved to No. 45 Fore Street until his move in 1796 to No. 5 Portugal Street. No example of ware has been seen with this scene or mark up to the present time.

39

a

About 1806-c1808. It is believed that this mark was introduced in 1806 after the visit to Spode's factory of the Prince of Wales in the company of his brother, the Duke of

Clarence (later to be William IV). The mark does not occur on the pieces of pattern No. 1112 which includes the Prince of Wales feathers in the decorative design (see Whiter pl. 156). The mark has been noted on examples of the following patterns: (LRW17) [GG 3659b]

500 Bowl, with sepia coloured Bat print.

981 Tea wares Bamboo and Rock pattern in red with gilding.

1122 Plate, Greek figures in centre, gilded bead at edge.

1168 Supper set and plate, red, blue and gilded design of great magnificence. (See Whiter pl.155).

1185 Square dessert dish, Bamboo and Rock, red and gold (see Whiter pl.157).

1224 Plate Ø 8½ ins., Swags of flowers painted in blue in the French style (Mark 39a)

1406 Plate, with cerulean blue rim, square frame in centre with exquisitely painted landscape. (39a).

Mark 39a is bat printed, whereas Mark 39, although also printed on the glaze, is transferred using tissue paper.

Although introduced in about 1806, it is evident from its presence on pattern 1406 that Mark 39a was still in use in 1810.

40

1821. The range of attractive marks for Felspar Porcelain are based on the design of Mark 40. When feldspar was introduced into the bone china body in 1821 by Spode, Mark 40 was used with its date and the addresses of Spode's premises. After 1821, the date was omitted. (LRW 18a).

a

1822. This mark is the same as 40 except that the date has been omitted. Note that Stoke upon Trent is in script type. Spode Felspar marks are usually printed in purple: sometimes this has faded to a grey colour, as the mark was printed over glaze and has been affected by acid or alkali attack. However on a few pieces a black printed mark is known; this occurs when the design is printed in black. (LRW 18b) [GG 3658].

b

1822. This is a rare mark. It differs from Mark 40a in that Stoke-upon-Trent is printed in 'upper and lower case' type (ie initial capital letter with small letters following) instead of script. The very few examples of Mark 40b that are known are smaller than 40a. An example on small tureen stand, pattern 3611 (WTC201).

c

1821. Another version of Mark 40 has Stoke upon Trent printed in a neater script, and STAFFORDSHIRE only in upper case letters, and spelt in full. Examples are known on patterns 3520, 3496 and 3502.

All four marks are rare.

41

1822-1833 The standard mark for Spode's Felspar Porcelain for which at least two sizes were engraved. (LRW 18c) [GG 3657]

Two recipes for Spode's Felspar Porcelain are quoted by Whiter (Whiter p 174):

	20 Nov 1821	
Bone	46%	49%
China clay	31	25
China stone	–	23
Felspar	15	3
Sand fritt	8	–

Several recipes are listed in Thos. Grocott's book, of which two which differ from the above are quoted alongside Marks 16 and 18.

42

About 1824 Whiter illustrates this mark as a print from an old copper plate engraving at the Spode Works. Since then a saucer in pattern 4920, with the Persian inscription of Mark 67, is on display in the Spode Museum. Printed in puce.

43 *Spode & Copeland*
LONDON
∴

This mark was recorded when a bowl was brought in to the Spode Works in about 1970. In 1986, two plates in Botanical pattern, 4565 in blue and 4833 in green, both with gilded tracing, were given to the author, and both have the Persian mark, 67. These are displayed in the Spode Museum.

44   SPODE & COPELAND,

This mark, with the two following, are recorded in a publication of the Company in 1902 entitled "Copeland's (Late Spode) China". Marks 44 and 45 are stated as being "both impressed and printed". Only one example of an impressed mark 44 (see Mark 11) has been seen up to now, [GG 3659a], and no example of a printed mark has been seen yet.

45   SPODE SON & COPELAND

Jewitt also records the same information, adding that 46 was also impressed or painted. [GG 3659].

46   S P O D E Felspar Porcelain

No example of either of these two marks (45-46) has been seen yet. There is no record of the firm ever being called 'Spode Son & Copeland', although it did have the title 'Spode Copeland & Son' from 1824 to 1826, in London only. (See Whiter p224).

47

Stone-China

About 1812-1833. This is believed to be the earliest mark used on Spode's Stone China (c1812). It was formed by superimposing Mark 36 upon a pseudo-chinese seal mark. This type of seal mark was popular among Spode's contemporaries, especially Miles Mason and J. Ridgway (LRW 19a) [GG 3651].

48

Stone China

About 1815-1833. Mark 48 was introduced a short time later, perhaps to avoid confusion with competitors who had adopted the same style, as, e.g, Clews. Both were used concurrently because they were engraved on the copper plates bearing the patterns: using these to date objects must be unreliable. (LRW 19b).

Examples of stone china which exhibit good translucency include Patterns 2038 & 2053. All of which carry Mark 47. Only the early wares were translucent probably due to the high proportion of Cornish Stone in the formula:

	Old Stone China		New Stone China	
Blue Clay Cornwall	180lbs	20.68%	100lbs	14.2%
Stone	624	71.72	240	34.28
Flint	46	5.287	160	22.85
Cornwall Clay	–	–	200	28.50
Patent Stone (Ironstone)	20	2.299	–	–
Blue Calx for Stain	7oz	2dm.	4oz	–

49

Spode's Imperial

1821-33 The ivory coloured earthenware was an improved form of cream coloured earthenware: the glaze was clear so that the body yielded the true nature of its colour. Spode named this improved body Imperial. The mark is printed in blue and has been seen on examples of Blue Rose pattern and numbers 3248 and 4176, the latter (LRW20) [GG3656] exhibiting considerable translucency. Pattern 4233 Frog pattern, painted in a plum colour is printed with this mark: an example rings like china and shows translucence. This example was white, not ivory. An example of pattern number 4290, printed in blue, coloured plum & gilded, also showed slight translucence. This might be due to the larger than usual proportions of china clay and stone.
A recipe dated September 13th 1826:

300	China Clay	33.186%
300	Vitrescent Stone	33.186
104	Blue Clay	11.504
200	Dried Flint	22.124

a

Imperial

Seen on a dessert dish of Union Wreath pattern, believed to be of Spode's manufacture, blue transfer-printed. Another example, printed with Union Wreath 1 Centre & Union Wreath 1 border, within the ribbons of the centre the words UNION CLUB.

50a

SPODE'S NEW FAYENCE

b

SPODE'S NEW FAYENCE

About 1826-33 Developments in body formulation were taking place continuously because of the variability of supplies of clays and cornish stone. The naming of bodies grew in popularity in the nineteenth century starting, perhaps, with Stoke China (Mark 6) and Turner's Patent. A body might be compounded specially for specific objects, like chamber ware or bowls, and the Earthenware Printed Body is often mentioned in the recipe books; the mix of January 17th 1826 was: (LRW21a)

290 gallons	Blue Clay slip	65.31%
78	China Clay slip	17.56%
58	Flint slop	13.06%
18	Cornwall Stone slop	4.05%

The percentage amounts can only be approximate because the recipe does not record the pint weight, that is, the weight of solid material in a pint of slip.

51a

Spode's NEW FAYENCE

b

Spode's NEW FAYENCE

The New Fayence is an ivory earthenware which in appearance is difficult to distinguish from Imperial, but the marks are more commonly found especially on ware with printed patterns which have added colours. Often seen printed in brown, pink and on an outline print coloured underglaze, pattern or black as well as blue.

The numbers serve to distinguish between the differences of type face or scroll work. (LRW21b) [GG 3655] (50 has SPODE's in upper case letters; 51 has Spode's in script letters)

B. N.°

1822 The B numbering series was started about 1822 and was introduced to distinguish patterns which were decorated underglaze. It may be presumed that the main series of numbers were then regarded as the A Series although no prefix was used. The B. No. mark is usually found with marks 50 & 51, when the pattern number has been added by hand. This mark is uncommon. The highest number is B959. (LRW22).

In the Book of B numbers, numbers 48-61 are prefixed C instead of B. This was an error. There is a Book of C numbers which record wholly hand decorated designs.

63

About 1830. Only two Spode marks are known to incorporate the name of the pattern; like the naming of bodies this was a practice which occurred towards the end of the Spode period. Floral pattern, 63, usually found printed in blue, was introduced *c*1830, while Aesop's Fables, 64, dates from about the same time and is commonly found as a green print as well as in blue. One example is known printed in black. (LRW23).

64

"Marks with the name of the pattern in an elaborate cartouche became popular among nearly all manufacturers of printed wares during the Victorian Period. They reveal an awareness of the importance of pattern names as a means of sales promotion as well as of identification. Earlier, patterns were known by a number, if they had one, or nicknames developed on the Factory and in the trade". Whiter p226 (LRW24).

For a list of the fables illustrated see Drakard & Holdway *Spode Printed Wares* p. 166.

65

This BLUE-WARE is printed from the CALX of British COBALT produced from Sparnon Mine in the County of Cornwall. August 1816.

a

This BLUE-WARE is printed from the CALX of British COBALT. produced from Wheal Sparnon Mine in the County of Cornwall. August 1816.

In the field of promotion, Spode applied the principle to the use of English cobalt. An inscription printed on the undersides of some objects records Spode's support for the native cobalt ore mined in Cornwall. Examples have been seen on Blue Italian and India patterns.

A correction to the mark was made by cutting off the word 'Wheal' from the transfer print and moving 'Sparnon Mine' closer to the centre of the line: In Cornwall, the word Wheal *means* Mine.

"Wheal Sparnon was worked for copper prior to 1760 and later from 1808-1827 when chiefly productive of copper, tin and cobalt. Cobalt was first recorded about 1809-10, found in a cross-course (a vein that runs at right angles to the main copper and tin lodes). Cobalt was produced mainly from 1814-27: rich ore was often worth over £200 per ton". Wheal Sparnon was situated in Chinton Road, Redruth. (Reference: Hamilton-Jenkin, A.K. *Mines and Miners of Cornwall Part II, Around Redruth*, pp 19-23).

66

DOOREAHS LEADING OUT DOGS.

This is an example of the titles used with a quite separate maker's mark on the various scenes of the Indian Sporting pattern P904 – this number refers to the catalogue of prints in *Spode Printed Ware* by Drakard and Holdway. The use of these titles, an added expense, appears to have gradually lapsed. Their use is less likely on the later productions of Indian Sporting prints.

67

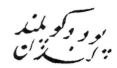

Mark on wares made for the Persian market, known on earthenware with mark 43, and on Felspar Porcelain with mark 42, on patterns recorded between 1827-31. Examples occur on Botanical pattern, 4565 in blue & gold, and 4833, green & gold.

The mark reads: Spode & Copeland, London.

Section II

COPELAND & GARRETT PERIOD 1833 to 1847

Impressed marks.

101   COPELAND
        & GARRETT

1833-47. This mark was used on all bodies throughout the period, though more often it is found on earthenwares and coloured bodies. Pattern number 5595 is of basalt body.

a   COPELAND &
      GARRETT
         8

Similar to Mark 101 except that the ampersand is on the upper line of type. [GG 1090]

Numbers are believed to be the workmans marks.

b

A third mark has the ampersand *between* the two names. This occurs on an encaustic tile: see illustration, page 25 where it is rather larger.

102

About 1833-1840. Rare mark of about 1833 found on earthenware, and on busts of MILTON and WELLINGTON made in felspar porcelain.

a

About 1833-1840. Similar to Mark 102 but with the numerals added. These numerals are probably the identification numbers of the clay makers, who could save time in impressing both marks of the factory and the workman, at one time. Compare Mark 4 of the later Spode period.

103

1833-1847. The new mark for the established earthenware body for prints, especially in colours other than blue.

a

An oval variation of this has been seen.

104

About 1840. A rare mark on earthenware. A formula for Common Body for December 10th 1838:
Measured wet by volume

Ball Clay Black ½	} 13 inches	24oz/pint
Blue ½		
China Clay	5,7/16	24oz/pint
Stanley Stone	3,1/16	31½oz/pint
Flint	4	31oz/pint

It may be that it was this Common Body which was marked New Fayence.

105

About 1839. The Blanche Body is recorded in September 1839 as follows: "If weighed dry, it is equal parts of Ball Clay, China Clay and Flint". This would yield a lightweight body: examples are numerous and show a white body with a clear glaze. John Cushion states that a crown on potters' marks occurs after 1840. The figure 40, in this instance however, is the workman's mark, not the date. The recipe book also calls this Chalk body.

106

About 1833-1842. A rare mark on white earthenware, it measures 14mm across. The formula for Royal Opal, if weighed dry, was:

Blue Clay	15 lbs i.e.	28.541%
China Clay	20 lbs	38.095
Flint	15 lbs	28.541
Cornish Stone	2½ lbs	4.762
Blue Calx	100 grains	

This record shows such small quantities

---

that it must have been a trial mixing, although larger mixings are recorded in another book of recipes (MSS 797/1).

This mark occurs on pieces of pattern 5135, decorated in the style usually associated with bone china, (c1833), also on pattern 6703 (c1842). Other examples seen on 5519 (c1835) and 6169.

107

About 1845. In 1845 the formula for Royal Alba Body is noted on February 7th. It gives wet measures by volume:

Blue Clay	8¼ inches at	24 oz/pint
China Clay	8¼ inches at	24 oz/pint
Flint	3³/₁₆ inches at	31½oz/pint
Cornish Stone	⅝ inches at	31½oz/pint

Examples are very scarce. One piece of white earthenware, of Portland shape, was among examples kept at the Spode factory as standards. The mark measures 22 mm across. The body is a high quality pearlware with a blue tinted glaze.

108

About 1845. Another very rare mark known on one piece of New Japan Stone, the formula for which is recorded by S. Garrett as:

Blue Clay	5 lbs	i.e.	32.258%
China Clay	5 lbs		32.258
Flint	2½ lbs		16.129
Vitrescent Stone	3 lbs		19.355

This, too, was a trial mixing, but production did extend over several years. See Mark 149. Another example occurs, on a white earthenware dish printed in green with Star Flower Sheet with narrow chequered bead. A large service of 5519 (recorded 1835) has this mark.

109

See mark 137.

110

A very rare mark with a crown inside the firm's name. Seen on a plate of pattern 6982 which also has the printed mark 143 usually seen on china.

Embossed Marks

111

Examples of embossed marks occur occasionally, especially on ornamental jugs and other items in coloured bodies made by the hollow ware pressing or slip casting method. The mark illustrated is on a jug, pattern number 5877, of Jackfield type appearance with blue enamel spots added. A toothbrush box in solid agate has a similar mark in white clay applied by sprigging it onto the darker clay (Fitzwilliam Museum). Also a cheese stand. See note on 227.

112 A similar mark with the name VINTAGE occurs on a set of parian jugs and jardinieres. [See illustration page 64].

Painted Marks

121

C & G
4952

The decorators were paid to apply the name SPODE onto some pieces in a service or set of ornaments, but with the longer title of the new proprietors this task was not practicable.

Marks were engraved within days of the taking over of the establishment on March 1st 1833. Until these were ready, the decorators used a temporary mark, examples of which have been seen on bone china patterns 4952, 4723, 4618 and 5052 painted in iron red.

Transfer Printed Marks

130

C & G

One example of this has been seen *printed* in green, on Portland Vase pattern. [GG 1088].

LATE SPODE

This meant 'until recently', and when the name of the proprietors changed was a means of keeping the goodwill of customers.

Marks incorporating

LATE SPODE

131

1833. Perhaps the earliest printed mark of the Copeland & Garrett period, swiftly executed on a Spode copper plate of Coral pattern.

132

1833-47. Printed on ivory earthenware, often already with the impressed mark 103, but also on ware with the impressed mark 4 made before March 1833. The mark was in use throughout the period, and occurs mostly in brown or green. It was engraved on the same copper plate as the pattern which is often an outline for later colouring.

133

1833-47. The earliest mark on C & G's Felspar Porcelain, often printed in green or brown. Minor differences may be noticed between individual examples. [GG 1093].

134

1833. This mark has been recorded as it appears on a piece of pattern 5127, printed in purple. Also seen on a dessert plate with the badge, nicely painted, of SERJEANT'S INN.

135

1833-47. The most common mark on all bodies at the early part of the period, often on wares impressed with the Spode marks 4 and 7. Printed in blue, black, green or brown, usually the colour in which the pattern is printed.

136

This mark is known from an engraving of 'Union Wreath, third', the earliest pattern number of which is 3839, c1825. The name of the new proprietors was engraved above Mark 49. An example has been seen on a service of pattern 4290. The formula remained the same as that used by Spode.

137

1833-38. Rarely found, but examples are known on patterns 4901, 4972 and 5564† which suggest that it was in use during the first five years of the partnership. Several objects have been seen with an impressed F: this, mark 109, was probably intended as an internal identification for a changed trial recipe. Note. Recipe for China Body F. July 1836.

† also seen on patterns 4780 (c1831) 5620 & 5644 (c1835).

360	Felspar	18.98%
700	China Clay	36.92
836	Bone	44.10
	Stain 27 drams Cobalt Calx	
	27 drams Calcined Manganese	

Best China Body May 20th 1847

394	Felspar	18.95%
749	China Clay	36.03
856	Bone	41.17
80	Cornish Stone	3.85
	Stain 2 oz Cobalt, 2 oz Calcined	
	Manganese	

The latest pattern recorded so far is number 5750 (c1837)

In 1836 A COPELAND & GARRETT recipe records:

Pearl Body called CROWN CHINA
600 lbs Bone

600	Cornish Clay
450	Cornish Stone
150	Blue Clay
6 oz	Zaffre Blue for stain

This was a white body.

Transfer Printed Marks

Marks which omit LATE SPODE

This series of marks may have started to appear in about 1838-9. Many of them incorporate a crown which John Cushion suggests became a popular feature after 1840.

141

About 1838-47. Not scarce but less common than Mark 142. The significance of the different crowns has not been discovered. Notice that the word AND is spelt out. Found on bone china and probably used on Felspar porcelain also. Example on pattern 5866.

a

Mark 141a occurs on pattern 3991, bone china or felspar. Both marks printed in blue-green, but also seen in dark pink on the bases of cups in pattern number 5783.

142

About 1838-47. The more usual form of this mark with the 'and' shown as an ampersand (&) and a third style of crown.

Although usually found on china, this illustration is printed from an engraved copper plate of the Field Sports pattern. Patented on 14 September 1846, Registered number 37254. This pattern included scenes after J F Herring, Senior and became the basis for The Hunt pattern. The Patent Mark is dealt with elsewhere.

143

About 1838-47. Usually printed underglaze in green or blue-green on china, but the mark has been seen in blue, pattern 5519, and brown, Arabesque pattern, both on the very white Royal Opal earthenware body and on crown earthenware. The design of the mark was probably influenced by the mark 41 used by Spode for felspar porcelain. This mark is engraved on copper plates of Field Sports, and occurs on green-printed Wellington pattern. It has been seen also printed in red with the AND GARRETT crossed out. [GG 1091]

Also seen in dark pink on pattern 5783, Louis Embossed shape teaware.

144

A compact mark with a crown inside the firm's name which is in sans-serif upper case letters with AND spelt out. It is rarely found and then only on white earthenware.

a

No example of this mark is available. It appears first in the Catalogue of an exhibition of Spode & Copeland wares at the Museum für Kunsthandwerk, Frankfurt-Main in February 1965, but is not included as being represented on any of the objects displayed. Origin doubtful. See note on page 87.

145

A rare mark found on earthenware. Examples are known on pattern 7611. Chatsworth, Old Nigel, and Lily patterns. Saxon Blue is recorded as a dark

'flow' blue, but two examples of this mark have been seen in light non-flowing blue – known in later years as Saxe Blue. Because the mark is engraved with the pattern (as for Old Nigel) it may have been applied even when the colour of the print was changed.

146

About 1845. The earliest report of this mark was on an earthenware shard excavated on a Hudson's Bay Company site in Canada. Some time was spent in trying to identify a pattern named ALBA, until Mark 107 was found when it was realised that this printed mark was probably used on the Royal Alba body. It is rare and engraved examples are found on copper plates of Antique Vase and Raphaelesque patterns.

147

About 1838-47. The successor to Mark 132 being the combination of impressed mark 103 with the crowned mark 142. Examples are engraved on copper plates of Antique Vase and Warwick Vase patterns.

148

About 1838-47. A common mark on earthenware of a white colour. Some examples have a + between the end of Garrett and start of Copeland, and some show minor variations in the detail of the crown.

Engraved examples appear on copper plates of the following patterns: Antoinette B606, Athenian, Aesop's

Fables, Lily, Wellington, Rad Sprigs, Pagoda, Macaw, Filigree, B700 & B772. It often occurs on ware with the impressed mark 105.

Two pieces of a dessert set of sage green type body, with a printed and painted pattern of birds, B591 & each marked with Mark 101a; one has printed Mark 147, the other Mark 148.

The printed mark cannot be an infallible guide to the body material.

149

About 1835-1845. An uncommon mark but one usually included in most books on marks. Applied on white earthenware, this print is from the engraving of Oak Wreath with rope bead pattern, first used for a dinner and dessert service for the Prince Regent† (see Whiter pl.158). See mark 108. [GG 1094].

A trial recipe is recorded:

5lb Blue Clay
5 China Clay
2½ Flint
3 Vitrescent Stone

† obviously the Prince's service was produced between 1811 and 1820.

150

About 1836. Although thought to be scarce, it has appeared on several shards excavated on three Hudson's Bay sites in North America. viz. at Fort Vancouver in Oregon on Geranium, Chatsworth & Rad Sprigs; at Fort Nez Percé on Broseley; at Lower Fort Garry near Winnipeg, on Beverley or Grecian Scroll pattern.

151

1846. Rare, seen on two pieces only; a New Shape Broth Bowl in pattern 7027 with crest and monogram in gold, border design B773 in flow blue traced in gold, the mark printed in blue; and the mark printed in green, bearing pattern no. 7441 in red, on a plate in

flow blue with pink and green, and white enamelling. The only dated tableware mark known to have been used during the partnership.

152

Unknown mark, which, like mark 144a is shown in the catalogue for an Exhibition in Germany in 1965. No other mark for Felspar Porcelain is known without the LATE SPODE reference. (This seems to be a tracing of part of a version of Mark 133).

153

Seen on a rectangular slab, possibly intended for a fireplace, with a gold printed decoration. The mark is 65mm wide and well printed in brown. Another example is recorded on a set of three slabs mounted as panels in a large wooden chest.

Printed Marks

Marks incorporating pattern names, &c.

161

About 1834-47. This mark occurs only on pieces decorated with the Byron Views pattern, each scene being named on the ribbon. In the example illustrated, The Tiber occurs on the covered vegetable dish. This pattern is on earthenware and

usually printed in green, blue or brown, but it was also printed in purple or pink. [GG 1092].

The appearance of The Tiber mark in a booklet *Copeland's (Late Spode) China* published by the firm in 1902 probably suggested the name Tiber as referring to the well known blue print by Spode which should properly be called 'Rome'. (See Whiter Fig.69, pp.168/9) (See *Ceramic View of Byron Country* by Robert Copeland, in *Country Life*, November 4, 1976, pp1296-7.) The engravings were destroyed* in 1868. A sauce ladle, with the same 'THE SIMPLON', has the mis-spelling GARRATT.
* 'Destroyed'. In a Print Record Book of c1865 et seq. the note "Engravings destroyed" occurs on several pages. Copper plates were expensive, so when a pattern was discontinued, engravings were re-used by 'knocking up' the pattern to level the surface on the reverse which was planished and on which a new pattern was engraved.

162

1833-47. Upon the change of ownership, mark 64 continued to be used except that the name SPODE was erased from the ribbon at the left. (This variety has been given the new number 162).

163

About 1842. An ornamental mark in the grand manner after the style of some armorial devices of European royalties. Used on earthenware for Seasons pattern in either blue, brown or green. Often the name of the scene is included in the ribbon. The term 'china glaze' must refer to an especially fine glaze which imparts the appearance of bone china.

This mark has also been noted by Godden printed in gold on bone china [GG 1095].

164

CONTINENTAL VIEWS
COPELAND AND GARRETT

1844. The addition of the name of the pattern to a standard mark seems to have commenced in about 1844-5 with this pattern and its similar one Louis Quatorze. The latter was Patented on December 2, 1844 and uses the identical border to Continental Views which was Patented on October 21, 1845. Statice pattern, patented October 14, 1844, is also named with Mark 164, which is the same as Mark 143 but more open, has a modified crown, and carries the pattern name.

165

NARCISSUS
BY GIBSON R.A.
Modelled by E.B. STEPHENS
and executed in STATUARY PORCELAIN
BY COPELAND & GARRETT
FOR THE
ART UNION OF LONDON.
1846.

1846. The special mark printed on the inside of the base of the first object of Statuary Porcelain, or Parian, to be commissioned by the Art Union of London. It became the practice to impress the marks into the clay on later productions, with the name of the subject often moulded into the cast base.

166

About 1838-47. The mark on wares destined for the Persian market, amounts of which seem to have been substantial. Many examples of bone china plates, richly ornamented with groundlaid colours, painted subjects and elaborately gilded, were available in Iran markets until 1939 and some have been collected since. The inscription reads COPELAND & GARRETT STOKE-ON-TRENT.

167

B. 773
S.

1833-47. The S mark appears on some earthenware patterns although the reason is not known. The S is engraved on several copper plates including those of patterns B773, Macaw, Louis Quatorze, Lily and Garland. See note on Mark 61 for the B number.

168

Executed by
Copeland & Garrett
at their Works
STOKE-UPON-TRENT.

1833-47. This large mark, recorded in an Engravings Record Book may have been intended for a large slab, possibly one supplied as a special commission. [It is numbered 1892 in the record book]. The date of engraving is not known.

169

MANUFACTURED
GARRETT'S
PATENT
MORTICE
Tiles
1846.
BY COPELAND & GARRETT

1846. Spencer Thomas Garrett, son of Thomas Garrett, of Cliff Bank Lodge, Stoke-upon-Trent, was granted Letters Patent, number 11,249, for his invention of "Certain Improvements in Cements, Bricks, Tiles, Quarries, Slabs, and artificial stones'. This patent, whilst including improvements to cements, is more particularly concerned with Garrett's Patent Mortice Tiles. The patent was enrolled on 16th December 1846 and granted on 22nd June 1847. It consisted of moulding bricks or tiles 'with fillets and grooves on certain of the surfaces thereof, and corresponding in dimensions the one with the other, so that when a number of such bricks, tiles, etc. are laid in single layers in several layers one above another, or in rows . . . the whole shall fit . . . into one another and any structure composed thereof be thereby greatly increased in compactness and stability."

No example of this form of tile has been noted yet. The engraving is number 1589 in the Engraving Book.

One of the Engraving Record Books contains prints of large marks to be applied under-glaze on earthenware 'scale plates' and 'butter stands' for use in shops purveying food. Many of these include the name of the manufacturer of the plate as well as that of the scales.

170

Butter Stand made for Juggins. See Mark 391 for similar mark.

171

H.R. CLARKE
MANUFACTURED
BY
COPELAND & GARRETT
SCALE PLATE

H.R. Clarke Scale Plate. Manufactured by Copeland & Garrett. Engraving number 1156.

The base of the covered vegetable dish in Byron Views pattern which carries Mark 161 with a view of 'The Tiber'.

Note. The sizes of some marks are larger than shown in this collection, especially numbers 168 to 173.

Robert Sangster. Butter Stands.
Engraving number 85.

F. Roe, Camberwell, London. No.   . By
Her Majesty's Letters Patent. Engraving
number 432.

*The official Alphabetical Index of Patentees
of Inventions, 1854, p. 487, indicates that
Freeman Roe held patents nos. 7398 of 7 July
1837 (water closets) and 10634 of 22 April 1845
(manufacture of pipes for conveying water and
other fluids). The business first appeared in
London directories in 1835 at 6 Brett's Buildings,
Camberwell. Other addresses include 2 Windmill
Street, Camberwell Road, 1838, 1840; 49
Strand, 1840; 11 Agar Street and 69a Strand,
1841, 1842; 70 Strand, 1844; 69a and 70
Strand, 1847. By 1852 the firm was listed as Roe
& Hanson, hydraulic and gas engineers, 70
Strand and Sumner Street, Southwark.*

*Roe's advertisement in Robson's Directory,
1839, describes him as 'plumber, &c, Camberwell
and No 69 Strand, patentee self-supplying water-
closet basin'.*

*It was probably the basin that was made by
Copeland and Garrett. It was said by my father,
Gresham Copeland, that the firm had made wash
basins – with holes for taps and waste plug – in
the years gone by.*

*Handled jardinière, or garden pot, in parian,
copied from a classical urn and offered by
Copeland and Garrett in 1846. The 'pad' mark
is a variation of Mark 111.*

*Handled jug, or pitcher, with similar studies of
young wine growers. Three sizes are known, one
(C & G) has a hinged parian lid, the others have
pewter lids. Mark 227.*

*Circular Stilton cheese stand in solid agate
marbled clay. Mark 111.*

*Trio in pattern 4952, Octagon shape, marked in
red with mark 121. Probably few examples were
so marked before engravings were prepared of
marks with the full names of the partners.*

*Sauce tureen stand of Spode's Peacock pattern on
high quality white earthenware, printed and
painted underglaze. Mark 149 is not commonly
seen. The impressed crown, Mark 5b, is very
rare, and its presence here suggests that it may be
a maker's mark rather than a factory mark. See
also pages 51 and 88 The pattern number, 625,
also shows a pitfall for collectors. This is not
Spode's 625 being made later, but B625, recorded
in 1840. Several cases are known where the prefix
letter has been omitted. See page 119.*

Section III

COPELAND PERIOD 1847 to 1969

Impressed marks.

201

1847-*c*1855. Seen on white earthenware, often with blue-tinted glaze as a result of the use of flow powder in connection with flowing blue or grey prints. Oriental pattern 8091 dates from 1847, Fern plain print dates from about 1852, Ruins, *c*1848.

This mark probably derives originally from Mark 5a and, more directly, from Mark 107 – Alba. The latest reference in the Fixing Book to the use of Alba is in December 1847, when some old stock was being used, perhaps. Early Copeland earthenwares have been found in a latrine at Upper Fort Garry, Manitoba, Canada.

202

COPELAND

1847-*c*1958. This mark is commonly seen especially on tiles but also on earthenware and statuary porcelain (parian). The size of mark varies, and some are in sans serif type.

It was in use up to the 1950s on meat dishes of New Stone, and was used on stonewares with sprigged ornaments: A large size (35mm) was used on plaques & slabs of saggar marl, and on tiles, and on majolica. [GG 1069]

Statuary porcelain, or parian.

The earliest recipe for statuary porcelain which has been found in Copeland recipe books is dated 1860. It consists of a glassy frit which is then added to the body:

Frit.
100lbs	Lynn Sand
60	Muntz's Felspar
20	Pearl Ashes

Body
94½lbs	Felspar, calc^d Glost
94½	Felspar, ground
189	China Clay
31½	Glass
63	Frit, as above.

Statuary Body for stands & large figures 1863.
112½lbs	Felspar, calcined
112½	Felspar, raw ground
235½	China Clay
37½	Glass
75	Frit, as above
77	Cornish Stone
77	Ball clay
10½	Flint

This is instead of the slip formerly mixed Jany 15 1864.

Ball clay and flint have been added probably to increase the 'green strength', ie the unfired clay article, while Cornish Stone was added to compensate for the otherwise lower fluxing materials.

a

An example of this mark occurs on a soup tureen and stand in 'Fern' pattern, which also exhibits a rarely seen printed mark for A.Kniajevsky of Moscow *c*1856. (see 201 above). See also Mark 304.

203

About 1890. The 'Spode Imperial' is an ivory-coloured earthenware: an early recipe states

6000lb	China Clay	i.e.	33.18%
6000	Vitrescent Stone		33.18
2080	Blue Clay		11.52
4000	Dried Flint		22.12

This recipe is the same as that dated Sept 1826 and quoted beside Mark 49. See also Mark 263. The similar printed mark was Registered 11 April 1890. Seen on a South African War Commemorative three handled loving cup.

204

About 1860-*c*1895. The B body was a cream coloured earthenware most often seen as dessert ware. No examples have been noticed to date from after 1891 – when the word ENGLAND might have been added to the printed mark – but its introduction is uncertain. It may have started *c*1860-70. Despite the above a recipe, dated 1894, records:

18¾	Ball Clay	78.94%
3⅝	Flint	15.26
1⅜	Stone	5.80
nil	China Clay	

Called 'Ivory Body', it was warmly applauded by Jewitt in his *Ceramic Art of Great Britain*.

B body, sometimes called Ivory
A recipe recorded *c*1881 by R P Copeland.

14 inches White Ball clay
		@ 24oz/pint
5	China Ball	25½
4	Flint	31
1	Stone	31

Ivory Body
Frit. Equal parts of Mow Cop sand and China biscuit pitchers ground together.
Body 1 inch of the above frit in the slip
@ 28oz/pint
4 inch Newton Abbott Ball slip
@ 24oz/pint

205

About 1888-1900. An example of the mark with the letter I occurs on a piece dated 1888, and another on a piece of Mandarin pattern dated 1896.

206

About 1859-1900. Another mark distinguishing a variation of the body recipe. Very rare. An example of Christs' Hospital No. 9 shows the body to be a heavy, white, semi-vitreous earthenware. Also a cup & saucer in 2/5660 (*c*1906) Pheasant pattern for Waring & Gillow. About 1859 a recipe for Y body is recorded in the slop (ie liquid) form:

11¹/₁₆ inches	Blue clay slip	24oz/pint
8⅛	China clay	26oz/pint
2³/₁₆	Flint	31oz/pint
3	Stone	31oz/pint

Stain same as Crown

Another is recorded 21 August 1894:

10½ inches	Ball slip	
9	China Clay	
3¾	Flint	
2½	Stone	

and Crown stain

About 1860-1969. The most frequently seen impressed mark of the Copeland period. The earliest example is known on a spoon warmer patented by Copeland in January 1869. Another early plate is date marked July 1882. It remained in use on 'Crown' body White earthenware until 1969. The mark is a straight development of Mark 201.

In May 1853 this recipe was recorded:
Common Body C. Crown

1694lbs	Blue Clay	30.76%
630	Stone	11.44
1920	China Clay	34.86
1260	Flint	22.88
3lbs 6oz	B Oxide	0.05

A recipe of about 1859 for Crown or Best earthenware:

$12\frac{5}{8}$ inches	Ball slip	24oz/pint
$7\frac{3}{4}$	China	26
$2\frac{3}{4}$	Flint	31
$1\frac{3}{8}$	Stone	31

11lbs stain ground & divided for 6 mixings of above.
Stain is
10lbs Black Oxide (of Cobalt)
11 Stone, flint or China clay.
Calcine the above in the glost oven.

The blending tub of the measurements
9 ft $2\frac{1}{8}$ inches long

4	9	wide
2	$3\frac{1}{2}$	deep

Two other recipes are of interest:
White Dip

80 lbs	Ball Clay
160	China Clay
80	Flint
40	Cornwall Stone
Stain	$3\frac{3}{4}$ oz Cobalt Blue well ground

Pearl White Glaze c1869.

110 lbs	Crown fritt
300	Cornish Stone
60	Flint
70	Glass
390	White Lead

In manuscript 'fixing' books which record the cost of decoration the type of body is always recorded: a frequent entry is WG, which may refer to the earthenware above, ie White Glaze.

208

Copeland's White body was used for hotel ware and may have been a modified Crown body. An example has been seen on a 'roll-edge' plate of Heron pattern made for the Canadian Pacific Steamship Co.

209

About 1857. The body looks like Crown earthenware but has a grey-tinted glaze. An example of the Richmond Views pattern (c1857) has this mark, and an example of pattern number D3145 of about 1863 is printed 'JUDGES LODGINGS' (York).

a

COPELAND COLLEGE IRONSTONE

This mark is known only from a pitcher mould in the Spode Collection which would have been used for making the impress marker. It may be assumed that catering ware for College and Hospital use might have this mark on a thickened ware of special formula.

These two marks with Mark 222 are the only references so far known to the use of the term Ironstone by Copeland on impressed marks.

210 Copeland Late Spode

Recorded by Hayden as being impressed, but so uncommon as not to have been seen by the compiler of this list.

211

1890-c1935. Ø This was a trade-mark registered on 11 April 1890 and is known on an oval meat dish of 1895. It remained in use for many years on the ivory earthenware body, one plate of which is

dated April 1929 $(\frac{A}{29})$ and decorated with Chinese Sports or Pastimes pattern, and others made in 1934.

Ø The Patent office kept a separate Register of Trademarks.

212

1910-11. A rare version of the Copeland mark, and found impressed on the stoneware decanters made for Usher's Whisky Distillers to commemorate the Coronation of King George V in 1911, and similar sprigged stonewares.

213

About 1930-1969. Impressed on Spode ivory body, and used subsequently to Mark 211 on earthenware.

214

About 1897. A variation seen on a piece of earthenware dated $\frac{F}{97}$ February 1897 and decorated with pattern number 2/4177. An example of Pheasant pattern, 2/5660, made for Waring & Gillow, is impressed $\frac{J}{08}$

a

COPELAND SPODE

About 1921. An example occurs on a bone china plate with the badge of the Royal Yacht Squadron, dated 1923: it has been seen also on pattern R5892 (Registered no. 657046 of 2 August 1916) date stamped $\frac{M}{22}$, and a Strawberry Embossed plate, white china is date stamped $\frac{N}{21}$.

215

About 1860. Several examples of this impression of the Copeland family crest have been seen usually on earthenware. Its significance is unknown, but it may have been used by one of the family on pieces which they had made, as it seems to have been produced by impressing a marker made from a ring into the clay. The impression is the same as on the ring, ie. it is facing the wrong way.

216

About 1870. The impressed bee mark may coincide with the use of a bee in printed marks which include the name of the pattern eg. Roma. It has been seen on earthenware very rarely.

217

a

About 1935-52. Used on the Spode Imperial ivory-coloured earthenware and seen on plates decorated with the hunting scenes after Lionel Edwards. It is also seen on Royal Jasmine glazed patterns of the 1930's, some of which were designed by Pinder Davis.

218

About 1879. Incised mark on the back of hand-made tiles. It is a monogram of W.T. Copeland & Sons. A series of tiles of Shakespearean characters have this mark, dated $\frac{N}{79}$.

219

COPELAND
FRESCO

About 1870-80. Impressed into the back of hand-made tiles, so far seen only on an ivory earthenware tile of a skater dated $\frac{O}{70}$.

220

About 1903. Impressed on a plate of very white earthenware with the appearance of fine bone china.

221

The signature of William Taylor Copeland has been seen scratched or moulded on several busts of statuary porcelain. There seems to be no obvious explanation for its occurence.

While laying out these pages I received a telephone call from a dealer who was enquiring about a portrait bust of Alexandra, sculpted by Mary Thorneycroft. The bust is of $1/16$th inch bronze with a white substance inside: it measures about $14\frac{1}{2}$ inches in height over the Socle, about the same as the parian examples. The detail is very well defined, and the usual inscription THE ART UNION OF LONDON appears on the back with this unusual mark.

It may be that the bronze was cast in a mould taken off a parian example. A figure of Marguerite cast in bronze has also been reported.

It is suggested that these are modern forgeries, especially as the filling of the bust seemed to be of an epoxy-resin.

222

About 1885-1932. This mark has been seen on a plate of white vitreous earthenware, with a badge of a naval emblem printed on the rim; and also on a plate with arms of the Corporation of the City of London, pattern 2/108, & date stamped $\frac{S}{95}$. A plate marking the Golden Jubilee of Queen Victoria is dated $\frac{S}{86}$.

223

1879. Impressed on the base of a toilet ewer with bamboo embossment at neck and base; it also has a raised pad or patch mark for Patent no. 301164, dated 9 June 1876.

227

About 1848. This type of pad or patch mark may be found on cast or pressed hollow-ware. The example occurs on a small parian jug embossed with convolvulus. A registration mark is also embossed but is unreadable: it may relate to Patent number 55174 registered Nov. 4 1848.

All marks seen so far have numbers which correspond to the trade sizes, e.g. 9, 18, 24, 30.

231　　　Copeland

About 1847. Infrequently seen on its own, the mark was probably introduced in 1847 and is known on earthenware. Sizes vary.

232　　　**Copeland Late Spode.**

a　　　Copeland Late Spode

1847-90. A common mark on earthenwares and also on stone china from about 1847-1890. The variation, 232a, has been seen on Garland pattern and Green Camilla.

233　　　COPELAND

Seen rarely on earthenware, in blue, on a ginger-jar printed Cracked Ice & Prunus with gilding. Also seen printed in gold on a plate with the arms of Monteath: of bone china it has ^P_F impressed also. Also on a lavender blue body water bottle with stopper, pattern 8186, printed green.

234　　　**COPELAND'S**

1847. Another mark seldom seen. On an earthenware model of a house, Shakespeare's Birthplace, with Registered Mark for 25 September 1847.

a

1847-8. Printed inside the base of early examples of Copeland's parian. A figure of Sabrina and two figurines probably made from Derby moulds are among the examples seen. Subsequently nearly every piece of Copeland's parian was marked with the impressed mark 202.

234b

Mark on one side of a circular slab made as the hygienic pan for a set of scales for use in a butcher's or fishmonger's shop. A date of 1850-60 is suggested because two other marks spelt COPELAND's are of this period. The slab, although pressed in clay, carries no impressed date mark.

235

About 1850-90. A commonly seen mark on bone china, usually printed in green or dark blue which sometimes shows a tendency to flow. [GG 1073]. The mark also occurs without COPELAND. Mark 235a

236

1847-56. Found on bone china and so far very rare. The mark with dates of use were published in the Copeland's China book of 1902. [GG 1071].

237

About 1847-90. Usually found on bone china, but also seen on white earthenware. It is usually printed in green on the biscuit, thus ensuring an indelible identification: green is a 'still' colour and does not flow in the glost firing. [GG 1072]

238

About 1851. Only one example of this mark is known to the compiler. It is on a bone china dinner plate painted with a scene 'Tower of Comares'. Probably painted by Daniel Lucas Junior and thought to have been exhibited at the 1851 Crystal Palace Exhibition in Hyde Park. Mark 237 has been adapted and carefully gilded over, with the belt in enamel blue edged with gilded lines.

239　　　COPELAND

This rare mark may be the start of the well known series of marks on bone china which became the standard until 1970. It seems that the name of the company, printed in sans serif upper case letters, was taken from mark 235.

　　No special significance can be seen in the choice of use of one mark in preference to another. Reference to 'Late Spode' occurs rarely between 1847-c1890: ie. most marks during the period name COPELAND alone.

240　　　COPELAND'S CHINA

About 1862-91. More common than Mark 239. The apostrophe shows the possessive use. The firm was known in the Potteries and the trade as 'Copelands'.

a

Similar to 240 but with serif upper case letters. Very uncommon.

241　　　COPELAND'S CHINA ENGLAND

1891-1920. Printed in green on bone china, underglaze. Also seen in a blue-green colour and in gold. The 'ENGLAND' was added to comply with the American McKinley Tariff Act of 1890 which required the country of origin to be stated on all imports into the United States.

242　　　SPODE COPELAND'S CHINA ENGLAND

About 1904-54. Following the readoption of the 'grid iron' or pseudo-Chinese seal mark for earthenware in about 1890, the value of the Spode connection was recognised and the name added to the mark on bone china. This mark, 242, remained standard for about fifty years. See Mark 274. Usually printed in green it has also been seen in gold. [GG 1077 refers].

243

COPELAND
LATE SPODE
160 New Bond Street
LONDON.

About 1858. This rare mark occurs on a white earthenware plate depicting a portrait of Albert Smith who offered entertainments in 'The Egyptian Hall', Piccadilly, London from 1852-58.

In about 1847 at the termination of the Copeland and Garrett partnership, the Portugal Street and Lincoln's Inn premises were vacated and a showroom and shop at 160 New Bond Street taken. A further move was made in 1881 to 12 Charterhouse Street.

a

COPELAND
LATE SPODE

b

COPELAND
LATE SPODE

The mark 243 is known without the address and may have been the source of the mark 243b which is illustrated in Jewitt, Chaffers and Copelands China 1902 but which has not been seen on an object.

244

W . T . COPELAND & SONS
160 NEW BOND St
LONDON
• • •
MAKERS

1868. A record of this mark is in the Engraving Book and dated 3 Nov 1868.

245

MANUFACTURED BY
W. T. COPELAND & SONS
– LONDON –
MANUFACTORY STOKE-UPON-TRENT

1890. An engraved copper plate giving instructions on the use of Queen Charlotte's Bed Bath has this mark. An

example of the utensil is in the Spode Museum Collection date stamped $\frac{J}{90}$, and with the inscription.

It is of ivory coloured earthenware, and was for use at Queen Charlotte's Hospital, London, and not for the personal use of Her late Majesty!

246

W. T. COPELAND & SONS.
STOKE-UPON-TRENT.

1869. Recorded in the Print Record Book, dated 25 June 1869.

247

1869-70. An example of the application of the name Copeland to a patent registration mark. Recorded in the Print Record Book in 1869 & 1870.

248

1868. Recorded in the Print Record Book as "Engd, Sep 24th/68 for Services". It is presumed that the mark was for use on heavy duty vitreous earthenware for hotel and shipping use.

249

1871. Another mark known only from the Print Record Book, dated 27 April 1871. At present there is no indication of its use.

250

1873. A printed form of Mark 209. This is recorded as Engraved in May 1873.

251

IRONSTONE

1883. Recorded in the Engraving Badge Book 4 April 1883.

a

IRONSTONE

Recorded in the Engraving Book.

COPELAND
PATENT JASPER

Seen on a white earthenware bowl, diameter 7.2cm, printed in blue, underglaze, with a simulation of marble veining.

252

1883. This earliest of the Copeland China seal marks is recorded as being engraved April 5, 1883. The omission of the Copeland name should not confuse collectors.

a

About 1883. More common than mark 252, and probably introduced shortly after it. [GG 1074].

253

SPODE
COPELAND
ENGLAND

1891-*c*1910. Seen often on bone china. printed in green or blue-green. See 412.

The span of years during which it was used has not yet been established.

See Appendix IV for notes on the McKinley Tariff Act and the addition of ENGLAND to trade marks.

254

SPODE
MANUFACTURERS STOKE ON TRENT
COPELAND
ENGLAND

About 1900-10. Printed in green, it has the addition of the words 'Manufacturers Stoke-on-Trent'. An example occurs on a Stone China plate of Pattern 1/3822 which is date stamped August 1906. (New Bridge pattern).

It is interesting that the name of the town is -on-, not -upon-, Trent, which has been used previously. Stoke-upon-Trent is the name of the town in the centre of which the Spode Works are situated. In 1910 the six towns of the Potteries, Tunstall, Burslem, Hanley, Stoke-upon-Trent, Fenton and Longton were federated to become a city, which took the name of Stoke-on-Trent. The mark is not seen often.

About 1880-90. This mark occurs on bone china and examples appear to have been applied by a rubber stamp in green onto the biscuit. Often the image is blurred and belies the high quality of the ware and its decoration. Examples date-stamped 1880, 1884, & 1888 have been reported.

a

1894. Engraved Jan 26, 1894. No example of the mark has been seen yet.

256

About 1890. The earliest form of the re-introduced seal mark, first used by Spode on Stone China (see marks 47 and 48). It was probably adopted to re-establish the Spode connection and occurs on earthenwares from 1890 onwards with variations. The early form has Copeland on a curve above the word 'Late'.

a

Mark 256a omits 'late' and COPELAND is in a straight line. Forerunner of mark 259.

b

1934 As 256 but with MADE IN ENGLAND seen on plate of 2/7725 dated August 1934.

257

ENGLAND

1891. As mark 256 but with 'England' added on a curve as a result of the McKinley Tariff Act. (See note on Mark 241).

This group of marks, 256-260, are known as 'grid irons'.

a

About 1906. Mark 257a is similar to Mark 257, except that all words are in straight, not curved lines and LATE is in capitals. Seen on Pheasant pattern, number 2/5660.

b

About 1907. Printed on earthenware, on pattern 2/5813, Maple Birds, date-stamped $\frac{M}{07}$. (See mark 415).

258

About 1920-60. Printed in green underglaze on Stone China. All stone china patterns were decorated on-glaze,† but the mark was applied on the biscuit before glazing. In later years the mark was applied by rubber stamp or by the Rejafix machine.
†Some were refired at glost temperature, so blue & black prints are usually in-glaze. [GG 1080].

259

About 1920-1957. Printed from the same engraving as the pattern and so it is usually in the same colour. In 1958 the method of date stamping earthenware with an impressed mark in the clay was discontinued because of the handicap to the makers who no longer had the benefit of mouldrunners to do the task. From

1958, a date letter was inserted in the top left corner of the seal:
A 1958   B 1959   C 1960   D 1961
E 1962   F 1963
[GG 1079].

a

1958-63

b

1933-69. Found on examples of Gainsborough, Romney & Raeburn patterns introduced in 1933. Also on Sorrento (Originally called Rome) pattern re-introduced about 1933.

260

X
COPELAND
SPODE
ENGLAND
Fine Stone

1960-69. In 1960 a new formula for Stone China was introduced after prolonged trials in the attempt to overcome the serious problems being experienced with the old body. The new body contained a high proportion of alumina which increased its strength, uniformity of colour and heat resistance. X indicated the body formula under extended trial, and when approved, was removed from the mark. The new body was renamed Fine Stone. [GG 1087].

From 1964 the date letter was placed in the top left corner (the example has B) and these letters represent:
A 1964   B 1965   C 1966   D 1967
E 1968   F 1969

From 1964 on earthenware, and 1970 on bone china and Fine Stone the date letters were joined with the craftsman number eg M15, the number being the identification for the craftsman. The dates follow the Fine Stone series:
G 1970   H 1971   J 1972   K 1973
L 1974   M 1975. See Marks 501 & following.

For dates of later years, see Marks 503, 506, 508. See also page 93.

261

Copelands
Jewelled Porcelain

About 1851-90. This mark appears occasionally on the very finely jewelled objects in bone china. It is printed in gold. Many of these richly enamelled wares are signed by the ornamenter. One such vase is signed and dated William Ball 1879. An account of the 1862 Exhibition states that Copeland's introduced Jewelled Porcelain at the 1851 Exhibition, and items are in that catalogue [GG 1078].

262

About 1882-94. Found on earthenwares especially those exported to the United States of America, from where several examples have been reported.

Printed in the colour of the pattern, dated pieces of 1883 and 1892 suggest the period during which the mark was in use.

263

Spode
Imp!
RᴰNº90067

1890. Ø Unexpectedly this mark includes no reference to Copelands yet was Registered. The Engraving is dated 11/4/90 and an item of ivory coloured earthenware is date stamped.

a

Spode
Imp!

Mark 263a omits the Trade Mark Registration number, which was registered on 11th April 1890. Ø

264

Copeland
Stone China

Recorded in Jewitt, Chaffers, &c, but never seen by the compiler. Examples of Stone China made by W.T. Copeland have been marked with Marks 252a – 254 and 232.

Ø The marks were recorded in the Register of Trade Marks and not in the Register of Designs. [Public Record Office Ref BT82].

265

About 1887-94. Frank's Boat Mark, sometimes seen with the words TRADE MARK beneath. The design seems to be based on pattern number 2/2927 designed by Frank Abraham (1858-c1933), son of Robert Abraham, Art Director. Francis Xavier Abraham also designed the Buttercup pattern. The pattern dates from 1887. Commonly found on earthenwares and stonewares of various colours. [GG 1076].

266

1894-c1910. The same as Mark 265 with the addition of the registered number 180288 & ENGLAND which was registered on 11 Sept 1894 and is for this trade mark and not for the pattern or design of object on which it occurs. Note the reference to 'Late Spode' and the reproduction of the simple entwined Cs of Mark 236.

a

About 1900-14. Several eggcup bases with this mark were excavated beneath the main offices in February 1984. Of white earthenware the mark was printed in brown, also seen in blue on Tower pattern, 1914.

267

About 1894-c1940. Without ENGLAND (Mark 267a) this mark has been seen on a piece of pattern D3335, but this pattern was introduced in 1863. Mark 267 probably dates from about 1894. Rustic pattern on Crown earthenware and date stamped 02 is the earliest example seen with ENGLAND up to the present.

a

About 1890-94. Without ENGLAND.

b

W.T.COPELAND
& SONS
STOKE·ON·TRENT
LEADLESS GLAZE

With LEADLESS GLAZE an example occurs on an object date stamped 1956.

c

As 267 with MANUFACTURERS over the top line.

A section of print pulled from the copper plate for pattern 2/2927 from which the 'Frank's Boat' marks are derived.

268

1892. This mark, the most elaborate of the Copeland period, is known only from the Engraving Book records where it is dated 19 Dec 1892. The internal 'gridiron' was used subsequently in association with pattern names. Notice that the positions of COPELAND and SPODE are reversed and the style of 'seal' is different from Mark 256 et seq. See Mark 411. An engraving of King's Sheet pattern, Registered No. 204193 (14 Dec 1892) is known also.

269

a

About 1874. Several examples are known. One on a five-necked tulip vase, or quintel, decorated in the Aesthetic style and of white china. Another vase 9in. x 6in. tall in the form of two pillars with the water container between, made of grey porcelain or stoneware (Reported to compiler). Other marks occur on an extremely rare bone china teapot and sugar bowl in the Japonesque style (15mm), and on a Reed Sparrow's Nest vase, pattern O325, dated 1874, in bone china.

270

Similar to Mark 166, an example occurs on a piece of Crown body with Indian Tree pattern printed in flow blue and coloured. This piece is date stamped Mark 207 and pattern number D4092.

The inscription written in Persian script reads COPELAND
LONDON

271

About 1901-c1910. Mark 271 appears on a plate with the arms of the Worshipful Company of Clothworkers: a service of this pattern was supplied in August 1887, but it is not known if the use of the mark dates as early as that. Mark 271a occurs on a plate date stamped with the badge of Government House, Australia. Mark 271b reproduced from an engraved copper plate, occurs on the Bicentenary Bowl made in 1933 to mark the 200th anniversary of the birth of Josiah Spode I. Six bowls were made for presentation.

a

b

1933. Alderman Copeland was appointed 'China and Glass Manufacturer to His Royal Highness The Prince of Wales' on 6 August 1866. The arms used in Mark 271 are those of the Sovereign.

No warrant has yet been found appointing Copeland supplier to the Queen. The Royal Warrant was granted by HM King Edward VII in 1901 and it is most likely that the mark 271 was used on bone china for specially commissioned services.

272

About 1935. No example of this mark is known. This print is from an engraved copper plate.

Royal Warrant appointing W T Copeland (known as Alderman) China and Glass Manufacturer to the Prince of Wales, August 1866. Copelands did not manufacture glass but acted as agents and distributors at that time.

Dessert plate, Festoon embossed, 1863, from the service commissioned by the Prince of Wales, with panels of roses and oranges, painted by C F Hürten.

274

SPODE
COPELAND CHINA
ENGLAND

1954-6. In 1954 it was decided to omit the 's after the name COPELAND. The mark was now applied with a rubber stamp or by the use of the Rejafix machine, (Compare Mark 242), which is an off-set printing device.

275

SPODE
BONE CHINA
ENGLAND

1956-60. The importance attached to the name BONE CHINA in the American market caused the mark to substitute BONE for COPELAND. This mark was in green, applied underglaze as before. [GG 1081].

276

Spode
BONE CHINA
ENGLAND

1960-70. In 1960, the old coal-fired bottle ovens were fired for the last time. Bone china was fired in the new Gibbons open-flame gas-fired tunnel kiln of advanced design. This kiln was called 'Jubilee' to mark the fifty years celebration of the City status of Stoke-on-Trent. A new mark with the SPODE in gothic-style type distinguished ware fired in this tunnel: it was applied in green. The style of Spode was derived from Mark 41, and had been used as a logotype on letter paper and advertisements for many years. [GG 1086].

a

Spode
BONE CHINA
ENGLAND

1965-74. A bolder version of 276, with serif capitals. Reserved for commemorative items, it often occurs in gold as part of the special descriptive backstamp. It was continued for a few years after 1970. Note the adoption of the new design of the Spode logotype, by John Sutherland-Hawes.

277

Spode
Impl.
ENGLAND

About 1913. Another version of mark 263 &c. with addition of the name ENGLAND. It is found printed in brown on items in the range of ornamental pieces. [GG 1084].

a

Spode's Impl.
COPELAND
ENGLAND
R.No667194

1919. Yet another mark. Seen on an oval meat dish of Ramsey shape to which the registration mark refers. This dates from 10.3.1919.

278

SPODE
COPELAND
ENGLAND

1919. A rare mark on a piece dated March 1919. Also seen on a piece of white china.

279

COPELANDS LEADLESS
GLAZE
ENGLAND
SPODE
COPELAND'S CHINA
ENGLAND

About 1910. An example of this LEADLESS GLAZE mark on bone china occurs on the 1910 Accession commemorative plate.

280

SPODE'S
Royal Jade
ENGLAND

1932. Royal Jade was a matt green glaze on Spode Imperial body. Ornamental wares like candlesticks, ashtrays and vases were produced. Short lived, to 1938 at the latest.

281

SPODE
COPELAND
ONYX
ENGLAND

1932. Onyx was the name of a pale grey coloured body, and animal sculptures by Eric Olsen were among the items available. Short lived.

The mark was in dark brown under the shiny glaze.

282

Spode's
Velamour
ENGLAND

1932-40. c1953-69. This mark was used for a matt vellum glaze of creamy-white

colour. It proved more popular than the Royal Jade and Onyx glazes, and was revived in about 1953, when it was permitted to manufacture ornamental ware for the United Kingdom market after the austere period of the 1939-45 war. A large number of objects were manufactured. [GG 1083].

On some items with embossed flowers, these were painted in colours.

On objects bearing marks 280-2, impressed numbers with the prefix letter K occur: these are the shape identification numbers which are in the mould.

283

Spode's
"Royal Jasmine"
England

1932. As in the former three marks, Royal Jasmine was a coloured glaze – pale jasmine yellow which gave a deep cream-coloured effect similar to early English creamware of the 1750-70's. The difference was that Royal Jasmine was used for tablewares and not ornamental items, but like them it was on the Imperial body.

The best known patterns were Strathmere, S2128 and Audley, S2401.

The close texture and extremely low porosity of the body after 1962 rendered it unsuitable for use with coloured glazes and Royal Jasmine was discontinued. This mark was often used in conjunction with Mark 259 and the pattern name and number.

There was no pattern called Royal Jasmine.

284

COPELANDS
EARTHENWARE
R.No159276
ENGLAND

1890-5. This mark is the only example of the mention of *earthenware* appearing on a Copeland mark. The registration is for the Charlotte shape. The mark appears on a dinner plate date-stamped 94[F], pattern 2/3867, and has a mark for MONA pattern. (See mark 426).

285

COPELAND
SPODE
ENGLAND

1941

About 1941. Printed on ware made to the orders of British Government departments. At present, no example is available and this mark is known from the entry in the Engraver's Record Book.

286

Spode
Copeland

1940-52. The mark used on undecorated earthenwares – Utility – the manufacture of which continued from early in 1940 to about 1952. The mark was rubber stamped in green or brown underglaze. A large A is sometimes printed beneath this mark, and was indicative of the top quality classification of Utility ware.

287

Spode
Copeland
England

1940-52. Another mark rubber stamped on Utility wares.

288

G$_{VI}$R
COPELAND
1945

1940-*c*1965. Mark applied by rubber stamp in black onto Spode Imperial earthenware made for the British Government. The most usual items were one pint handled mugs, lipped bowls, and roll edge plates for use by the armed services and in government institutions.

289

Spode

a

Spode
Impl.

About 1950-60. Used occasionally on Spode Imperial ware when left undecorated. No explanation is known why the country of origin was omitted.

290

1949-65. Four years after the end of the 1939-45 war it was permitted for coloured stains to be added to the bodies used for Utility wares. Spode chose a medium tone green and produced the same range of tablewares in both the ivory and green bodies.

From 1955-1963 a few patterns were used on Flemish Green, especially Moondrop and Jacinth. The letter B indicates the year 1959 (See Mark 259a) [GG 1082]. See page 93.

291

Spode
FORTUNA
England.

1955-60. Ornamental wares, especially containers for flowers were produced in a dual-tone of Flemish Green on the outer surface and Spode Imperial ivory on the inner. Also some embossed wares were made in which the ivory clay slip was painted on the embossed design in the mould before casting in green slip. This two-tone was called 'Fortuna'. [GG 1085].

292

SPODE'S
English Lavender
ENGLAND
B

1958-*c*1965. A blue coloured body had been made in the nineteenth century, and a similar product was reintroduced in 1958. Of fine earthenware it was named English Lavender. Some ornamental items were made especially with Chinese-style prunus blossom embossments in white with a matt glaze. A two-tone tableware was made in 'Tricorn' shape for a few years. A limited range of tableware in 'Hamilton' pattern was offered as a premium with a washing-up liquid.

293

Spode
ENGLAND
Alenite
FLAME-PROOF
OVENWARE
B

1960-66. The Fine Stone body was found to have excellent thermal properties which were suitable for oven proof and flameproof ware. In order not to associate this culinary aspect with the high prestige decorations, a new name, Alenite, was adopted for a range of embossed items called Henri IV. The name was created to recognise the Alumina base of the formula

and to honour the Chief Chemist, Cyril Allen, who developed it. In 1962 a white version was introduced with a new range of cooking pots which were flameproof. Due to insufficient production capacity for both white and grey, the white was discontinued. Mark 293, with the FLAMEPROOF legend applied to the white only. The B letter is for 1965.

294

SPODE
Meadow Sweet
ENGLAND

About 1958-65. A two-tone earthenware with Flemish Green rim & back, and yellow centre. Teacups were yellow with green handles, on plain green saucers.

295

About 1963-. Double S mark used on wares which were rejected as best quality, but because of only slight faults were sold as sub-standard. Applied on-glaze when the decoration was applied to the slightly sub-standard white china. Used occasionally even in the 1980s and 1990s.

296

Spode
FINE STONE
ENGLAND

1964-6 Rare mark used on a small bowl made for the Society of the Cincinnati Triennial Meeting in Boston. May 1965.

Section IV

W T COPELAND 1847 to 1867
W T COPELAND & SONS 1867 to 1932
W T COPELAND & SONS LTD. 1932 to 1970

Printed marks.

Retailer Marks which incorporate the Copeland name.

Marks incorporating *both* the names of the Company and that of a retailer or distributor. These were engraved and applied specially at extra cost to the client.

In some cases, only the record in the Engravers' Record Book is available. Gaps are left in the numbering to allow for marks which are discovered later.

Milk jug from the set supplied to HMS Alert, Mark 309. Similar ware was supplied for use on HMS Discovery.

304

About 1852. This mark occurs on a soup tureen decorated with Fern pattern, the original service being purchased in Moscow. See 202a.

305

About 1855. Mark 305 is known from a copper engraving.

306

About 1870. Recorded in the Engravers' Book, with an alteration to Dawidon, but no indication of location.

307

1869. On a saucer, Registered Design No. 232307

308

1876. A small saucer decorated with the American flag is known with this mark. A grotesque vase formed of three bald – and mean-looking – eagles was produced to mark the Centenary of the Declaration of Independence. Both plain & coloured versions are known. See page 138.

309

The Arctic Expedition of 1875 aimed at reaching the North Pole before anyone else. Two vessels, the 'Alert' and 'Discovery' set out on May 29th 1875 and returned in 1876. Although they did not achieve their goal the expedition was considered to have been a success; certainly it was very well equipped! Items of tableware manufactured by Copelands include milk jugs, teacups and saucers, and plates. Some are printed in black, others in blue, with the badge prominently displayed and the name of the ship printed on the underside.

310

A pseudo Sèvres mark applied as a lithograph to a few objects which were replicas of Sèvres pieces. This particular mark occurs on a plate made for the Russian Czar Nicholas II to replace original Sèvres plates made in 1779 for Empress Catherine II. The mark is pale blue, and only on pieces made for Thomas Goode & Co.

311

This pale blue lithographed mark occurs on some bone china plates decorated in the style of Sèvres with floral/fruit subjects painted by Arthur Perry, and commissioned by Thomas Goode & Co. The gilding was by C J Deauville.

Reproduction of Sèvres plate supplied in 1779 to the Empress Catherine II of Russia. Painted by J Arrowsmith and C B Brough, 1906. Marks 311 and 341.

315

1880. The earliest reference in the Engraving Records to this famous store in New York.

316

About 1881. A shard, bearing the date 81 was excavated in the 1970's on a site in Stoke-on-Trent, but not on the Factory. No record is available in the Engraving Book.

320

1882. Gilman Collamore. An emporium in New York. This mark was engraved 15/6/82.

321

MANUFACTURED
BY
W. T. COPELAND & SONS
FOR
RICHARD BRIGGS.
BOSTON.

1883. No example has been seen by the compiler. The dealer was in Boston, Massachusetts, USA.

322

1884. John Mortlock established his business of retailing china in 1746. The principal shop was in Oxford Street, London, with a Studio in Orchard Street. The mark of the manufacturer might be in the centre, as here. Engraved 27/3/1884.

323

1887. Davis Collamore is now at 921 Broadway, New York. A more sophisticated mark than No. 315 used in 1880.

324

1889. A new style of mark almost identical to that of Davis Collamore. Engraved 22/8/1889.

325

1890. The same mark as Mark 324 except that the address of Gilman Collamore is 5th Avenue & 30th St. 25/4/1890.

326

1889. Thomas Goode founded his china and glass store in 1827 in South Audley Street in London. In 1844, he moved to 19 South Audley Street, where they have remained ever since.

327

1889. A B & R P Daniell was a china and glass retailer in Wigmore Street, and in New Bond St. London, for whom a mark was engraved in 1872. The business was founded in c1825 and continued to 1917. Mark engraved 23/10/1889, but examples have been seen rarely.

328

1892. Mark 328 is as Mark 327, but the address is 129 New Bond Street. This was engraved 30/5/1892.

329

1889. Ovington Brothers was an important china and glass store in Brooklyn, New York. Mark engraved 5/6/1889. Copelands were supplying Ovingtons in 1871.

334

1891. William Whiteley was an important drapery store. Started in 1863 in Westbourne Grove, London, it grew rapidly adding many departments until china and glass were included by about 1878. This mark of the 'Universal Provider' was engraved in December 1891.

(Ref. Alison Adburgham (1964) Shops and Shopping 1800-1914, Allen & Unwin).

335

1892. No information is available on this dealer. Engraved in November 1892. The mark has been seen on ware date-marked 1902.

336

1893 To mark the occasion of the wedding of George, Duke of York and the Princess May on July 6th 1893 the Brighton china and glass shop of Cheesman commissioned an earthenware mug. (See page 79).

338

W.T.COPELAND & SONS
STAFFORDSHIRE
J.McD.& S
Importers

1896. This mark is probably that of Jones McDuffee & Stratton of Boston, Mass. USA up to 1950. The firm was founded in 1810 by Otis Norcross.

339

1897. Engravers' Record Book. Most likely a commemorative plate or mug to mark the Diamond Jubilee of Queen Victoria.

341

1342

1899. Thomas Goode founded this famous firm in 1827. Copelands were privileged to supply many very important people with bone china and earthenware through Goode's, including many services for the Royal Family.

(Ref. Philip M Rayner (1977) Thomas Goode of London 1827-1977).

This practice of producing wares specially commissioned continues to this day.

345

James Green & Nephew. Retailers in St Paul's Churchyard, London from 1834-42 under the name J Green & Co. In 1841 and 42 the firm was styled J Green & Sons. An address in Upper Thames St. & 62 Cornhill dates from c1879. This mark dates from 1899.

346

The Savoy Hotel in London, one of the world's greatest hotels, chose Copelands Nigel pattern for one of their restaurants. Engraved on copper plates. Pattern registered 11th September 1907.

349

1892. The Columbus Pitcher is similar in appearance to the Chicago Pitcher, but with a large sprig of the Landing of Columbus on each side. This panel was registered 11th August 1892.

350

1913. This mark occurs on two unusual objects – the handle for a razor strop and a china cover for a cut-throat razor. It is not known at present if Charles M. Van Heusen was the firm associated with the shirt makers. The Engravers' Record Book date is 24th August 1894.

351

1902. The pattern consisted of Chinese dragons chasing round the object, while inside was the message "We'll tak a cup o' kindness yet for days o' Auld Lang Syne".

The wine pot shape is a near copy of an Yi-Hsing Chinese red stoneware wine pot. The design was registered at the Patent Office 7 Jan 1879. It is not known why the shape is called Crichton.

352

MADE EXPRESSLY FOR
HOTEL ST REGIS
Copeland China
IMPORTED BY
DAVIS COLLAMORE & Co Ltd
5TH AVE AND 37TH ST

1903. This mark incorporates the words 'Copelands China' in the handwriting of Ronald Copeland who had recently joined his father in the firm.

353

1904. Recorded in the Engravers' Book.

354

1906. The Chicago Pitcher is of coloured clay – buff with a coating of clay slip of a different colour – matt blue – onto which are sprigged embossed scenes depicting the history of Chicago from 1673-1893. (See page 169).

355

COPELAND
ENGLAND
A.T.WILEY & C° L?
MONTREAL.

1907. A T Wiley & Co. Ltd. was an important distributor in Canada.

356

This mark occurs on pieces made for the Canadian Pacific Railway Company's hotel 'Glacier House' in the Rockies. It is not known yet to what the name Regal refers.

367

1920. Recorded in the Engravers' Book. A. French & Co. were the Boston specialist importers who supplied the Algonquin Club.

368

RP Nº. 691240.

No 7
"HOMEWARD"
BY
LIONEL EDWARDS

1922. Soane & Smith commissioned a set of paintings by Lionel Edwards which were reproduced on earthenware by Copelands, See mark 425.

There were twelve different subjects on the plates, which depicted scenes of twelve famous hunts:–

1 Full Cry
   The Beaufort
2 Gone Away
   The Warwickshire
3 Going to Halloa
   The Old Berkeley
4 A Check
   The York & Ainstey
5 Off to Draw
   The Pytchley
6 The Find
   The Atherstone
7 Homeward
   The New Forest Buckhounds
8 Gone to Ground
   The Hursley
9 Stag at Bay
   The Devon & Somerset Stag Hounds
10 Drawing the Dingle
    The Flint & Denbigh
11 The Kill
    The Cotswold
12 The Last Draw
    The Vale of White Horse

369

"SUTHERLAND"
SPODE
COPELAND CHINA
ENGLAND
R8920 V
TIFFANY & Cº
NEW YORK

1925. Copelands had been supplying Tiffany & Co. Fifth Avenue, New York since at least 1883. This mark was engraved all together with the name of the pattern, SUTHERLAND, on the Stafford shape with ivory groundlay all over and

blue leaves and rich gilded lines on the moulded rim. The pattern number R8920 was written with a brush.

370

Harrods in Brompton Road was founded in 1849. From a grocery shop, Charles Digby Harrod began to develop a department store. In the 1920s or 1930s the address (but not the location) was changed to the more fashionable one of Knightsbridge. Copelands made many patterns exclusively for Harrods including: CHELSEA Rd. No. 568949 [26th August 1910] Earthenware 2/6247, Bone China R4073 PEPLOW Rd. No. 568948 [26th August 1910] Earthenware 2/6246, Bone China R4075 OLD BOW Rd. No. 599813 [17th April 1912] Earthenware 2/6418, Bone China R4730 ROCKINGHAM Rd. No. 659905 [24th March 1917] Earthenware 2/7012, Bone China R6434. These patterns remained current until about 1963.

371

1929. A mark used on ware made for the Admiralty for use in His Majesty's Naval establishments and afloat.

376

1933. Heal & Son Ltd. used this mark on a few patterns, the name being inserted where here is 'Silver & Jade'. This ware was earthenware with the matt Royal Jade glaze trimmed with silver lines, strokes. etc. Heal & Son have a store in Tottenham Court Road, London.

377

W T COPELAND & SONS LTD
MANUFACTURERS OF
Grosvenor China
ENGLAND

1933. In 1932 W T Copeland & Sons bought Jackson & Gosling Ltd., whose trade name was 'Grosvenor China'. It was sold in 1955. All records of patterns and other papers were transferred to the new owners, Thomas Poole & Son.

380

About 1933 This mark is known so far from an engraved copper plate and the compiler cannot date it although it may have been used on hotel ware in the 1930's.

Juggins's Butter Stand.
Engraving number 1350.
A similar mark, 170, was used in the
Copeland & Garrett period.

392

Only known from the Engravers' Book,
where these entries are not dated.

Earthenware mug commissioned by Cheesman of Brighton to commemorate the wedding of George, Duke of York and May, Princess of Teck, 1893. Mark 336.

Earthenware mug commemorating the coronation of Queen Elizabeth II, 1953. Mark 259.

'Going to the Derby', the claret jug which carries Mark 404.

Plate from the Field Sports pattern, depicting the grandstand at Epsom.

Ionian pattern, registered 11 June 1851. Every item of dinnerware depicts a different altar, gravestone or other monument. Copper plates have the name CONNAUGHT HOTEL engraved on them: one wonders what diners thought of the results after enjoying a meal in the dining room! The marks include a variation of 427, 215, 231, and a good example of a printed registration mark.

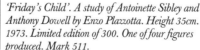

'Friday's Child'. A study of Antoinette Sibley and Anthony Dowell by Enzo Plazzotta. Height 35cm. 1973. Limited edition of 300. One of four figures produced. Mark 511.

The Coronation miniature teaset on tray, Marks 430 and 431. The shapes are copied from an original Spode teaset in a private collection.

Miniature tea and dinner sets were made throughout the nineteenth century by many manufacturers. They were intended as 'toys', and are described as such in Spode's shape book of 1820. Depending on their elaborate or simple nature they were intended for cabinet display or as children's play sets. They are not travellers' samples.

Strathmere pattern, S2128, marked 259 and 283, with the pattern name printed below the 'gridiron' and the handwritten pattern number.

Items of teaware made exclusively for Heal & Son Ltd.

Section V

COPELAND PERIOD PATTERN NAMES

Printed marks.

During the Copeland period the naming of patterns assumed considerable importance and many of these names enjoyed specially designed marks while others had to be content with a number. Some B and D patterns are marked with a printed number, e.g. B772 and D95.

The letter S occurs on wares and is engraved on copper plates. At present its significance is not known. See Mark 167.

401

About 1847. Louis Quatorze border (patent number 22919) and full pattern (22920) were patented on Dec. 2 1844 – numbers in brackets. The border design is the same as that for Continental Views, patented Oct 21, 1845, number 30699. Mark 401 is a renewal of Mark 164 – if not so well engraved.

402

About 1895. Copeland and Garrett introduced the pattern in about 1842 (Mark 163). It remained popular in the later years of the nineteenth century when mark 402 was used.

403

About 1938. The pattern was re-engraved about 1938 but the war prevented its wide distribution. After the war the sizes of ware were different due to changes in material causing the engravings not to fit properly. Mark 403 was the later mark.

404

1868. This mark occurs on a claret jug on which is depicted a man on a cart driving a donkey – possibly a costermonger on his day off. It is well printed and embellished with gilding "Going to the Derby". The pattern number is D5985 and dates from 1868.

Alderman W T Copeland was a keen horse-racing man having a number of racehorses of his own.

405

About 1903. Landscape pattern was a Chinese porcelain design copied by Spode for replacements. It continued in production throughout the nineteenth and up to mid-twentieth century. The letters N.T. are often printed on the back of this pattern. So far it is not known why. (See Copeland *Spode's Willow Pattern* pp 125, 128-9).

406

1870. Recorded in the Print Record Book of Badges. The earliest pattern number is D8920 dated to early in 1872, but as a plain print it would not have been recorded; only when additional colouring and/or gilding was added would it be entered in the Pattern Book.

(Illustrated p166, Sussman.) Engraved 15/12/1870.

407

About 1880. This 'Bee' mark occurs with several different pattern names. Those known so far are: Nineveh, Delhi, Venetia, Connaught. They date from the 1880s. [GG 1075].

408

Known only from an engraved copper plate, which has the appearance of being of some other firm's, as the style is different from the traditional 'handwriting' of the Spode factory designs and engraving techniques. (The pattern is strikingly similar to that of W Adams & Son.)

409

About 1880. A set of engraved coppers for this pattern are still in good condition. No piece has been seen yet. The style suggests a date of about 1880. It was a Davenport pattern, though not one of the copperplates has the Davenport name. It was registered on 10/12/1924, number 709821.

410

About 1890. This Mark 256 with the addition of the pattern name engraved with the mark.

In other instances Marks 257 and 259 were accompanied by a pattern name with a registered number when appropriate. This registered number is for the shape or, more usually, the engraved design. Many different coloured versions of such a pattern were often produced each with its own pattern number, applied by hand. King was registered on 14/12/1892; George III was registered as 'Raleigh' on 9/8/1920.

KING
Rᵈ Nº 209193

Sometimes a pattern name may be printed separately, either with or without a registered number.

Note. The marks illustrated are meant to be representative, and not confined to the patterns named.

411

About 1892. The other version of the 'gridiron' or pseudo-Chinese seal, noted at Mark 268. Mimosa was a later name for Antique Vase. Shards have been excavated in North America. Earthenware. Other patterns using this mark include: Corinthian, Mandarin.

412

About 1891. The seal mark, 253, showing how the pattern name and registered number were placed. Bone China.

413

COPELAND
ILIUM
ENGLAND.

Variations of pattern marks derived from engraved copper plates.

414

"Crete"
COPELAND
ENGLAND.

Typical of marks incorporating the name of the pattern – mostly on earthenware.

415

1906 The Devonia shape of Dessert ware was registered on 22 December 1906. This mark, 415, was drawn from one on a plate of pattern 2/5943 date stamped $\frac{O}{89}$. It was on earthenware. (See mark 257b.)

416

"DEVONIA"
Rᵈ Nº 493287
SPODE
COPELANDS CHINA
ENGLAND

The same information but in association with the bone china mark 242. The mark was engraved on March 18, 1907.

417

1894. Engraved in June 1894, this mark has been seen on an elaborately embossed tall bottle. The mark probably relates to a range of ornamental wares.

418

An example has been seen without ENGLAND but this may be because it would not fit on!

419

COPELAND
Spode's Tower
ENGLAND

420

Spode's
"Camilla"
Copeland
ENGLAND.

About 1891. It is not certain when marks 418-420 were introduced. The patterns had been in continuous production since their first appearance. No examples of these names on the wares are known before these marks, which are not printed in the 1902 catalogue. The use of a similar oval cartouche for Spode's Trophies was recorded in the Engravers Book in March 1900. Italian pattern was introduced in 1816. See pages 154-159.

Tower pattern, based on The Bridge of Salaro near Rome, appeared in 1814.

Camilla may be dated to 1833-35, very early in the Copeland and Garrett period. Usually seen on earthenware, the mark was still applied on bone china when the pattern was so used.

421

1930. The Hunt pattern dates from about 1930 when a series of incidents which occur on the fox hunting field were engraved for a full range of tablewares. Usually on earthenware, there are many versions on bone china. Most of the scenes are after drawings and paintings by J F Herring, Senior, some of which were first engraved for use in the Field Sports pattern, patented on September 14, 1846 number 37254. See also Mark 510.

The scenes on the 10in & 8in plates:
1. Full cry
2. The find
3. Throwing off
4. Off to draw
5. Gone away
6. The huntsman
7. The meet
8. The death
9. Going to halloa
10. Drawing the dingle
11. The kill
12. The last draw

The scenes on smaller plates:
1. First over
2. Gone away
3. A check
4. The find
5. The last draw
6. The huntsman
7. Homeward
8. The meet
9. Going to halloa
10. In the spinney
11. Full cry
12. Drawing the dingle

Other subjects on cups, saucers & c include: Leaping the brook, Taking the lead, The chase, Well cleared, The hounds.

See page 163 for a fuller account.

422

Y. 7144
SPODE
Rᵈ Nº
COLONEL
395839
COPELAND

About 1930-70. On bone china it is more usual to find the name of the pattern neatly printed below the standard mark in the same colour as the printed pattern. Colonel is an exception. It was registered on August 23, 1902, and is a copy of a popular blue and white Chinese decoration of the early 15th Century AD. It was brought back by Colonel Alfred Copeland after his service in Persia and a set of ware was made for him and his army rank gave the name to the pattern.

423

SPODES JEWEL
COPELAND
SPODE
ENGLAND
REG Nº 70392
U.S. PATT. JUNE 15ᵀᴴ 1926
SPODE'S BILLINGSLEY ROSE

SPODE'S MANSARD
COPELAND
SPODE
ENGLAND
US PATENT 88688
Rᴺ Nᵒ. 777266
CUP HANDLE
US PATENT 102458

1924-70. A typical layout for several shape names with the London registration numbers, which refer to the embossed shape design and not to the decoration. The shapes registered included:

Jewel   Rd. No. 70392
                  Registered 15/6/1924
Mansard   Rd. No. 777266
                  Registered 6/10/1932
Centurion Rd. No. 762857
                  Registered 21/3/1931

424

Blanche de Chine
REG Nº 785542.
U.S.A. PATENT PENDING
Spode
BONE CHINA
ENGLAND

1934-70. The Blanche de Chine shape, inspired by Chinese porcelain, was registered 5/8/1933, number 785542, and was made in Bone China from 1934-1973. The best known pattern was Geisha, Y3456. The mark was associated with the current factory mark, in this example Mark 276 (1960-1970).

425

SPECIALLY DESIGNED BY LIONEL EDWARDS. MANUFACTURED BY W.T. COPELAND & SONS. ENGLAND.

Rᴺ Nᵒ. 691840.

1922-c1955. Engraved Sept. 1922 when the words "Solely for Soane & Smith, Oxford St, London W1" were (also included as No. 368) incorporated. The pattern consisted of very many scenes of fox hunting, those on the 10″ plates also naming the hunt which was depicted. The scenes show various stages in the hunt and are named, e.g. 'Homeward' with the number of the scene. After Soane & Smith discontinued the pattern, Copelands continued it but omitted their name.

426

COPELANDS
MONA
ENGLAND

1894. This mark appears on a 10″ plate, Charlotte shape, impressed marked Spode Impl (Mark 203) and date stamped $^F_{94}$, with Mark 284. Pattern 2/3867. The pattern CYRIL also occurs on this style. The mark also occurs on Hawkweed, No. 206165, 1893; and also for a plate commemorating the wedding of George, Duke of York & Princess May of Teck, 1896. No. 212545.

427

IVY

Several other patterns have their names in similar panels.

428

1852. The manner of applying names to the backs of objects varied widely. Strawberry was patented on 1/10/1852, patent number 86931.

429   "SPODE'S GINGHAM"

1929. Gingham pattern was registered on 26/2/1929. Rd. No. 743842. Several patterns are called Spode's . . . . . . but this does not necessarily mean that the pattern predates 1833.

430

SOUVENIR BY SPODE COPELAND TO COMMEMORATE THE CORONATION OF QUEEN ELIZABETH II JUNE · 2ᴺᴰ · 1953
SPODE COPELAND CHINA ENGLAND

1953. Apart from specially commissioned commemorative items and standard mugs and beakers, the rarest Coronation item was a miniature teaset on a round tray. The latter was marked in gold as Mark 430, the individual items also marked in gold with Mark 431. Only 108 sets were sold, none was specially numbered.

431

CORONATION SPODE COPELAND CHINA ENGLAND JUNE · 2 ND · 1953

1953. The mark applied to the individual items of the miniature teaset, which consisted of the tray, teapot, sugar box, cream jug, plate, two teacups and two teasaucers.

259

COPELAND
SPODE
ENGLAND
STRATHMERE
Spode's
"Royal Jasmine"
England

283

S2128

The name 'Royal Jasmine' (Mark 283) refers to the glaze. This whole mark is duplicated here as well as earlier because it includes the pattern name, and number which is applied by hand.

When seeking for information about a pattern it is very important to quote this number. The mark below it is the decorator's personal mark.

1894. The significance of HB is not known at present although it has been suggested that the pattern, known originally as HB border, and later as Wicker Dale, may have been made for the Hudson's Bay Company. It was registered 30/1/94.

441

Spode's "Royal Jasmine" England Autumn by Ronald Copeland Rᴰ Nº 798464

1934. In the nineteen-thirties Copelands introduced many patterns to appeal to the new fashion in design which has become known as Art Deco. Few of these patterns are seen these days, but the pattern books record scores of designs which were right up-to-date at the time. Autumn was registered on 4 Dec. 1934. Its pattern number was S475, a later version being pattern O 809, the O indicating at that time that the pattern was decorated on-glaze.

442

COPELAND
SPODE
ENGLAND
REQUEST
DESIGNED BY
T. Hassall.

443

Spode's "Royal Jasmine" England "DIANA." DESIGNED BY
Pinder Davis

At this time some patterns carried the name of the designer. T. Hassall was Art Director, while Ronald Copeland was Chairman. Pinder Davis was commissioned to design several patterns which included Diana (443), Shepherd's Hey, and Country Souvenir. T. Hassall's name is associated with Request (442), Isles, Grass and Arrow, and Anemone.

444

"Cutie-Kitten" SPODE COPELAND ENGLAND S.3243

1957. A group of pieces designed by Christopher Boulton for children. Transfer-printed and painted under-glaze.

445

BARBECUE SPODE COPELAND ENGLAND

1957. A set of four Tricorn shape plates with comical pictures entitled 'No comment'.

S3244   Lampost and dog's paw prints.
S3251   Cockerel bemused with duckling by hen.
S3252   Black cat being propelled to the moon by an old boot.
S3253   Steeplechase with monkey as jockey on kangaroo.

446

Away in a manger. Designed by JCBoulton Hand Engraved by J Longmore SPODE COPELAND ENGLAND

1957-8. Two coupe shape plates intended as Christmas plaques. This one is pattern S3245, and the second "where is he that is born" is S3250, and shows the three wise men riding camels.

Section VI

SPODE LIMITED 1970 – the present

Printed marks.

On July 1st 1966 the firm of W T Copeland and Sons Limited was sold to The Carborundum Company Limited, but the old name was retained and no changes were made to the marks.

In 1970, the Company celebrated the 200th Anniversary of the founding in 1770. To mark this event the name of the firm was changed to Spode Limited and an extended exercise was conducted by the London designer, John Sutherland-Hawes, to present a uniform image of excellence.

501 **Spode**
ENGLAND

1970-76. The special logotype of Spode, which he had drawn in 1963, and ENGLAND was common to all bodies and patterns. BONE CHINA (502) or FINE STONE (503) were added where appropriate. Most popular patterns had the pattern number, name and details of design history – if earlier than 1900- added below, eg 503a.

a

Earthenware marks were as 501 with the pattern details added as in 503a where appropriate. Usually printed in black, other less suitable colours were used until a stable and clear image could be obtained.

It should be noted that smaller items like cups and saucers might be marked only with the shorter mark with no pattern details.

502 **Spode**
ENGLAND
BONE CHINA

a **Spode**
ENGLAND
BONE CHINA
Y8085
PERSIA

The Bone China mark was in red and gold, the logotype and pattern name being in red, the other details in gold eg Mark 502a.

The suffix 'a' is given to the marks which include the pattern name, number and date.

The basic mark has no suffix 'a'.

503 **Spode**
ENGLAND
FINE STONE

a **Spode**
ENGLAND
FINE STONE
W128
TRADE WINDS
FROM A DESIGN
C.1805

The Fine Stone mark was in black, with details in gold when the decoration had to be fired in the enamel kiln. This practice ceased in about 1973 when black only was used.

Both the Bone China and Fine Stone marks were applied as water slide-off transfers (decals).

504a
Y7332-B
CONSUL
Spode
Fine Bone China
ENGLAND

505

1976. In 1976 the marks for Bone China and Fine Stone were changed. The china mark (504) being in Red and Black, the stone mark similar (505) in black only. A letter after the pattern number indicated the date –A 1976; –B 1977; –C 1978. Fine Bone China was now used.

In 1976 on July 1st, Spode Limited joined with The Worcester Royal Porcelain Company Limited to form Royal Worcester Spode Limited.

506

1978. A further change to the Fine Stone mark was made to incorporate the OVEN TO TABLEWARE legend. The date letters were discontinued on newly introduced patterns on Jubilee shape.

507a **Spode**
Fine Bone China
ENGLAND
Y6235-E
BLUE COLONEL

1979. The Bone China mark was modified in 1979 to bring it smaller, and to place "Fine Bone China" above ENGLAND. Now it was red and black. The date letters continue: –D 1979; –E 1980; –F 1981.

508

1980. This special mark was introduced to identify distinguished services with armorial bearings, badges and monograms, as well as very special hand painted wares.

509

1981. A range of oven-to-table ware of vitreous stone ware was introduced in 1981. An ivory coloured ware matched the colour of Spode body earthenware, and a white ware matched the Crown body earthenware.

510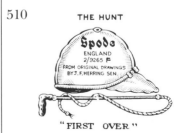

1980. The Hunt pattern continues to be popular, but the range of scenes has been shortened. Moreover, Kibblestone Hall was pulled down in the 1960's so the mark 421 has been revised.

511

1973-1976. In 1972 the distinguished sculptor Enzo Plazzotta was invited to allow some of his studies of ballet dancers to be manufactured in porcelain. He consented to this request and the result was a series of figurines, being studies of Antoinette Sibley and Anthony Dowell. Made in a special body – studio porcelain – the finished effect was similar to parian. Only four studies – two singles and two double figures – were marketed as numbered limited editions of 500 and 300 each respectively.

512

1990. This mark is applied to items whose origins lie in examples in the Spode Museum Trust Collection. Two series of six dessert plates inaugurated the scheme: the Fruit and Flower series after a design *c*1825, and the Edwardian series after floral subjects painted by Arthur Perry, *c*1912.

513

1990. A revival of mark 295 for use on ware rejected at the undecorated stage, but which suffered from only slight defects and was decorated with patterns selected for the purpose of providing inexpensive ware. Applied on-glaze in black on fine earthenware.

514

1990. A mark similar to 513 but with Spode in red, the remainder in black, and used for the same purpose.

515

1987. This simplified version of mark 508 appears on some of the series of 8in scene plates issued in numbered limited editions of 2000. These series include the Armada, and Great Explorers Collections.

Unknown marks

SPODE & COPELAND,

44

SPODE SON
& COPELAND

45

SPODE
Felspar Porcelain

46

is a sketch of mark RC42, omitting
LONDON.

is meant to reproduce mark 41, as is this
one, but the squiggle lines are not quite
right.

144a   152

Copeland
Stone China   Copeland Late Spode

264   210

Certain marks have been attributed to Spode and Copeland without satisfactory proof. This has probably arisen because a mark has been drawn somewhat sketchily, and sometimes the cartouche and embellishment has been omitted: these omissions, however, have not been explained in all cases. The expense of photographing every mark is very great and, in earlier times, the accurate drawing was expensive also.

Moreover, Jewitt may not have had access to a comprehensive range of objects with different marks, and he may have assumed that a mark would reflect the title of the Company. He lists two marks:

SPODE, SON or SPODE & COPELAND, both impressed and printed.
& COPELAND

Only in 1989 has an impressed example of the latter mark (11) been noticed, although the names occur printed in italic with LONDON on marks 42 and 43. The former is listed as 45.

"It must be true; I've seen it in print!" Once a mark has appeared in a publication, it is likely to be copied ever after by writers wishing to list makers' marks, but they usually cannot possibly have seen examples of all that they illustrate. So these two marks were reproduced in the Catalogue to the Spode-Copeland 1765-1965 Exhibition mounted by Dr P W Meister of Frankfurt, and repeated in the catalogue for a similar exhibition held in Oslo in 1966. Godden includes both as 3659 and 3659a.

The title 'Spode, Son & Copeland' occurs on page 502 of John Ward's *The Borough of Stoke-upon-Trent* when referring to the London trade. The London business was never given this title, although it was listed in the London Post Office Annual Directories of 1813, 1814, 1821, and 1827 as Spode & Copeland, and in 1826 as Spode, Copeland & Son.

The marks which appear to be rough drawings are those which refer to Felspar Porcelain. The Company publication, *Copeland's (Late Spode) China* of 1902, reproduces Jewitt's selection of marks, but adds:

SPODE
Felspar Porcelain   This combination of upper case and lower case does not occur on any piece known to me. (46)

Godden shows mark 3649 ⊗, but this must be a maker's mark and not a manufacturer's mark.

It is expensive to employ an artist to draw marks accurately or photograph them, so these complicated ones were drawn roughly and printed in the Frankfurt and Oslo catalogues.

Jewitt includes C & G with the name of the pattern. This is an extremely rare mark, only one example being known in 1990, printed in green underglaze on Portland Vase pattern but without the pattern name included in the mark.

The Frankfurt catalogue includes two doubtful marks, for which no example is known so far; they are illustrated as marks 144a and 152. This catalogue also illustrates badly drawn examples of the impressed body marks, 204 and 205.

Makers' marks

The method of payment to the workers was known as 'good from oven'. The maker or decorator was paid only when the object had been selected and found to be perfect after the firing process. It was essential, therefore, that he could identify the ware which he or his team had worked upon, so that proper payment could be made. If an object or pattern was produced only by one maker or decorator there was no need for a mark, but some items would be so popular that they were worked on by several people, and this needed each worker to have a distinguishing mark. The method was unfair in at least two ways: after the mark had been applied, other hands would do work on the object; for example, in clay, the piece needed to be fettled and sponged to remove the rough edges and to smooth the surface, it had to be placed in a saggar, and it was fired. A transfer-printed item, after the mark had been applied, was 'washed-off' and 'hardened-on', dipped, placed in a saggar and fired.

Some less than scrupulous owners often claimed that ware was not up to standard, so paid less than the proper amount for the work, but later proceeded to sell that ware at full price. Despite these serious shortcomings, the manufacturers succeeded in rejecting the change to 'good from hand' until 1872.

The clayworkers' marks on the Spode Works in the years to at least 1847 usually took the form of a number beneath the name SPODE, or was incorporated into the COPELAND & GARRETT impressed mark. A degree of analysis of many of these marks shows what class of craftsman used which numbers. The two usual marks were the upper-case SPODE, 4, and the lower-case Spode, 3. These are designated either WMI, workmens impressed mark, WMI/UC (upper-case) or WMI/LC (lower-case).

The Copeland & Garrett mark may be of several sorts from 101 to 110.

Mark 19a has been recognized as being an identifying mark on a cover and a base, especially of teapots and covered sugar boxes in Old Oval shape. Mark 19b almost certainly identifies China Body No. 16. These two marks, therefore, are not makers' marks.

Until September 1990, mark 5b had been observed only on objects of bone china and felspar porcelain. However, a sauce tureen stand made by Copeland & Garrett, marked NEW JAPAN STONE (mark 149), and decorated with underglaze pattern B625, one of many versions of Peacock pattern, has appeared.

New Japan Stone is a superior quality earthenware, and it brings into question whether marks 5b and 5a are manufacturer's marks or clayworker's marks.

Mark 5b has been seen on items which would have been made by a hollow-ware presser, as the sauce tureen stand might have been.

Mark 5a has been seen on garden seats, a large foot bath, and a large salmon dish (platter); all items made by a big ware presser.

Marks applied by transfer-printers began by being painted on by the transferrer. The simplest marks were used at first and for this reason, and also because a printer and his team might work for more than one manufacturer, such marks cannot be said to be an infallible proof of attribution. They are merely a guide, but other features of a piece must conform to known characteristics of the manufacturer's wares if an object is to be attributed with any degree of certainty. Two patterns, examples of which corresponded to the quality expected of Spode, Long Bridge and Damsel with Parasol, carry makers marks the same or similar to those found on known Spode wares; they cannot be claimed as Spode, however, because not one single copper engraving has been found among the 25,000 or so copper plates in the Spode Museum Trust's Collection.

19a Impressed

19b Impressed

5b Impressed

5a Impressed

Warning.
The presence of a maker's mark on its own is no guarantee that the object was made at the factory usually associated with that mark.

Workmens' impressed marks

SERIES WMI

SPODE PERIOD TO 1833
WMI/UC   MARK 4

SPODE

PRESSERS (DISHES,
PLATTERS, WINE BIN
LABELS, DESSERT DISHES &C)

1   5   9   10   11   13   14

15   18   19 21   22   23 24

39   42   48

FLAT PRESSERS (PLATE
MAKERS)

4   7   12   16   19   20

27   28   30   31 44   50

54   60

HOLLOW-WARE PRESSERS
(TUREENS, COVERED
VEGETABLE DISHES, SAUCE
BOATS &C)

11   17   23   24   25   37

40   49

WMI/LC   MARK 3

PRESSERS (DISHES,   *Spode*
PLATTERS, &C)

29   A B Ǝ F L N

2   3   69   ✳

FLAT PRESSERS (PLATES, &C)

1   2   3   3   5   8   9

*Where the same number occurs it may
be assumed that the same maker was
versatile!

COPELAND & GARRETT
PERIOD 1833 TO 1847

Claymakers' numbers are found
associated with several impressed marks:
101a, 102a, 103, 104, 105, 106, 110.

PRESSERS (DISHES, &C)

1   2   7   9 10   19   22 70

FLAT PRESSERS (PLATES, &C)

3   4   6   10 12 13   15 19

20   29   80

COPELAND PERIOD
1847-C1855

COPELAND

FLAT PRESSERS

4   6   9   18

Workmen's marks –
painted

SERIES WMP
SYMBOLS, STROKES ETC
PAINTED IN BLUE.

Pattern names are those on which
examples have been found.

WMP1	/	Willow II, Mandarin, Buffalo, Pearl River House.
WMP2	//	Caramanian, Buffalo B, Love Chase, Flying Pennant, Pearl River House.
WMP3	///	Pearl River House.
WMP4	////	Pearl River House.
WMP5	+ ✗	Buddleia, Buffalo, Caramanian, Willow II, Forest Landscape II, Pearl River House.

Later marks were transfer-printed:
copper plates were engraved with a
number of the same symbols from which
the printer would take several prints
before starting to print the pattern, so one
mark could be applied to each piece. In the
Copeland period – and indeed at the
present time – numbers were used instead
of symbols. Today this applies also to
slide-off transfer operators.

Relatively little information may be
derived from makers' marks on Spode
wares. The identities of individual
craftsmen in the forming and decorating
processes are not known, although
painters and gilders often did mark their
work for the reasons stated earlier. The
highly skilled artists and gilders seldom
marked their work – they did not need to.
After about 1860 some artists were
allowed to sign their work on the front,
though some preferred the back. In the
early years of the twentieth century
transfer-printed outline prints of varied
subjects, like flowers, fish, birds and
landscapes, were used to lessen the
expense of completely hand painted ones
and thus widen the market for these rather
nice services. Some of these prints include
a signature: this might have been that of
the original artist, like James Fenn, or it
may have been a fictitious name or that of
one of the paintresses who painted it.
Some of these names are: A Ball, R Wood,
N Simpson, J Price, P Hall, G Cholerton.

Collectors and dealers should be
thorough in the inspection of such
signatures to determine whether they are
printed or the artist's own.

Samples of printed signatures:

J.Price

A Ball

P. Hall

m Edge

P enn.

G Cholerton

WMP6	井	Bridge, I, Trophies, Tall Door, Forest Landscape II
	井	Tower, Rock
WMP7	卌	
WMP8	卌	
WMP9	⌇	Caramanian, Buffalo B, Blue Italian, Milkmaid, Botanical, Common Wolf Trap
WMP10	O	Trophies – Nankin, Caramanian
WMP11	⸓	Flying Pennant, Net
WMP12	ρ	Temple with Panel
WMP13	ϙ	Temple with Panel, Mandarin
	↻	Buffalo B
WMP14	⊕	Woodman
WMP15	8	Willow I
WMP16	✳	Bridge I, Buffalo B
WMP17	⸝	Tower
WMP18	Ϝ	Temple with Panel
WMP19	✓	Net, Forest Landscape II
WMP20	∽	
WMP21	•	Forest Landscape I, Bridge I
WMP22	••	Mandarin II (bone china)
WMP23	∾	Willow I, India, Blue Italian
WMP24	V	Forest Landscape I
WMP25	刀	Forest Landscape II
WMP26	⅄	Caramanian

WMP27	井	Flower Cross
WMP28	✗	Temple-Landscape, Buddleia
WMP29	⸜	Flower Cross, Greek
WMP30	⸪	Caramanian
WMP31	⸬	Buffalo B
WMP32	×	Japan
WMP33	◿	Fence, Willow I, Forest Landscape II
WMP34	⸫	Net

Note. Marks 1-28 correspond to those illustrated on page 166 of *Spodes Willow Pattern*.

Workmens' marks – transfer-printed

SERIES WMT

Symbols, letters, etc printed in blue.

WMT1	♂	Caramanian, Net, Willow III (C & G), Greek, Blue Group
WMT2	⸜	Caramanian, India, Old Peacock, Net, Waterloo
WMT3	6	Blue Italian
WMT4	⟋	Chatsworth (C & G), Lily (C & G)
WMT5	4	Pattern 2141 (C & G Saxon Blue)
WMT6	⟁	Botanical
WMT7	⸀	Flying Pennant
WMT8	⸂	Willow III
WMT9	Ⱳ	Fitzhugh

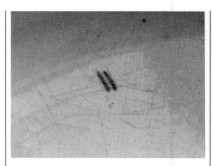

Example of mark WMP2.

Example of mark WMT11.

Mark	Pattern
WMT10	Greek
WMT11	Lily, many patterns
	Lily, Botanical
WMT12	Lange Lijzen, many patterns
WMT13	Greek, Castle
WMT14	Caramanian, many patterns
WMT15	Aesops Fables, Convolvulus border pattern 1171 (C & G)
WMT16	Blue Camilla (C & G), Botanical (C & G)
WMT17	
WMT18	Caramanian, Buffalo B, Botanical
WMT19	Marble
WMT20	Old Peacock, Lily (C & G)
WMT21	Old Peacock
WMT22	Pattern 2053 Stone Japan, Willow III, Leaf
WMT23	Net
WMT24	Gloucester, Gothic Castle
WMT25	Greek, Japan, Pattern 5519 (C & G)
WMT26	Bridge I, Daisy
WMT27	Lily (C & G)
WMT28	Lily (C & G)
WMT29	Botanical
WMT30	Geranium
WMT31	Botanical (C & G)
WMT32	Botanical, May
WMT33	Tower
WMT34	Bridge I
WMT35	Aesops Fables
WMT36	British Flowers
	Marble Sheet
WMT37	Jasmine
WMT38	Aesops Fables
WMT39	Blue Rose
	Greek
WMT40	Camilla (C & G)
WMT41	Italian (Copeland)
WMT42	Japan
WMT43	Floral, Aesops Fables
WMT44	Floral, Aesops Fables
WMT45	Blue Camilla (C & G)
WMT46	Botanical
WMT47	Botanical

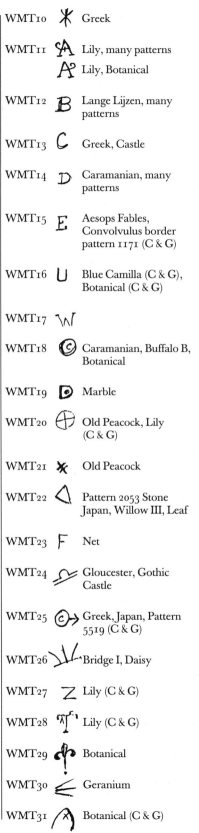

Datemarks

The dating of objects

Some patterns retained their popular appeal for very many years after their introduction. It is not unknown for objects made at the end of the nineteenth century to carry an early Spode number: eg. 967 pattern, introduced in 1807, was being made in 1870's, and an invoice dated February 12, 1862 lists items in pattern 3767, only a couple of years before pattern D3767 was introduced, yet it was the Spode design which was referred to.

Pattern numbers were usually applied with paint, by hand, although in rare cases the numbers were printed. They are not easy to read sometimes especially when applied underglaze, but without the number it is difficult to establish the identification of the pattern.

Before 1870, no standard system of datemarking is known. In 1870, Copelands adopted a very simple system of datemarking their wares. A letter over two figures were made into 'markers' which claymakers impressed into the bottom of the clay object. Because some pressure was required to push the marker into the clay, datemarks are generally found on pressed ware – that is, flatware objects made by pressing plastic clay onto a plaster mould, like plates, soup plates, saucers, platters, meat dishes, dessert comports and plates. It is impractical to press a marker into the surface of most hollow-ware objects because the base would be deformed by the pressure.

However most examples of parian made after 1870 are datemarked with the date of manufacture, as well as the date of the original sculpture which is so .etimes seen, although this latter date will have been in the mould.

The letter represents the month. The initial letter for the first & last four months of the year being obvious:—

J January	A April	L July	O October
F February	Y May	T August	N November
M March	U June	S September	D December

A close study of the underside of a plate or other object may reveal such a mark, but they are not always clear; being applied quickly, an impression might be incomplete due to the marker not being stamped properly. Objects like plates and saucers were made by 'flat pressers', or platemakers, who had the assistance of mould runners. Mould runners, usually young boys, had to bring to the maker empty moulds which, after the plate was made he would stamp the date on the back, perhaps the manufacturers mark and the maker's mark. He then had to run with the moulds into the 'walk-in stove', place the mould on a shelf and bring out dry moulds, remove the dry plate and place the empty mould ready for the maker. All this activity meant that he had to be 'on the go' constantly so it is not surprising that impressed marks were applied hastily and sometimes are difficult to read.

When walk-in stoves began to be replaced by modern driers with fan-blown air, the makers emptied the moulds first then handled them directly with no need for a mould runner. This meant that the act of impressing marks was inconvenient; it was time-consuming, and interrupted the flow of work. For earthenware, therefore, which was the first product to be affected, impressed date marks were discontinued in 1957: later, datemarking on Fine Stone and Bone China was discontinued in 1963.

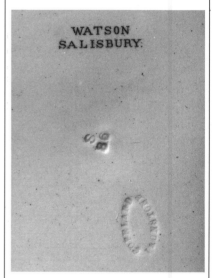

Plate commemorating the Golden Jubilee of Queen Victoria in 1887. It includes the rare Mark 222, the retailer's name, and the date mark for September 1886.

Date marker for June 1891

Marks and dating since 1957

Fine bone china

1957-9
**SPODE
BONE CHINA
ENGLAND**

Mark offset-printed on 'Rejafix' printing machine in green underglaze. Date impressed in clay with letter for month as shown, page 92 (to 1963).

1960-9
Spode
**BONE CHINA
ENGLAND**

Same printing method as previous mark. From 1964 a printed date – letter (followed by the code-number of printing team or operative) was introduced, as follows:

1964	A	1968	E	1972	I
1965	B	1969	F	1973	J
1966	C	1970	G	1974	
1967	D	1971	H	to June	J

1970-5
**Spode
ENGLAND
BONE CHINA
Y8085
PERSIA**

Water-slide transfer in red and gold. No date letter applied in 1975.

1976-8

Y7332-B
CONSUL
Spode
Fine Bone China
ENGLAND

1979 onwards

Spode
Fine Bone China
ENGLAND
Y6235-E
BLUE COLONEL

Water slide transfers in red & black. Date letters are added to the pattern number, as indicated:

1976	A	1984	I	1992	R
1977	B	1985	J	1993	S
1978	C	1986	K	1994	T
1979	D	1987	L	1995	U
1980	E	1988	M	1996	V
1981	F	1989	N	1997	W
1982	G	1990	P		
1983	H	1991	Q		

Fine stone

1957-9

COPELAND
SPODE
ENGLAND
New Stone

Mark applied by rubber stamp or 'Rejafix' machine. Date impressed in clay with letter for month (omitting I) as shown, until 1963. In 1960 re-formulation led to re-naming of the body and a new mark, applied by rubber stamp in green underglaze.

1960-9

X
COPELAND
SPODE
ENGLAND
Fine Stone

From 1964 a printed date-letter was introduced, as for Bone China (see above), similarly discontinued in June 1974. But from 1965 the code letter is also seen within the 'gridiron' mark.

1970-7

Spode
ENGLAND
FINE STONE
W128
TRADE WINDS
FROM A DESIGN
C.1805

The new mark was printed in black or applied as a waterslide transfer in black and gold. After the ending of the previous dating system in June 1974, no date was given in 1975. From 1976 a date letter was added to the pattern number as for Bone China.

1978-80

OVEN TO TABLEWARE
FINE STONE
Spode
ENGLAND
Y4973 C QUEEN'S BIRD

1981 onwards

In 1981 the date letter following the pattern number was inadvertently omitted. From 1982 to 1992 the date letter was added after the pattern name. The Fine Stone body was withdrawn in March 1993 and the Lowestoft range of items was made in earthenware, adopting Mark 501, but due to an oversight the two patterns Summer Palace, W150, and Queen's Bird, Y4973, retained their original pattern number. New numbers were allocated in 1997: Summer Palace S3588, and Queen's Bird S3589.

Fine earthenware

1958-63

COPELAND
SPODE
ENGLAND

Mark printed from engraving using Murray backstamp machine. The previous dating method (impressed) ended in 1957: from 1958-63 a date letter was (often) inserted into top left corner of the gridiron.

1958	A		1961	D
1959	B		1962	E
1960	C		1963	F

From 1964 a new dating system was introduced – a letter printed with the code number of operative or printing team, eg M3. Applied as a print or waterslide transfer depending on the pattern.

1964	A	1968	E	1972	J
1965	B	1969	F	1973	K
1966	C	1970	G	1974	L
1967	D	1971	H	1975	M

1970-5

Spode
ENGLAND
ITALIAN
SPODE DESIGN
C.1816

1976 onwards

Spode
ENGLAND
ITALIAN
SPODE DESIGN
C.1816 E

The new mark, printed from engraving (rollers), was revised in 1976 and from then on has had the date letter added to the pattern number exactly as on bone china.

Josiah Spode II. 'The Spode factory was without doubt the most important factory in the early nineteenth century.' Hallé, Nineteenth Century European Porcelain.

Retailers/importers named on backstamps

DATE
1869

UNITED KINGDOM	NORTH AMERICA	EUROPE/OTHER
F. Abrahams & Son, Canterbury.		English Earthenware, 87 Rue St. Lazare, Paris. Jacquel, Rue de la Paix, Paris. Callinan & Son, 25 Suffolk St., Dublin.

1870

J. Spicer, 6&7 High West St., Dorchester.		A. Deseulle, English Earthenware, Depot 89 Rue Neuve des Petits Champs, Paris. Depot Central, Place de l'Eglise, St. Germain des Pres., Paris. Alexander Davidson, (altered to Dawidon) (place unknown).

1871

S. Chittenden, China Rooms, Cardiff. Sandbach & Co., Manchester. Barrett & Son, Cambridge.	Ovington Bros, Brooklyn.	Au Bon Marche, 29 Rue Chateaudun, Paris.

1872

Messrs. Daniell, 129 New Bond St., London.		Depot 17, Rue Drouet, Paris. J. Marquerie, Prix de Fabrique, 31 Rue de 4 Septembre, Paris.

1873

Heuser & Bein, 94 London Wall. F. H. Twyman, 12 King St., Ramsgate. F. Warner, Melton Mowbray.	Chas W. Hind, Silver St., Gainsburg.	Au Vase Etrusque, 20 Boulrd, Malesherbes.

1874

J. Parker, China Dealer, Hitchin W. Mabey & Sons		

1880

	Davis Collamore & Co., B'way Cor. 21st St., New York	

1881

F & C Osler, 100 Oxford St., London	Bailey, Banks & Biddle, Philadelphia A. French & Co., Boston	

1882

Thomas Gibson, Southport. James Pearson, Blackpool. Jacobs, Sandwich. Hudson, Southsea. W. O. Cheeseman & Son, Brighton. Leuchars & Son, 38 & 39 Piccadilly, London. Brown & Mackay, 23 Fenchurch St., London.	J. E. Caldwell & Co., Philadelphia. Gilman Collamore & Co., Union Square, New York. James M. Shaw & Co., 25 Duane St., New York.	Leuchars, Paris. Biston, Toussant. Chalons, Marne.

Copelands supplied wares direct to the Royal Family and the royal yacht, governments, armed forces, hospitals, schools and colleges and many institutions as well as commercial concerns.

| 1883 | |

1883

Philip Ashberry & Sons, Sheffield.

Richard Briggs, Boston.

Whyte & Sons, Dublin.

J. Abrahams, Canterbury.

Tiffany & Co., New York.

T. Goode & Co., 19 South Audley St., London.

Theadore B. Starr, New York.

F. C. Osler, 100 Oxford St., London.

Frederick Aldis, Belgravia, London.

1884

John Mortlock, Oxford St., & Orchard St., London.

Whyte & Sons, 4 Marlborough St., Dublin.

John Rose & Co., 39 & 41 King St., Manchester.

T. R. Grimes, 83 New Bond St., London W.

Coldwell & Kemp, Portsea.

1885

W. Hill & Son, 60 Bishopsgate St., EC.

Bigelow Kennard & Co., Boston.

Au Bon Marche, A. Dupeyrat, 29 Rue de Chateaudun et Rue Saint-George, 32. Paris, Terre de Fer.

G. Jennings, 155 Edgware Place.

1886

Spiers & Son, Oxford.

G. C. Shreve, San Francisco.

E. Eschle, 18 Commercial Palace, Aberdare S. W.

Burley & Co., 83 & 85 State St., Chicago.

1887

Osler, 100 Oxford St., London.

Davis Collamore & Co., 921 Broadway, New York.

Royal Yacht Osborne.

Pellatt & Wood, 25 Baker St., London W.

Made for J. E. Caldwell, Philadelphia.

Watson, Salisbury.

Ovington Bros.

Advance Australia.

J. Remus, 14 Piccadilly, London.

1888

Algonquin Club
A French & Co.

Hudson's Pottery Gallery, Southsea.

Tyndale & Mitchell, Philadelphia.

1889

Kitchen Dept.
Trinity College
Cambridge
St Bartholomew the Great

Down Bros., 3&4 St. Thomas St., London SE.

Ovington Brothers, Brooklyn.

A. Parsons, Devizes.

Shreve, Crump & Low Co., Boston.

Designed by W. J. Goode. Daniell, Wigmore St., London.

Gilman Collamore & Co., Union Square, New York.

1890

SS America

Hendersons China Stores, Sunderland.

Gilman Collamore & Co., 5th Ave & 30th St., New York.

Commercial Union Assurance

R. P. Daniell & Co., 129 Bond St., London.

Tice & Huntington, Importers, Cincinnati.

Daniell, Wigmore St. & New Bond St., London.

C. L. F. Huntington, Importers, Cincinnati.

Copestake Moore, Crampton & Co., London.

1891

Albert Barker,
5 New Bond St., London W.
William Whiteley,
Universal Provider.

Mermod & Jaccard,
Jewellery Co., St. Louis,
Made in England.
Bolling & Co., Louisville KY,
Made in England.

Baker & Co., Cork.

1892

Daniell, 129 New Bond St.,
London.
F. Crook, Motcomb St.,
Belgrave Sq., SW London.

Burley . . . Columbus 1893.

1893

Haskell & Co.,
Glass & China, Bournemouth.

1894

J. T. Godwin,
Dorchester & Weymouth.
Tredwin Dobbs, Bath.
Haskell & Co.,
Bournemouth.
Bennett & Co., Exmouth.
G. Fox & Son, Leicester.
Land & Co., Southport.

The Bailey, Banks & Biddle
Company, Philadelphia.
Chas. M. Van Heusen,
Importer, New York.

1895

Phillips, 175-9 Oxford St.,
London.
Heybourn & Co., 62 High St.,
Maidenhead.
Crook, Motcomb St.,
Belgrave Sq.

Davis Collamore & Co. Ltd.,
Broadway & 21st St., New York.
Gillman Collamore & Co.,
5th Ave. & 30th St., New York.
Tiffany & Co., New York.

1896

Treadwin Dobbs,
20 Milsom St., Bath.

J. McD & S. Importers,
(Jones, McDuffee &
Stratton, Boston).

1897

Sneddon & Sons,
Union St., Glasgow.

1899

Made for H. P. Munnings
China Rooms, Hertford.
Supplied by R. Hogg & Co.,
Belfast.
Presented by
T. Goode & Co., London.
James Green & Nephew,
London.

Burley & Co., Chicago.
The New Algonquin Club,
J. McD & S Co.

La Ceramica Inglesa,
39 Alcala 39, Madrid.
Magasins de L'Union des
Grands Fabricants,
Albert Blanchet,
12 Avenue de l'opera,
17 Rue Auber, Paris.

COPELAND SPODE'S TROPHIES

1900

John Ford & Co.,
39 Princes St., Edinburgh.
H & H (Hukin & Heath).

Davis Collamore & Co. Ltd.,
Fifth Avenue & 37th St.,
New York.

1901

Livingstone's China, Oban
(BURNS PATTERN)
John Ford & Co., Aberdeen.

Leuchars & Son,
Geffroy Sercet, Paris.

Government House SA
South Africa

Cadburys Cocoa

Cambridge University

St. Johns Coll. Cambridge

Royal Canadian Dragoons

Watch Weel
Who burnt the tablecloth?

Rideau Club, Ottawa

OTHER BACKSTAMPS OF INTEREST

Victoria & Albert
    HM Yacht

Presented by the High Sherriff
    (Mr. R. Copeland)
      June 26th 1902.

HM Yacht Osborne.

G
Marlborough House
    1903.

RHS (Royal Horticultural Society)

Hodsons Horse.

1902

Algonquin Club
(repeat of 1899?).

La Ceramica Inglesa
(as above).
D. Sheehan, Cork.
Treacher & Co., Ltd.,
Bombay & Poona.
Imported, chez A La Paix
34 Avenue de L'Opera,
Paris.

1903

Made expressly for Hotel
St. Regis, Copeland China
imported by Davis
Collamore & Co., Ltd.,
5th Ave and 37th St.

1904
Townsend & Co.,
22 Holmiside, Sunderland.

Nizam of Hyderabad &c.
Maison Toy,
10 Rue de la Paix 10, Paris

1905
Temple & Crook,
Motcomb St., Belgrave Sq,
London.
H. C. Reynolds Ltd.,
Wolverhampton.

C. A. Selzer, Cleveland.
Shreve & Co.,
San Francisco.
Cowell & Hubbard Co.,
Cleveland.
Richard Briggs Co.,
116 Boylston St., Boston.

E. Bourgeois,
Faience Porcelains
Cristaux, Grand Depot,
21 Rue Drouot, Paris.
33 Rue St. Fereol, Marseille.
NFV Gelder & Co.,
25 Prins Hendrikkade.
Staffordshire Warehouse,
Amsterdam.

1906
J. L. Fox & Co.,
4 New Briggate, Leeds.
Chas Mumby & Co. Ltd.,
Portsmouth,
(Makers of Table Waters)
T. F. Lumb & Co.,
39 North Parade, Bradford.
Waring & Gillow Ltd.,
Oxford St., London.

Dulin & Martin Co.,
Washington D.C.
Burley & Co., Chicago,
(Chicago Pitcher).
Made for Bullard Brothers,
St. Paul, Minnesota.

1907
Thomas Wallis & Co. Ltd.,
Holborn Circus.
Henry Rogers, Sons & Co.,
Wolverhampton.
R. Hogg & Co. Ltd., Belfast
Asprey, London.
White & Wright, Liverpool.
Heal & Son, London W.

J. Dalfinger & Co., Louisville.
Hudson's Bay Company.
A. T. Wiley & Co. Ltd.,
Montreal.

1908
Mumbys Table Waters.
Phillips Ltd., 43,44,
New Bond St., London W.
Pearce & Sons Ltd,
Silversmiths, Leeds, York &
Leicester.
Tate & Oglesby Ltd., Hull.

1909

Jacobs Zweena, London.	Brock & Feagans,	H. J. Linton,	
Hospitals & General	Los Angeles, California	30 Rue Feydeau, Paris.	
Contracts Co. Ltd.	for ET Sherer.	E. Cardenal & Co., Madrid.	
33&34 Mortimer St.,			
London W.			
Phillip's Arcadian,			
43&44 New Bond St., London.			
Hampton & Sons, London.			
Townsend Galleries,			
Newcastle-upon-Tyne.			
Frain's Ltd., Dundee.			
H. G. Stephenson Ltd.,			
Manchester.			
Simpson & Son Ltd.,			
Halifax & Blackburn.			
G. W. Darby,			
30 Market St., Nottingham.			

1910

Letheby & Christopher Ltd.		Le Rosey, 5 Boulevard	Ontario
Robert Hogg & Co. Ltd., Belfast.		Malesherbes, Paris.	Osborne EVIIR
T. F. Lumb & Co., Bradford.			

1911

Maple & Co. Ltd. London.	Bigelow Kennard & Co.,	E. Cardenal & Co., Madrid.	
James Howell & Co. Ltd.,	Boston.		
Cardiff.			
Waring & Gillow Ltd.,			
Deansgate, Manchester.			

1912

D. J. Allams & Sons,		Whyte & Sons Ltd.,	
Torquay.		Dublin.	
Lewis & Cooper,		La Hispano Inglesa,	
Northallerton.		41Cª de San Jeronimo 41,	
H. C. Reynolds Ltd.,		Madrid.	
Wolverhampton.			

1913

Down Bros Ltd.,	Gimbel Brothers, New York.		
Leadless Glaze,			
St. Thomas St., London SE.			
Messrs. Read, China Road,			
Brierley Hill.			
Joseph W. Bridge Ltd.,			
Accrington.			

1914

	Wright, Tyndale & Van	Dillons, Coleraine, Ireland.	Holyrood Palace
	Roden Inc., 1212 Chestnut	Hall & Anderson, Calcutta.	1915
	St., Philadelphia.		
	Made for Charles R. Lynde,		
	Boston.		

1916

Maple, London.	The Hodgkins Co. Inc.	Maguire & Gatchell Ltd.,	
Robert Hogg & Co. Ltd.,	Buffalo.	Dublin.	
Belfast.	The Regnier & Shoup		
	Crockery Co.,		
	St. Joseph, Mo.		
	Bullard Bros, St. Paul.		
	R. H. Stearns Co., Boston.		
	T. M. James & Sons,		
	Kansas City, specialists in		
	English Bone China.		
	C. Reizenstein Sons, Pittsburg.		
	The Bailey Banks & Biddle		
	Co., Philadelphia.		

	1917		
	From Alfred Dunn, 6 New St., Birmingham.	C. Hall, Springfield, Massachussetts. G. L. Emerson, Boston. L. Bamberger & Co. Newark NJ.	
	1919		
City of London.		William Junor, Toronto.	
	1920		
	Marsh, Jones & Cribb Ltd., Leeds.	Gilman Collamore & Co., 15 East 56 St., New York.	
	1922		
	Soane & Smith (Lionel Edwards). Temple & Crook, Motcomb St., Belgrave Sq.		
	1923		
	Robert Hogg & Co. Ltd., Belfast. Asprey & Co. Ltd., Bond St., London. F (. No. 701655.		
	1924		
Victoria & Albert Royal Yacht.	Sir Joseph Causton & Sons Ltd., London.	Sandor Decsenyi, Pasadena, California.	Simons & Co., 853 Au de Mayo, Buenos Aires.
	1925		
Goldsmiths' Arms	Eccles, Jones.	Martin, Washington D.C. Geo. L. Emerson, Boston, Massachussetts. Sander Decsengi, Pasadena, California. Expressly made for Mrs. Anita M. Baldwin.	
	1926		
RAF wings			Hardy Brothers, Canberra & Melbourne.
	1927		
	Scotts Ltd., Newcastle. Windsor & Firth Ltd., Ossett.	Made expressly for The Hardy & Hayes Company, Pittsburgh. Eldridge, Omaha.	
	1928		
GvR Royal Yacht Matching	James Green & Nephew, London. Stonier & Co. Ltd., Liverpool	Rich & Fisher Inc., New York.	
	1929		
Lloyds		Lynde Sanger & Co. Inc., Boston, Massachussetts. The FE Sherman Co., Bar Harbor, Maine.	
	1930		
Clothworkers			EB Lattorff, Hamburg.
	1931		
Cincinnati badge Fishmongers	Apsley Pellatt & Co., 3 Bloomsbury St., London WC1. J. H. Awmack Ltd., The Headrow, Leeds. Tréron et Cie, Glasgow.		Coombes Company, Ltd., Rangoon & London.

1932

Spaulding Gorham, Chicago.

1933
Heal & Son Ltd.,
Silver & Jade.
Fortnum & Mason Ltd., London.
Fribourg & Treyer, London.
Barkers, Kensington.

1934
Apsley Pellatt & Co. Ltd.,
3 Bloomsbury Street WC1.

1936

Richard Briggs China Co.,
Boston.

1937
1938
T.H. Lawley & Co. Ltd.,
London.
Payne & Son Ltd.,
Southampton.
James Green & Nephew
Ltd., London.

Robert Anstead,
Los Angeles.
The Bailey Banks & Biddle
Co. Ltd., Philadelphia.
Eldridge, Omaha.

1940
J. H. Awmack Ltd.,
The Headrow, Leeds.

Supported by Robert Anstead,
Beverley Hills
Dirigo, Chicago.

1953
Mabey & Johnson Ltd.,
54 Victoria St.,
London SW1

1962
Fortnum & Mason Ltd.,
London.

Jackson's China & Furniture,
Leamington, Ontario.

OTHER BACKSTAMPS OF INTEREST

Blanche de Chine
Reg. No. 785542

Newcastle-on-Tyne

Goldsmiths

Mansard
US Patent 88688
Rd No. 777266

Salters Co.

1957 Royal Exchange
1958 New York Trust Co.

Group of objects in fine bone china relating to Winchester. Left, pitcher in the shape of a leathern bottle; centre, bowl in the style of the Winchester Bushel; right, model of the Trusty Servant, with the appropriate verse.

Advertisement in the 1926 Annual Review listing overseas agents.

Patent Office registration marks

In 1842 designs started to be registered with the British Patent Office, and numbers allocated to each design. The mark on the ware is in the form of a diamond surmounted by a circle in which there is a roman numeral which shows in which class the product is registered: Class IV includes the ceramic wares. Each of the corners of the diamond contain a letter or numeral which indicate the date of the registration, but the registration number is seldom added to the mark applied to ware. The diamond, or 'kite', mark might be applied to clay ware if the registration applied to the shape of the article; this might be formed in the mould, added as a pad mark or impressed into the clay. In some cases a printed mark was applied on the biscuit ware which related to the shape. The Chelsea shape, for example, was registered on the 15th November 1879 and the kite mark occurs on items of this range of items which are decorated with a variety of different patterns. Most transfer-printed marks, however, relate to the printed pattern.

One or two instances occur where the registered number does not relate to Copelands' design, but to that of a retailer or the manufacturer of, say, metal goods, for whom Copelands made the essential ceramic part.

The diamond mark system ended in December 1883 and was replaced by one in which all designs were numbered consecutively and ceramic objects had to take pot luck with everything else – lace, garden tools, hurricane lamps, textiles, glass, etcetera. It would take years of unrelenting and tedious research to list all the numbers of ceramic designs with the names of the manufacturers and descriptions of the product. Fortunately, a record of the Copeland designs registered after 1884 was kept at the Works, and details of the earlier diamond marked designs was built up from the information listed in John Cushion's book of *British Ceramic Marks* [1976].

Patent Office registration marks (Class IV) 1842-1883

Date + period	Parcel No.	Patent No.	Description of Design + pattern number if known
COPELAND & GARRETT			
1844			
14 Oct	4	22158	Statice pattern 7139,2/2641
2 Dec	3	22919	Louis Quartorze border pattern 7328
		22920	Louis Quartorze pattern, with centre
1845			
5 Mar	1	26608	Egg & Dart border patterns 7260,8237,B786
25 Apr	2	27350	Raphaelesque pattern 7384,9847,B801
19 June	1	28150	Lobelia pattern [George Phillips, Longport]
4 Sept	3	30161	Royal Stuart plaid } mosaic pattern for
		30162	Cameron plaid } tiles, toilet ware,
		30163	Macduff plaid } teaware etc.
21 Oct	1	30699	Continental Views pattern
1846			
17 Apr	3	34684	Door Finger Plate design, pattern 7427
21 July	1	36278	Caledonian pattern
			[Francis Morley & Co, Shelton]
		37171	Border pattern
		37172	Border pattern
14 Sept	4	37254	Field Sports pattern
		37986	Phillips pattern
17 Dec	2	39544	Broad pointed border pattern 7611
		39545	Bell flower panel pattern 7534
1847			
9 Jan	7	40110	Etruscan shape tureen & vegetable dish
15 Feb	4	41459	pattern of small circles
		41460	Wax mortar night shade
12 May	4	43154	Stone porcelain edge for flower garden border

1847

Date		No.	Description
17 Aug	2	45091	Round dish
		45092	Jug with Portland Vase design embossed
9 Sept	3	45730	Rose Wreath pattern 7803, Piccadilly D6361
16	3	45822	Lily & Rose pattern
13 Oct	1	46299	Ewer and basin

1848

Date		No.	Description
18 Jan	2	49040	Rose spray in centre, small sprays & bead
14 Mar	2	50798	Border of flowers with convolvulus wreath
15	2	50803	Covered vegetable dish and stand
30 June	2	52529	Alhambra pattern 8163
15 Sept	3	54438	Ruins, or Melrose, pattern D415
4 Nov	2	55174	Convolvulus embossed jug
13	4	55337	Vine embossed jug

1849

Date		No.	Description
10 Apr	4	59400	Bold coloured border scrolls pattern 8021
11 Aug	4	61865	Embossed covered jug
17	2	62003	Garland pattern 8031
9 Nov	4	63523	Lily of the Valley embossed jug
22	2	64319	Syringa†, or Mock Orange, pattern 8371
6 Dec	3	64739	Ewer and basin, embossed holly

1850

Date		No.	Description
9 Mar	3	67987	Japonica pattern, 9269, 2/2712, 2/3564, R7097
19 Sept	2	71989	Rural Scenes pattern, Duncan Scenes, Priscilla Alden
17 Oct	6	72544	Embossed wall bracket
20 Dec	6	75148	Lotus pattern 8627

1851

Date		No.	Description
30 May	4	79085	Lotus embossed jug
11 June	2	79183	Ionian pattern, 2/6205, 2/6734
19	5	79300	Byron border of grapes, Girl giving drink to boy
14 July	3	79684	Covered tureen, embossed with hawthorn
1 Oct	1	80827	Sweet Pea pattern
8 Dec	8	81960	Bead like Osborne with floral festoons, and 'Plight thee my troth, for better or worse . .'

1852

Date		No.	Description
14 May	5	85081	Tuscan Embossed Tea & dessert ware
16			Fleur de Lys pattern in green
14 June	4	85354	Tuscan pattern 9098 This is on the shape of dessert plate used for the Goldsmiths Company
4 Aug	3	86070	Fleur de Lys pattern 8910
		86071	Jasmine border pattern, 4540, 8945, 8978, 9275, 1/7784, B118, R982
1 Oct	6	86931	Strawberry pattern D2612, B305, 9581, 1/988

1853

Date		No.	Description
3 Jan	3	88808	Scroll border and centre pattern 9077, D96, D98
		88809	Lozenge bead D95, D129, D255
26 Feb	5	89958	Embossed wheat on barrel shape jug
		91579	Arabic script plate
26 Nov	2	93452	Embossed panel 3x1 Swan & Acanthus

Index to the letters used for years and months from 1842 to 1883

Two arrangements of letters and figures were used. From 1842-1867 the year letter was at the top of the diamond. When all 26 letters had been used the year letter was moved to the right of the diamond.

The first series from 1842-1867 with the year letter at the top

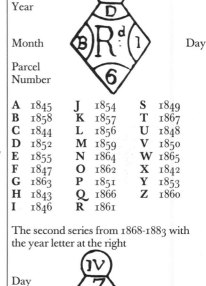

	A	1845	J	1854	S	1849
	B	1858	K	1857	T	1867
	C	1844	L	1856	U	1848
	D	1852	M	1859	V	1850
	E	1855	N	1864	W	1865
	F	1847	O	1862	X	1842
	G	1863	P	1851	Y	1853
	H	1843	Q	1866	Z	1860
	I	1846	R	1861		

The second series from 1868-1883 with the year letter at the right

A	1871	J	1880	W	1878
C	1870	K	1883	(March 1-6
D	1878	L	1882	ONLY)
E	1881	P	1877	X	1868
F	1873	S	1875	Y	1879
H	1869	U	1874		
I	1872	V	1876		

THE MONTH LETTERS WERE THE SAME FOR BOTH YEAR SERIES

A	Dec	G	Feb	M	June
B	Oct	H	April	R	Aug (also
C or O	Jan	I	July		Sept 1-19 1857
D	Sept	K	Nov (&	W	Mar
E	May		Dec 1860		

†The Mock Orange, Philadelphus, was known (wrongly) as Syringa some years ago. Syringa is the botanical name Lilac.

Once the registration mark was engraved on the copper plate it could continue to be applied on ware many years after the date when it was registered; registration only protected the design for three years, so sometimes the registration of a design was renewed. Moreover some of the designs registered by Copelands were of patterns introduced first in the Spode period, but then recoloured and thus the altered version justified protection. The presence of a diamond mark or registration number can only state an approximate date when the item or pattern was made. Several instances have been noted of patterns which have been registered some time after the original design was recorded in the pattern books.

Rural Scenes pattern, from watercolours by E. Duncan. Registered 19 September 1850. Many versions were produced, usually as plain prints. This one is on the Amiens embossed shape, c. 1879.

Ruins pattern, registered 1848, and also called Melrose. A different scene was used for each piece.

1854			
23 Feb	3	95163	Embossed jug in form of oak tree, inscribed VICTORIA WELLINGTON
12 Sept	2	96826	Hops embossed jug
1855			
7 Apr	7	99814	Honeysuckle Empire pattern 9775, Crystal Palace 3299, B855, 7187, D317, 2/4345
1856			
1 Sept	3	106161	Union border pattern with large thistle leaves and roses and small shamrocks
22 Oct	3	106770	Tulip embossed jug
11 Dec	4	107955	Lattice pattern 3958, D434
1857			
29 Apr	1	109810	Richmond Views pattern, Border only Lace pattern
19 Jun	1	110160	Grenada pattern D622
7 Sept	2	111105	Christmas pattern D579, with panels of holly, mistletoe centre, wheat, hops and ivy, D8540 1/8132
1858			
17 Dec	6	117443	Sardinia pattern D1489, 2/9663
23	9	117530	Ewer and basin, rope handle & embossed edge
1859			
25 Jan	4	118119	Lorenzo pattern
2 July	2	120560	Atlantic Royal Mail pattern
14 Oct	4	123116	Persian pattern
1860			
10 Jan	4	125365	Etna pattern
14 Feb	9	126446	Embossed vase
		126447	Embossed vase on pedestal, with handles and lid
1861			
19 Mar	3	139053	Parthenon pattern
3 May	8	140367	Beads – short lengths either side of twisted ribbon
11 June	2	141326	Jug with Tiffany handle
		141327	Coventry pattern
17 Sept	2	143702	Shamrock pattern D2548, 1/5264, R9048, 2/7618
18 Oct	3	145157	Souvenir pattern D2807
1862			
13 Mar	6	149938	Nymphea pattern, 1372, D2928, 2/1213
1863			
22 May	4	162618	Corn & Poppy pattern, 9457, D3252, toilet ware, 2/2317, 2/3488, 2/5494, 2/4449
		162619	Jug with curious handle
24 July	3	164468	Elcho pattern, D3301
		164469	Denmark pattern D3402, D6068, 1/2544, 2/865

1864

13 Feb	6	171673	Embossed jug
6 Sept	5	178264	Pekin pattern D4013, B582, 2/123, 2/355, 2/6462, 2/6561, ›/9591, R6114, R6470
1 Nov	7	180695	Ornamental handled pot

1868

2 Feb	7	194949	Covered butter dish, oblong
12 Nov	3	203538	Childrens' plate designs with gnomes, &c.

1867

24 Apr	2	207636	Teapot shape

W T COPELAND & SONS

1867

26 Oct	1	212881	Mug & saucer design "A Merry Christmas to You"
28	4	212956	Nursery Rhyme designs
3 Dec	3	214618	Embossed jug

1868

25 Mar	7	217615	Acorn pattern

1869

24 July	4	231222	Tennis set – cup on long saucer
2 Aug	6	231504	Nautilus shell Spoon Warmer
19	6	232307	Non-drip saucer; ridges for cup to sit upon
26	6	232474	Jam pot with knob in the form of a child's head
31	12	232598	Embossed grass tea & coffee service
8 Sept	5	232878	Embossed fern tea & coffee service

1870

15 July	1	243207	Embossed jug

1871

4 July	8	253796	Embossed cup & saucer
		253797	Embossed cup & saucer
		253798	Embossed cup & saucer
19 Oct	6	256907	Embossed jug

1872

30 Jan	7	260081	Embossed leaves cup & saucer
11 June	12	263348	Jug with 'built in' handle

1873

13 Jan	4	269621	Ewer & basin – panels a Chine

1874

21 Jan	7	279964	Bamboo embossed teapot
1 Dec	5	287598	Nightlight holder on pedestal

1875

8 Nov	8	295803	Jug

1876

9 June	6	301164	Ewer & basin THE WATFORD
5 July	7	301641	Parrot model, hanging on a ring

Nautilus shell spoon warmer, for keeping the silver sauce ladle in hot water so that fatty gravy would not congeal upon it. No. 231504.

Jug embossed with Celtic motifs. Stoneware. Although registered in 1871 this example bears Mark 266, showing it was made after 1894. Height 19 cm. Registered October 19th 1871.

Queen Anne shape was made in bone china and earthenware and remained in production for over thirty years. No. 393103.

A page from the pattern book. Aesop's Fables pattern 2/1356, one of several versions.

1877			
24 Jan			Fairies
21 Feb	9	307909	Pair of parrots on a ring
8 Mar	14	308329	Lantern
2 July	3	311523	Embossed jug
1878			
24 Jan	6	318041	Cupid wall bracket for flowers
5 June	14	322223	Covered vegetable dish and draining grid
		322224	Handled asparagus basket
14 Oct	8	327625	Robin (tail up) handled mug, with mistletoe
		327626	Robin (tail down) handled mug, with holly
1879			
7 Jan	7	330920	Crichton shape teapot
28	11	331597	Aesops Fables pattern 2/1351, Stork & Frog
12 Mar	12	333235	Aesops Fables pattern Eagle & Tortoise
		333236	Aesops Fables pattern Pot & Kettle
15 Nov	16	342925	Chelsea shape covered vegetable dish, oblong
		342926	Chelsea shape plate
		342927	Chelsea shape soup tureen & stand, oblong
1881			
28 Apr	12	364488	Primrose pattern 2/1683,1/2722
30 July	15	367590	Ornamental tureen
1882			
4 Jan	2	375426	Bowl
		375427	Jug
9 Oct	3	387771	Curious jug, with lugs for cane handle
1883			
8 Jan	5	392590	Queen Anne shape Covered vegetable dish
23	10	393102	Queen Anne shape Bowl
		393103	Queen Anne shape Jug
25 Oct	15	406030	Satchel Biscuit Jar (W W Harrison & Company, Sheffield, metal designers & manufacturers).

Satchel biscuit jar. No. 406030.

Crichton shape teapot, modelled after a Chinese Yi-Hsing red stoneware wine pot, copied by Josiah Spode c. 1810. Mark 351. Famed for the Burns pattern, other decorations were applied on this shape. No. 330920.

Number	Date	Name of Design – Shape or Pattern No.	
90067	11 4 90	Trade Mark for Spode Imperial, ivory earthenware	
180288	11 9 94	Trade mark earthenware. This is a felucca, a small sailing boat used on the River Nile, derived from the border of pattern 2/1889 and known as Frank's Boat.	
26070	1 5 85	Walpole shape, later called Centurion Shape	2/2682
87603	17 11 87	Westminster shape dinnerware,	1/8265
89620	13 12 87	Iris Basket pattern	
97940	12 4 88	Gong pattern	
113989			
137935	9 11 89	Slop & Commo Pase [It is not clear what this means!]	
142592	14 1 90	5 thistle pieces made for T Goode & Co	
142593	15 1 90	Old Crow pattern	1/6105, 2/3420
142594	15 1 90	Meadow pattern	1/6403, 2/3329
143192	31 1 90	Venice shape dinnerware	
159275	20 10 90	Floss pattern	1/6653, 2/3368
159276	20 10 90	Charlotte pattern	1/8742
159843	27 10 90	Chester pattern	1/6542
159844	27 10 90	Clarence pattern	2/3415
159997	29 10 90	Chelsea Wicker shape tableware	
160319	4 11 90	Plain Louis uncovered ewer,	
160320	4 11 90	Louis XV Embossed uncovered ewer } or chocolate jug	
165006	20 1 91	Hapsburg pierced dessert plate	
165883	5 2 91	Louis XV Embossed tableware	
168716	25 3 91	Campkettle	
176982	21 8 91	Goodwood Entree Dish	
178065			
178266	15 9 91	Beatrice pattern	1/7002
189802	24 3 92	Istria pattern	2/3719
190477	4 4 92	Cyril pattern	1/7223, 1/8029
193677	7 6 92	Victoria toilet bowl (ewer 1/8231)	
196703	11 8 92	Columbus panel for the Columbus Pitcher	
198288		Reported on a printed pattern of rabbits, ? as 1/8182	
204192	14 12 92	May pattern with centre	
204193	14 12 92	King pattern (an old Spode pattern)	3875, R6469
206164	19 1 93	Mortimer shape tableware	as 1/7951 &c
206165	19 1 93	Hawkweed pattern	2/3818, 1/7608
206166	19 1 93	Victoria plate, ivory earthenware for A. B. Daniell	
212545	23 5 93	Teck pattern	2/4042
213963	23 6 93	New Fluted Milkpan	

Registered Numbers

This record is the best information available at present. The Spode Works record lists a minimum of details, and many of the registered designs have not been identified to pattern numbers. Where pattern numbers have been found, at least one is listed here.

The numbers are usually printed below the mark, or backstamp, with Rd.No. in front, as for example, Chinese Rose Rd.No.629599.

Two registered numbers, 90067 and 180288, which are frequently seen on Copeland earthenwares, are registered trade marks, recorded in the Register of Trade Marks, and they are not designs or patterns.

Hapsburg pierced dessert plate. Derived from a Derby mould of the Bloor period, 1825-30, which was among those bought by W T Copeland in 1852. No. 165006. See Twitchett, J, Derby Porcelain (1980), plate 72.

Ashantee footstool, No. 235780.

Savoy shape bowl, underside. No. 248670.

NUMBER	DATE	NAME OF DESIGN — SHAPE OR PATTERN NO.	
226335	30 1 94	H B border & Game centre.	
		Wicker Dale pattern	2/4088
226336	30 1 94	Delft pattern, with Tower border	2/3993
226431	31 1 94	Ship or Bertha pattern	
		(Old Spode)	3067, 2/15
228637	7 3 94	Danish shape teaware	as 1/8058 &C
233767	11 6 94	Chatsworth pattern (C & G 5889)	1/1490, 2/9043
235081	25 6 94	Chrysanthemum or Molyneux	
		pattern	B282, 1/8039
235082	26 6 94	Wild Rose pattern	1/285, R7847
235083	26 6 94	Japanese pattern	2/3947, 2/3913
235780	11 7 94	Ashantee foot stool (often in	
		Tower pattern)	
235781	11 7 94	Abdul pattern	2/4005
235782	11 7 94	Foxglove pattern	2/4002
236891	30 7 94	Basil pattern, or Festoon, 1/8086	1/8060
236892	30 7 94	Violets pattern	1/8068
236893	30 7 94	Carlyle shape tableware	as 1/8084 &c
236894	30 7 94	New Jasmine pattern, or	
		Jessamine	1/8070
242006	11 10 94	Heart shape teapot, sugar,	
		cream jug & tray, as	1/7943
243298	30 10 94	Leeds shape tableware	as 1/8374
248670	30 1 95	Savoy shape tableware &	
		serving pieces	as 1/8267
257404	3 7 95	Mountford teacup & saucer,	
		as 1/8403	1/8450
258025	12 7 95	Exeter pattern	
265772	15 11 95	Leighton shape tableware	as 2/5219
265773	15 11 95	Hastings pattern	2/4150
265774	15 11 95	Morocco pattern	1/8279, 1/8342, 2/6632
265775	15 11 95	Mask bead, laurel &	
		festoons pattern	1/8287, 1/8402
268689	8 1 96	Lothian saucer	
268690	8 1 96	Atlantic chamber pot	
270229	1 2 96	Egg & Bird shape	
270230	1 2 96	Clarendon embossed shape	
		dinnerware	as 1/9390
276022	11 5 96	Louis XV shape for G Gyori,	
		Vienna	
285413	3 10 96	Jubilee Embossed jug	
287959	10 11 96	Grant shape teapot	
290166	12 12 96	Pineapple shape table ornaments	
290167	12 12 96	Cymbaline pattern	1/9363, 2/4410
291232	31 12 96	Goode's new morning set	
295195	5 3 97	Pineapple shape – more table	
		ornaments	
301576	15 7 97	Grosvenor shape, festoon	
		embossed, tableware	

NUMBER	DATE	NAME OF DESIGN – SHAPE OR PATTERN NO.	
306407	9 10 97	Gadroon oval ewer and bowl	
309589	23 11 97	Holly Embossed Mountford shape teaware	
317544	20 4 98	The Seven Wonders of the World pattern	2/4506
317815	26 4 98	Hamburg shape teaware	as 1/9859
319321	23 5 98	Hanging Lamp	
319322	23 5 98	Wildflowers pattern for toiletware	
339809	16 6 99	Sutherland shape dinnerware	as 1/9862
342853	8 8 99	Pearl shape dessert ware & candelabra	
345322	16 9 99	Golf embossment for a slab	
346636	5 1 99	Tudor Lions pattern for toiletware	2/4822
	1900		
351929	16 1 00	Elmo pattern	2/7573
353027	8 2 00	Burley's Oyster Plate	
382297	29 10 01	Ivanhoe pattern	2/4925, R699
382972	9 11 01	York shape teacup & saucer	
386590	1 2 02	Sheraton pattern	
395839	23 8 02	Colonel pattern	R994, 2/5061
425264			
425456	27 1 04	Guelph shape dinnerware	
434243-			
435142			
448091	12 1 05	Crinkled Paper Flower Holders	
449865	8 2 05	Claridge's Hotel border pattern	
453872	7 4 05	Verbena pattern	2/5445, R2153
454624	15 4 05	Nelson Centenary Loving Cup	
455224	27 4 05	Burley border pattern, Stafford Blue Leaf	1/9688
461740	31 7 05	Bradford pattern	R2298, 2/5597
462111	4 8 05	Treve's Sickfeeder with Spout	
462112	4 8 05	Sutherland shape Chocolate Jug & Coffee Pot	
462113	4 8 05	Wicker Embossed Salad Bowls, Fernpots	
466535	5 10 05	Treve's Sickfeeder	
466536	5 10 05	Games (?) Embossed on Toiletware	
467171	14 10 05	Spode's Garden pattern	2/5624, R2501
467172	14 10 05	Herald pattern	2/5970, 2/7569
470195	2 12 05	Florial pattern for toiletware	
470196	2 12 05	Rugby bead pattern (L & NW Rly)	
471342	27 12 05	L & NW Railway special shape saucer	
471342	27 12 05	Gresham pattern	R2496
471343	27 12 05	Basket of Roses pattern for toiletware	R2583, 2/5583
474683	24 2 06	Bridal Festoon pattern also called Blackstone	2/7173
477282	11 4 06	Port shape teaware	

Nigel 2/5793. No. 512488.

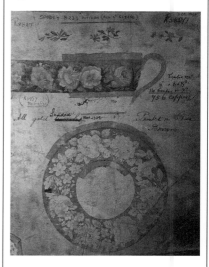

R3827, so called Spode's B233, although no evidence has yet been found for this number. No. 553455.

Wildflower pattern. A sheet pattern also popular on tableware. No. 319322. The pattern number for tableware is 2/6748, but toilet ware was T862.

Maple Birds 2/5812. No. 494242.

NUMBER	DATE	NAME OF DESIGN — SHAPE OR PATTERN NO.	
487290	18 9 06	Chippendale on Queen Anne shape toiletware	R2680
487291	18 9 06	Gadroon Cheese Stand, Hygienic	
487292	18 9 06	Cheshire Cheese Stand, Hygienic	
487358	19 9 06	Nora pattern	
493287	22 12 06	Devonia shape Dessert ware	
493476	31 12 06	Evesham Asparagus Plate	
494242	17 1 07	Maple Birds pattern	R4622, 2/5812
511316	11 9 07	Waldorf Hotel pattern for toiletware	
511317	11 9 07	Waldorf Hotel pattern for tableware, for Waring & Gillow	
512488	24 9 07	Nigel pattern for Waring & Gillow	2/5793, B252
516551	29 9 07	L & NW Railway non-spilling cup	
525497	5 6 08	Lowestoft pattern	R3912, 2/5438
526380	19 6 08	Spode's 2794 pattern	
526381	19 6 08	Flower Embossed shape table and toiletware	as 2/7067
528065	23 7 08	Marathon pattern	R3471, 2/5988
531630	16 10 08	Spode's 3127 pattern	
536718	6 2 08	Oriental pattern on toiletware	
544807	26 6 09	Eggstand with hot water pan, for H & H	
546207	21 7 09	Spode's B89 pattern	
548466	2 9 09	Cat-handled jug	
552715	17 11 09	Cup & Saucer designed to avoid cup falling over	
552716	17 11 09	Teddy Bear handled jug and mug	
552768	18 11 09	Vienna pattern on Flower Embossed shape	2/6137
553455	1 12 09	Spode's B233 pattern	R3827
553963	11 12 09	Blue Scale and Bird pattern on vases etc.	R3896 ?
554297	18 12 09	Stoneware Teapots, Sugar Boxes and Cream Jugs with embossed Vine border and medallion for badges	
560515	9 4 09	Shirley pattern	R3912
561065	19 4 10	Ingestre pattern	2/5918, 2/7574
561066	19 4 10	Delft Trellis pattern	
561636	3 5 10	Sauceboat with hot water pan for Hukin & Heath, London	
561943	3 5 10	Single egg holder with hot water pan	
564547	13 6 10	Lyon pattern for William Whiteley	R4112, 2/6248
564548	13 6 10	Cornwall pattern	R548
567326	25 7 10	Rose shape tableware	
568948	26 8 10	Peplow pattern for Harrods	R4075, 2/6246
568949	26 8 10	Chelsea pattern for Harrods	R4073, 2/6247

Chelsea pattern. No. 568949.

NUMBER	DATE	NAME OF DESIGN – SHAPE OR PATTERN NO.	
572093	11 10 10	Memorial vase of the late King Edward VII	
572093	21 10 10	Angus pattern for toiletware & vases	2/6401
572659	1 11 10	Swansea Rose pattern	2/6284, 2/7577
575389	20 12 10	Coronation Vase for King George V	
575390	20 12 10	Individual covered Jam Pot (for Hukin & Heath)	
575763	31 12 10	Shagreen or Parrot pattern, Spode 5742	R8654, 2/6178
575764	31 12 10	Peacock and Parsley pattern, Spode 4079	R4619, 2/6105
576929	21 1 11	Lowestoft or Famille Rose pattern for Connaught Regiment	
580303	14 3 11	White Star Line pattern	R416, R4332
580796	22 3 11	Woodpecker pattern for Heals	T745
586209	1 7 11	S border pattern	R3930, 2/7213
591441	25 10 11	Karra shape Lamp	
591442	25 10 11	Plain shape Lamp for T Goode & Co.	
596271	13 2 12	Rose Chintz or Patricia pattern	2/9051
596272	13 2 12	Bordeaux Sweets	
596273	13 2 12	Crete Sweets	
596274	13 2 12	Coventry Sweets	
599813	17 4 12	Old Bow pattern for Harrods	R4730, 2/6418
508158	26 9 12	Grasshopper pattern, Spode 2372	D9821, 1/2134
608159	26 9 12	Hanging Bell Push	
608594	5 10 12	Brompton pattern	BD135, 2/6497
608585	5 10 12	Stuart or Pearl & Laurel pattern for Stonier & Co. Liverpool	
609025	15 10 12	Table Bell Push	
615911	12 3 13	Bird & Border or Eden pattern for Gorringes	S2629, S2655 2/6518, Y4584
615912	12 3 13	Spode's Berries or Currants pattern	B100, 3966
616247	19 3 13	Heron pattern	2137, 8683, 2/468, 2/6256
618135	26 4 13	Spode Sprig & bead pattern	R1694
620281	12 6 13	Ilkley Swastika pattern	R4927
621192		Hancock's Rockery & Pheasant pattern	
622027	10 7 13	Electric Light Shade	
623209	29 7 13	Brick and Festoon pattern	
627672	5 11 13	Crossbar Border & Vase pattern	2/6574
629599	13 12 13	Waring's Rock or Chinese Rose pattern for Waring & Gillow, London	Y7416, 2/9253, R5008
630909	19 1 14	Brick & Curl Border or Pembroke pattern	
631483	27 2 14	No. 114 Shape Vase	

Peacock and Parsley 2/6105, No. 575764.

Coffee cup and saucer, with marks, of the cobalt blue and gold pattern used in the First Class dining rooms of the Titanic *and her sister ship the* Olympic.

Character jug of the Duke of Wellington.
No. 646176.

Blighty 2/6921, No. 658632.

Chelsea Birds 2/6837, No. 651133.

NUMBER	DATE	NAME OF DESIGN – SHAPE OR PATTERN	NO.
637555	26 5 14	Avondale pattern for Hamptons	2/6544
637556	26 5 14	Chinese Figures pattern	2/6655, 2/6810
637852	3 6 14	Portland Vase or Grecian pattern	2/6553
639277	2 7 14	Greek pattern (Spode pattern)	1111, S3110
643560	7 11 14	Tongking shape covered pieces	
643561	7 11 14	Single Inkwell on tray	
643562	7 11 14	Single Dresden Inkwell on tray	
644931	2 1 15	Tudor pattern	2/6698, R7978
644932	2 1 15	Octagon Inkwell with compartments for stamps & sealing wax	
646036	13 2 15	Randall's Birds pattern for Harrods	2/6616
646176	18 2 15	Wellington character jug, helmet as cover	
646542	3 3 15	Spode's Imari pattern	
648815	26 5 15	Plain Round Covered Box with Rose Knob	
649410	22 6 15	Table electric bell push, square plinth	
650526	3 8 15	Marlborough shape tableware	
650527	3 8 15	Marlborough Sprays or Luneville pattern	2/6770
651133	1 9 15	Chelsea Birds or Exotic Birds & Flower pattern (Blackbird)	B595, 2/6837
651617	22 9 15	Foot Soldier Grenadier Guards	
651618	22 9 15	Mounted Soldier 'Scots Greys'	
653635	11 1 16	– pattern (un-named)	2/6886
653908	25 1 16	Sèvres pattern dessert ware	C1887
654734	4 3 16	Sèvres pattern dessert ware	C1872
654735	4 3 16	Sèvres pattern dessert ware	C1903
655338	12 4 16	Chaplet pattern	R5936, 2/6903, 2/6873
657046	2 8 16	Bead & Festoon pattern	R5892
657047	2 8 16	Lens pattern	R7754, 2/7054
657048	2 8 16	Chippendale pattern	R5893
657049	2 8 16	Adams pattern	R5801, R5870
658630	4 12 16	Dragon (Cat's Face) pattern	R5955, 2/3154
658631	4 12 16	Shields pattern with Scale border	R5954
658632	4 12 16	Blighty pattern	2/6921
658633	4 12 16	Bristol pattern	
658634	4 12 16	Kensington pattern	
659202	22 1 17	Kestrel bird figure	
659203	22 1 17	Woodpecker bird figure	
659204	22 1 17	Marne pattern	R6034
659205	22 1 17	Ming pattern	
659270	30 1 17	Poppy Leaf pattern	

NUMBER	DATE	NAME OF DESIGN — SHAPE OR PATTERN NO.	
659271	30 1 17	Water Lily pattern, Repro Spode beads	
659905	24 3 17	Rockingham pattern for Harrods	R6434, 2/7012
660026	10 4 17	Adams Lead Vase pattern	R6834
660465	19 5 17	Song Bird (Tomtit) pattern	
660466	19 5 17	Grecian border pattern	2/7053, 2/7102, 2/7414
661351	19 5 17	Adams Queen pattern	
661352	7 8 17	Pirie Cupid pattern	
661353	7 8 17	Adams Marguerite pattern	
661354	7 8 17	Adams Sunbeam pattern	
661355	7 8 17	Adams Katherine pattern	
661356	7 8 17	Adams Griffin pattern	R6142
661702	13 9 17	Adams Bedspread pattern	R6141
661703	13 9 17	Adams Gower pattern	R6102
661704	13 9 17	Adams Bride pattern	
661705	13 9 17	Adams Festoon pattern	R6514
661706	13 9 17	Beetle pattern	2/7575
661766	20 9 17	Ledoux pattern	R6350, 2/7093
662840	31 12 17	Foot Soldier '95th Rifle Regt'	
662841	31 12 17	Mounted Soldier 'Royal Horse Guards' (The Blues)	
662842	31 12 17	Mounted Soldier 'Life Guards'	
662843	31 12 17	Foot Soldier 'Gordon Highlanders'	
662844	31 12 17	Adams Truro pattern	
662845	31 12 17	Spode's Latin pattern	R6247 or R6235
662846	31 12 17	Daisy Scroll pattern	
662847	31 12 17	Wristlet pattern	
662848	31 12 17	Adams Fan or Honeysuckle pattern	R6248
662849	31 12 17	Fruit Pickers for Heals, London	2/7076
662868	2 1 18	Italy or Poplar pattern	2/7087, R7423
662869	2 1 18	Spode's Carnation pattern	2/7969
662870	2 1 18	Roumania or Leaf pattern	1/7506, 2/3834
662871	2 1 18	Open Book pattern	
662872	2 1 18	Greek shape covered pieces	
663505	27 2 18	Foot Soldier 'Scots Guard'	
663507	27 2 18	Flying Duck bird figure	
663567	6 3 18	Waverley Shell Sweet Dish	
663568	6 3 18	Belfry Sweet Dish	
664060	26 4 18	Chanticleer pattern	2/7104
664843	7 8 18	Trincol pattern	2/7147
664844	7 8 18	Scale & Crossbar border with rose sprigs	2/7148
664845	7 8 18	Runnymede pattern	2/7468, R7341
664846	7 8 18	New Lens pattern	2/7146
664847	7 8 18	Brick & Curl border with landscape pattern	2/7145

Rockingham 2/7012.

A mounted soldier of the Royal Horse Guards: a very fine study in earthenware.

George III or Raleigh, is cherry picker with sheet pattern 2/7342.

NUMBER	DATE	NAME OF DESIGN – SHAPE OR PATTERN NO.	
664848	7 8 18	Chelsea Feather pattern	2/7140
666459	23 1 19	Haig shape teapot with fruit knob	
666460	23 1 19	Dutch shape, square candlestick, Chinese model	
666461	23 1 19	Blue Diaper & Bird Centre pattern	T1056
667193	10 3 19	Key Border for Trust Houses	R6628
667194	10 3 19	Ramsey Embossed Dinnerware	
667195	10 3 19	Plymouth Basket pattern	2/7199
667947	2 4 19	Fallen Leaves pattern	R6869, 2/7613
667948	2 4 19	President shape ewer	
669773	24 6 19	Battersea pattern	R6760, 2/7215
671378	9 9 19	Claridge pattern	Y2565
671880	6 10 19		2/7123
671881	6 10 19	S Groups	
672284	24 10 19		T1070
672577	10 11 19	Grapes pattern	2/7255, R7252
672578	10 11 19	Scroll Border & Bird Centre pattern	
672579	10 11 19	New Strawberry pattern	
672580	10 11 19	Ming pattern	
672808	20 11 19	Scroll Border, fruit Group Centre pattern	
674815	26 2 20	Blue Pheasant pattern	
674819	26 2 20	Spode shape teapot	
674817	26 2 20	Narrow Fruit Bead pattern	R6074
675601	6 4 20	Adams Border pattern	
675602	6 4 20	Spode Centre & Background pattern	
675603	6 4 20	Small view centre pattern	
675604	6 4 20	Jack ewer	
675605	6 4 20	Fruit Border pattern	
676564	4 6 20	Bradford pattern	
676566	4 6 20	Spode's Wreath pattern	
676567	4 6 20	Audley Asparagus Tray	
676568	4 6 20	Kensington pattern	
677525	9 8 20	Chungking pattern	
677526	9 8 20	Raleigh pattern. Later called George III for Harrods	2/7342
677527	9 8 20	Persian Scale pattern	
677528	9 8 20	Milford pattern	S2106
677899	1 9 20	Dover pattern	?Y3114
677900	1 9 20	Calais pattern	
677901	1 9 20	Lichfield pattern	
679151	6 11 20	Persian style pattern on dinnerware	
679152	6 11 20	Persian style pattern on dinnerware	

NUMBER	DATE	NAME OF DESIGN – SHAPE OR PATTERN NO.	
679153	6 11 20	Persian style pattern on dinnerware	
679154	6 11 20	Persian style pattern on dinnerware	
679155	6 11 20	Persian style pattern on dinnerware	
679156	6 11 20	Tulips & Scrolls pattern on dinnerware	
679157	6 11 20	Persian style pattern on dinnerware	
679158	6 11 20	Persian style pattern on dinnerware	
679159	6 11 20	Persian style pattern on dinnerware	
679160	6 11 20	Persian style pattern on dinnerware	
680210	7 1 21	Spencer pattern	2/7393, R7482, 2/7548
680211	7 1 21	Persian Rabbit pattern	R7751, 2/7459, 2/7634-5
680212	7 1 21	Persian style pattern on toiletware	
684594	12 8 21	Persian style pattern on toiletware	
684595	12 8 21	Persian style pattern on toiletware	
684596	12 8 21	Persian style pattern on toiletware	
685868	26 10 21	Vine Border	
688176	15 2 22	Windsor Flower Bowl and Stand	
689265	30 3 22	Worcester Bird Scroll Border ?	
689265	30 3 22	Teapot with sunk Knob and small spout ?	
691234	3 7 22	Feather Sheet, Chelsea Bird Centre	1/7746
691235	3 7 22	Leeds pattern	2/7641
691236	3 7 22	Ming pattern	2/7593
691240		Lionel Edwards Hunting Scenes for Soane & Smith	2/7636
692518	28 8 22	Fish and Water Lilies Border pattern	2/3487
692519	28 8 22	Spode's Landscape & Grasshopper pattern	2/5211, R1669
692520	28 8 22	Nymphea pattern	2/1213, D2928
692521	28 8 22	Duncan Scenes pattern on round dish	R4479, 2/6865
694729	11 12 22	B723 pattern (Mr. R. R. J. C.)	1/1827
695226	13 1 23	Flower Sprays	1/9969, 2/1092
695227	13 1 23	Persian style pattern	
695228	13 1 23	Grass & Bell Border pattern	
695529	26 1 23	Chinese Centres pattern on plate	1/9645

1922. Plate from the dinnerware set illustrating different stages of a hunt and depicting twelve well known packs, from paintings by Lionel Edwards. See page 78. No. 691240.

Gobelin pattern, bone china, R8150, one of several versions. No. 739639.

NUMBER	DATE	NAME OF DESIGN – SHAPE OR PATTERN NO.	
695560	26 1 23	Ribbon & Spot pattern	1/228
695993	16 2 23	Egyptian Border pattern on dinnerware	
696118	22 2 23	Lotus Flower Border pattern	8627 ?
696119	22 2 23	Egyptian Border on teaware	
696296	28 2 23	Luxor pattern	2/7691
697305	11 4 23	Ribbon & Laurel Border pattern	
697306	11 4 23	Laurel Bead pattern	9104
697307	11 4 23	Laurel Festoon & Fruit Border pattern	
697308	11 4 23	Bude pattern (Spode design 2219)	R8081
700093	23 8 23	Egyptian Bird pattern	
701333	19 10 23	Chanticleer pattern	2/9001 ?
701656	7 11 23	Spode's Hamilton pattern	
705474	10 5 24	Fruit Border pattern	
709821	10 12 24	Persian Bird border pattern	2/4404
712186	2 4 25	Bird on Tree pattern on toiletware	D9918, 1/180
713890	12 6 25	Aviary pattern	2/7972
713891	12 6 25	Carnation & Bird pattern	2/7969
715957		Cube shape teapot, etc. for Cunard Line	
723365	20 8 26	Teapot, Ship shape	
723366	20 8 26	Teapot, Ship shape	
730502	6 7 27	New Japan pattern	W34, S1739
739639	4 8 28	Gobelin pattern	R7955, R9641
739640	4 8 28	Spring or Shoolbed New Bird pattern	R7779 1/4874, 2/8730
740865	2 10 28	Chinese Hunting Scene pattern after K'ang Hsi original for Spode Bicentenary	C2032, Y2181
743841	26 2 29	New Seagull pattern	
743842	26 2 29	Gingham pattern	2/8142
750152	18 11 29	Koro pattern	2/8700, Y1692
754074	17 4 30	Belhi shape cup	
756846	30 7 30	Hereford pattern	2/9350
762857	21 3 31	Centurion shape tableware	
766049	11 7 31	Chocolate Cup Set	
767614	22 9 31	Florida pattern for Drew's Restaurant	1/3369, 2/3044
767994	13 10 31	Varsity or Madonna pattern	
767995	13 10 31	Bermuda or Wheatian pattern	2/9379, S798
769284	4 1 32	Silver Birch pattern	2/9810
776474	2 9 32	Merrie England pattern	2/9604
777264	6 10 32	London Cries Cherries figure	
777265	6 10 32	Utility vegetable dish	
777266	6 10 32	Mansard shape tableware Lawrence pattern	S1482
778046	6 10 32	London Cries Milk Below figure	

The Churchill Toby Jug, 1941. Earthenware, hand coloured.

NUMBER	DATE	NAME OF DESIGN — SHAPE OR PATTERN NO.	
778047	6 10 32	London Cries Primroses figure	
778048	6 10 32	London Cries Turnips & Carrots figure	
778049	6 10 32	London Cries Fresh Peas figure	
778050	6 10 32	London Cries Strawberries figure	
785542	5 8 33	Blanche-de-Chine shape	
791877	26 4 34	Grosvenor pattern	Y3297 ?
798464	4 12 34	Autumn pattern	s809
807855	12 11 35	Hounds pattern Earthenware teaset, Melba shape	
838714		Churchill Toby Jug	K745, F447
861241	11 2 50	Andromeda pattern	Y7498
861242	11 2 50	Rannock pattern	Y7596
861243	11 2 50	Split Leaf pattern as Kingston	Y7326
861245	11 2 50	Studley pattern	Y7316
861246	11 2 50		
861247	11 2 50	Dover pattern	Y3114
861248	11 2 50	Vine pattern	
873465	1 4 54	Sherwood pattern	s2853
873466	1 4 54	Rembrandt pattern	s2580
884662	15 5 57	Cigarette Lighter Base for Ronson Products Limited	
884663	15 5 57	Cigarette Lighter Base for Ronson Products Limited	
884664	15 5 57	Cigarette Lighter Base for Ronson Products Limited	
886590		Smudge pattern	2/4854, 2/6451
909685	19 1 63	Golden Celtic pattern	
909686	19 1 63	Golden Dolphin pattern	
915427	3 3 64	Hamilton pattern for Colgate-Palmolive	s3379
918116	16 10 64	Chalice and Paten	K1286
918117	16 10 64	Candlestick in bone china	K1287
918119	16 10 64	Mallow pattern (Summerfield)	Y8103

1941
Patent No. 558911 Utility Teapot

Strawberries.

Cherries.

Pattern numbers

Most Spode Factory patterns were allocated pattern numbers which correspond to the designs recorded in the pattern books: indeed, there are records of some 70,000 patterns. Not all patterns are illustrated; examples might include a small variation in gilded 'finish', a different colouring, or the same pattern but on a different shape. The pattern book record will be a manuscript note like "R5060 as R4915 but printed in 294 green, rest same".

The pattern numbers were frequently painted on the objects, often in conjunction with the painted name 'Spode', or with one of the printed marks. The lists which follow give the approximate date when the designs were recorded in the pattern books, but some popular patterns were produced over a long period of several years, sometimes many decades, so that a pattern number should be read in conjunction with the manufacturer's mark in order to estimate the actual date of production of a particular object. Of all manufacturers, perhaps Spode, and especially Copeland, used more marks than any other, with little regard for any form of disciplined plan. This random choice of marks has yielded an interesting assemblage of designs which now help to date the wares on which they occur.

The very early designs seldom bore a pattern number, and it is not known if the numbering system commenced in the 1790s or when the factory pattern books were instituted for on-glaze decorations by Henry Daniel in about 1800. The discovery of an un-dated, un-named pattern book in 1988, however, suggests that Josiah Spode I had started this pattern book in the decade before his son employed Daniel. Several patterns in this early book correspond exactly with some of the few patterns on the first two pages of the factory's first book of Daniel.

Summary of pattern numbers

DATES	NUMBERS + PRINCIPAL CONTENTS
c1794 to 1800	*14-710 Very early series recorded in un-named book, mostly neat border patterns, on-glaze.
c1800 to 1857	*133-9999 Mostly patterns decorated on-glaze: all bodies.
1822 to 1848	*B1-B959 Under-glaze patterns, including 'peasant' ware
1833 to 1857	L1-L121 Lustre decorations.
1837 to 1851	G1-G30 Gold transfer-printed patterns on-glaze.
1845 to 1870	C1-C138 Wholly hand painted, sponged or spatter ware.
1852 to 1874	*D1-D9999 All decorative methods, all bodies.
c1840 to c1900	1-1411 Tile patterns, including jug stands.
1867 to 1927	01-0657 Ornament designs.
1874 to 1900	*1/1-1/9999 Bone china, including Stone china; 'C' books.
1874 to 1933	*2/1-2/9999 Earthenware patterns; 'E' books.
1880 to 1956	C200-C2240 Patterns for Thomas Goode & Co; C & E numbers run consecutively.
1900 to 1927	*R1-R9999 Bone china, including Stone china.
1904 to 1918	TB1-TB531 Bone china and earthenware table and toilet wares. The meaning of TB and these patterns is not clear; they may have been produced at the request of the London manager, Mr. Bennett.
1906 to 1938	T500-T1100 Toiletware patterns.
1910 to 1917	SC1-SC8. BD9-BD565 Patterns for Bawo & Dotter, New York CS566-CS625.
1911 to 1941	A1-A502 Acid etched patterns on bone china.
1927	H1-H25 Bone china patterns, including stone china.
onwards	*Y26-Y8555.
1932 onwards	K1-K1653 Shape designs.
1933 onwards	*S1-S3421 Earthenware patterns; some on-glaze designs have the prefix O instead of S.
1934 onwards	F1-F1664 Fancy items, ornaments, figures, etc.
1936	P1-P40 Pencilled ground decorations.
1936 to 1971	N1-N400 Scene plates for colleges, commemoratives.
1938 onwards	*W1-W161 Stone china and Fine stone patterns.
1973 to 1975	NF501-NF519 Bone china designs for the Carborundum manufacturing unit in the Museum at Niagara Falls.

1980 onwards	DI-*D428* Designs specially commissioned.
1987 onwards	MI-*M62* new series of numbers for sample designs.
c1896 *to* c1960	X721-X5539 Patterns produced speculatively for consideration by agents and retailers. Only records are in manuscript, written in small Black books. Missing numbers are 1-720, 2075-2873.

*indicates a principal series. Note that a number in *italics* is that reached by June 1990; the series is still having patterns added to it.

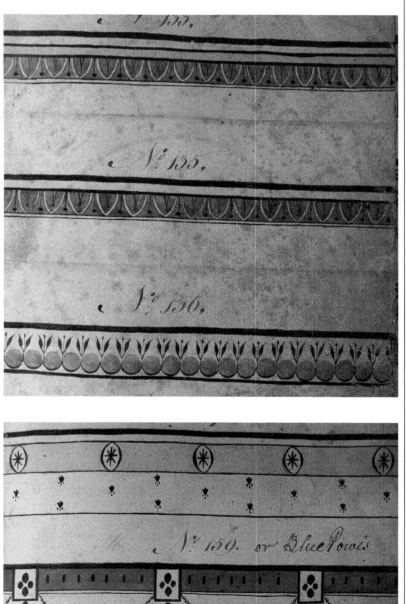

Moreover, the style of painting, writing and layout point to the probability that they were both by the same artist. One suggested explanation is that Daniel only recorded the few of Spode's earlier patterns that he was called upon to decorate, perhaps as repeat orders. In the next few years, when an order for a 'matching' was needed for an earlier Spode pattern, a new number was allocated; the likelihood being that no number had been painted on the particular piece sent as a sample, or that that number had already been applied to a different pattern in the meantime.

I suggest that it was Spode I, rather than Spode II, who instituted the earlier pattern book that has been discovered recently. Leonard Whiter showed that during the lifetime of Henry Daniel's tenure as decorator about 150 patterns were recorded in each year. In the Copeland period, following the expansion of the business, it was usual for about 500 pattern numbers, including colour and gilded variations, to be recorded in each year. Working backwards to when the business was smaller, it seems reasonable to suppose that *less* than 150 patterns were recorded in each year. The earlier book contains details of 403 patterns, almost every one illustrated, the last one numbered 710. At 150 per year dating back from 1800 yields the year 1795, but at, say, an average of 100 per year, the year 1793 or 1794 seems to be when the book might have been started. In either case, Spode I was directing the factory in Stoke-upon-Trent where the decorations may be assumed to have been applied and fired. [If, however, the decorations were applied in London at that earlier period, then Spode II would have been responsible for the book!].

Another fact, however, suggests a date after 1796 in which year Spode invoiced W. Tatton for a great variety of 'English China' as well as a dinner service in 'Queensware', but none of the entries includes a pattern number.

The schedule of dates in the following lists is as accurate as possible. The Spode period details are derived from the excellent research of Leonard Whiter [see *Spode,* pages 80-89]. There is still no certain evidence that the system of numbering in the factory books began

The first two pages of Spode's master copy of the first pattern book. Note the link between some of these numbers and those of the very early pattern book.

earlier than 1800, even though some of the earlier pages are water-marked 1794.

Perhaps the paper had been bought by Spode for his own pattern book and the early numbers of Daniels records were on the surplus paper which Daniel took over from Spode.

The patterns from 1833 onwards have been determined from records of costings and price fixing books. These entries were made at periodical sessions and dated when entered. It is possible that some patterns were introduced up to twelve months earlier, as special commissions and only given a pattern number later.

There are seven principal series of pattern numbers, with many supplementary series recording specific types of patterns, or those for special customers.

Dates of introduction of patterns

Spode period to March 1833

The first series of numbers, apart from the very early book, includes patterns on all bodies, and only those which have some on-glaze decoration. The numbers are mostly continuous from number 300, although there are 136 missing or blank numbers, and 158 numbers for which only written directions are given; a further 10 numbers which are missing from the Spode Master Pattern Books were found to have illustrations or directions in among some sheets of Mr. Daniel's working copy. These sheets were sold at Sotheby's, Chester, in January 1989.

Before number 300, the only numbers recorded are 133, 135, 136, 146, 147, 159, 236, 241, 251 up to 254, 256 up to 271, 273, 276, 289.

The dates are for the full year January to December, and can only be approximate, so, for example, up to December 31st 1801 pattern numbers up to number 150 were recorded; in 1802 a further 150 pattern numbers were used, that is 'up to number 300'.

1801	up to 150	1818	up to 2700
1802	up to 300	1819	up to 2800
1803	up to 450	1820	up to 3000
1804	up to 600	1821	up to 3250
1805	up to 750	1822	up to 3500
1806	up to 900	1823	up to 3750
1807	up to 1050	1824	up to 4000
1808	up to 1200	1825	up to 4150
1809	up to 1350	1826	up to 4300
1810	up to 1500	1827	up to 4450
1811	up to 1650	1828	up to 4500
1812	up to 1800	1829	up to 4600
1813	up to 1950	1830	up to 4700
1814	up to 2100	1831	up to 5050
1815	up to 2200	1832	up to 5200
1816	up to 2500	1833	up to 5350
1817	up to 2600		

On the page recording pattern number 5192 the name 'Copeland & Garrett' is written. This suggests that this was the first pattern number recorded on or after March 1st 1833.

Underglaze patterns. B numbers

In 1822, probably coinciding with the departure of Henry Daniel, a new series of pattern numbers was recorded for patterns decorated wholly under-glaze, either as plain prints, as print and paint, or as painted only. These B patterns run to B959 which was recorded in 1846, so covering the Spode and Copeland & Garrett periods. Examples which have the B number clearly marked are uncommon, if not actually scarce. Some examples have been seen with the correct number but omitting the B pre-fix. Sometimes the printed 'B No' occurs without the hand-applied number. In the front of the B Pattern Book are some cup patterns numbered C1 up to C31: these are duplicate entries of the C Pattern book and were added after 1845. Later in the B series are patterns C48 up to C61; these are not duplicated, and may have been wrongly prefixed. Most B patterns were on earthenware, but an example of B773 is known on china, printed in blue.

The dating of B patterns is no easier than it is for the first series.

The schedule is based on the two pieces of information available at present: the watermarked paper and the few entries of when pattern sheets were sent to London (marked L).

Spode period B patterns

1823	up to B40	1829	up to B265
1824	up to B70	1830	up to B300
1825	up to B110	1831	up to B330
1826	up to B150	1832	up to B365
1827	up to B185	1833	up to B388
1828	up to B220		

Copeland & Garrett period & Copeland B patterns

1833	up to B388	1841	up to B711 L
1834	up to B420	1842	up to B748 L
1835	up to B430	1843	up to B770 L
1836	up to B445	1844	up to B800
1837	up to B459	1845	up to B830
1838	up to B576	1846	up to B906
1839	up to B600 L	1847	up to B930
1840	up to B654 L	1848	up to B959

Plate in pattern B68 painted in blue and yellow, c. 1824.

Plain blue prints on earthenware seldom have a pattern number. After 1822, many plain underglaze prints in other colours were given B numbers. Sometimes, an underglaze print has some enamel decoration added, and this may be recorded: it is from this information that approximate dates may be calculated for the original plain print.

Copeland & Garrett period 1st March 1833 to 30th June 1847

The dating of pattern introduction from 1833 is more accurate because of the preservation of additional records at the Spode factory. The range of numbers during this period is from about 5192-7600.

1833	up to 5350	1841	up to 6700
1834	up to 5466	1842	up to 6819
1835	up to 5662	1843	up to 6991
1836	up to 5738	1844	up to 7128
1837	up to 5841	1845	up to 7342
1838	up to 6138	1846	up to 7547
1839	up to 6367	1847	up to 7747
1840	up to 6508		

Many examples of Stone china bear the impressed mark SPODE'S NEW STONE (mark 7) but also a printed Copeland & Garrett mark. This implies that a large stock of undecorated ware remained in the warehouse at the time of Copeland's purchase of the business.

Lustre patterns
L numbers

A thin book, begun in 1833, records patterns decorated with lustre, although lustre was used on patterns recorded in the regular series of numbers before this date. Some patterns are pre-fixed F, referring to the use of French Gold.
F14-17, 36-8, 45, 48, 52.
Dec 1833 L1
Jan 1834 up to L24
Sept 1834 up to L30
Mar 1835 up to L39
23 Feb 1836 up to F4184 & L49, also F3008, F3390, F1039.
10 Jan 1857 up to L112
23 Sept 1857 up to L121

Gold transfer-printed patterns
G numbers

The existence of G numbers is attested to from references in the Fixing Books and from two examples which are marked G29 and G30, and have the border of Aquatic pattern. The fixing book quotes G1 on

June 12th 1837 and G30 on April 3rd 1841. Previous to 1837, gold printed subjects may be assumed to have been achieved by the bat-printing method.

Tile and Jug Stand patterns

Tile and jug stand patterns are recorded in six volumes beginning in 1840. Earlier tile designs were recorded in the first series of pattern numbers along with tablewares and ornamental objects. Few dates are given, but the books provide a wealth of information about tile designs and the extensive trade in jug stands for the brewery and distilling trade as advertising material, much as beer mats do today.
Numbers do not have prefix letters.

1840	Tile Book I 1 to 149
	No. 30, dated Nov 2 1840
	No. 90, as 7196, c1845
	Tile Book II to 304
	No dates
1852	Tile Book III to 738
	No. 309, Dec 29 1852
	No. 716, Dec 16 1867
1868	Tile Book IV to 969
	No. 739, Dec 2 1868
	No. 969, Oct 14 1878
1878	Tile Book V to 1272
	No. 1037, Feb 11 1880
	No. 1141, Dec 16 1880
c.1884-	Tile Book VI to 1411
c.1900	No dates, but No. 1395

shows a brewer's jug stand decorated with medals awarded in 1894 and 1895.

Hand painted, Sponged and Spatterware patterns C numbers

In 1845 a series of numbers was introduced to record patterns decorated without the use of transfer-prints and solely on earthenware. These are pre-fixed with the letter C, and run from December 1845 to March 1870. A few pattern sheets were sent to London, and these dates form the basis for this schedule. Examples of C number patterns have been found in South Africa and Indonesia, these exhibiting the sponged technique; shards of several patterns of the 'peasant' ware have been excavated at St. Jerome's Convent in Mexico City, but these have been identified as having B numbers. No example has been notified to me that has the pattern number applied to it. These wares were relatively inexpensive to produce and met the need for 'cheap and cheerful' strong table and toilet ware.

Dec 1845 to C4	Dec 1854 to C83
July 1849 to C45	Jan 1857 to C96
June 1853 to C63	Mar 1870 to C138

Pattern C65 showing hand painted centre with sponged border. c.1854.

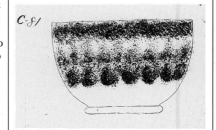

Two pattern book records of spatterware designs. c.1854.

Copeland period

W. T. Copeland period
1847 to 1867

The first series of numbers, started in about 1800, was exhausted in about 1857. A new series, the D numbers, had been started before the earlier series had been completed. There is evidence to suggest that the first D numbers were begun in 1852, because a bead, or narrow border, was patented on January 3 1853, and this is recorded as pattern D95.

The D numbers, like the first series, embrace all bodies, processes including under-glaze decorations. By December 1857, when the first series had reached number 9999, the D series had reached D655. Detailed information on patterns produced between 1852 to 1855, and 1864 to 1867, is not available, so the numbers are estimates in these periods.

1847	up to 7747	1853	up to 9250
1848	up to 7983	1854	up to 9475
1849	up to 8301	1855	up to 9700
1850	up to 8521	1856	up to 9880
1851	up to 8734	1857	up to 9999
1852	up to 9033		

D patterns

1852	up to D90	1860	up to D2091
1853	up to D180	1861	up to D2500
1854	up to D290	1862	up to D3016
1855	up to D400	1863	up to D3466
1856	up to D524	1864	up to D4048
1857	up to D655	1865	up to D4430
1858	up to D967	1866	up to D4810
1859	up to D1412	1867	up to D5200

W. T. Copeland & Sons period
1867 to 1932

In 1874, when the D series ended, separate series were introduced to distinguish the different bodies: 1/ for Bone china and Stone china, and 2/ for earthenwares. Most earthenware patterns required copper plates to be engraved so were introduced less frequently than those on china, which could be a record of just a different coloured band or groundlay, a different gilded treatment, or other hand applied decoration. Thus the china soon exhausted the 1/numbers, and needed two more series; the R numbers from 1900 to 1927 and the Y numbers from 1927 to the present. In 1927, at the end of the R series, the next series was pre-fixed with the letter H, but as the numbers were applied by hand painting, the H was easily confused with R, and so it was changed to Y.

D numbers

1868	up to D5600	1872	up to D8973
1869	up to D6930	1873	up to D9523
1870	up to D7690	1874	up to D9999
1871	up to D8475		

1/China numbers

1874	up to 1/104	1887	up to 1/5268
1875	up to 1/454	1888	up to 1/5610
1876	up to 1/863	1889	up to 1/6120
1877	up to 1/1230	1890	up to 1/6536
1878	up to 1/1425	1891	up to 1/7105
1879	up to 1/1847	1892	up to 1/7491
1880	up to 1/2193	1893	up to 1/7859
1881	up to 1/2708	1894	up to 1/8199
1882	up to 1/3041	1895	up to 1/8457
1883	up to 1/3500	1896	up to 1/8802
1884	up to 1/3975	1897	up to 1/9186
1885	up to 1/4366	1898	up to 1/9540
1886	up to 1/4891	1899	up to 1/9930
		1900	up to 1/9999

2/Earthenware numbers

1874	up to 2/56	1904	up to 2/5417
1875	up to 2/349	1905	up to 2/5569
1876	up to 2/472	1906	up to 2/5820
1877	up to 2/748	1907	up to 2/5923
1878	up to 2/1047	1908	up to 2/6057
1879	up to 2/1473	1909	up to 2/6173
1880	up to 2/1613	1910	up to 2/6287
1881	up to 2/1884	1911	up to 2/6368
1882	up to 2/2117	1912	up to 2/6502
1883	up to 2/2323	1913	up to 2/6613
1884	up to 2/2501	1914	up to 2/6721
1885	up to 2/2675	1915	up to 2/6808
1886	up to 2/2856	1916	up to 2/6966
1887	up to 2/2967	1917	up to 2/7107
1888	up to 2/3096	1918	up to 2/7194
1889	up to 2/3258	1919	up to 2/7346
1890	up to 2/3472	1920	up to 2/7433
1891	up to 2/3652	1921	up to 2/7562
1892	up to 2/3787	1922	up to 2/7658
1893	up to 2/3946	1923	up to 2/7790
1894	up to 2/4049	1924	up to 2/7955
1895	up to 2/4172	1925	up to 2/8039
1896	up to 2/4341	1926	up to 2/8218
1897	up to 2/4451	1927	up to 2/8320
1898	up to 2/4564	1928	up to 2/8498
1899	up to 2/4704	1929	up to 2/8816
1900	up to 2/4807	1930	up to 2/9204
1901	up to 2/4932	1931	up to 2/9401
1902	up to 2/5121	1932	up to 2/9721
1903	up to 2/5248	1933	up to 2/9999

R China numbers

1901	up to R750	1915	up to R5682
1902	up to R1205	1916	up to R5959
1903	up to R1595	1917	up to R6378
1904	up to R2127	1918	up to R6584
1905	up to R2467	1919	up to R7023
1906	up to R3003	1920	up to R7257
1907	up to R3279	1921	up to R7506
1908	up to R3552	1922	up to R7710
1909	up to R3834	1923	up to R7908
1910	up to R4188	1924	up to R8478
1911	up to R4503	1925	up to R9170
1912	up to R4815	1926	up to R9778
1913	up to R5106	1927	up to R9999
1914	up to R5409		

Y China numbers

1927	H1 to H25	1948	up to Y7067
	Y26 to Y398	1949	up to Y7126
1928	up to Y1222	1950	up to Y7193
1929	up to Y2030	1951	up to Y7229
1930	up to Y2484	1952	up to Y7296
1931	up to Y2807	1953	up to Y7361
1932	up to Y3069	1954	up to Y7480
1933	up to Y3525	1955	up to Y7607
1934	up to Y3948	1956	up to Y7688
1935	up to Y4414	1957	up to Y7772
1936	up to Y4884	1958	up to Y7930
1937	up to Y5336	1959	up to Y7985
1938	up to Y5881	1960	up to Y8001
1939	up to Y6253	1961	up to Y8006
1940	up to Y6439	1962	up to Y8026
1941	up to Y6597	1963	up to Y8070
1942	up to Y6681	1964	up to Y8084
1943	up to Y6737	1965	up to Y8105
1944	up to Y6775	1966	up to Y8112
1945	up to Y6813	1967	up to Y8122
1946	up to Y6881	1968	up to Y8138
1947	up to Y7004	1969	up to Y8155

W.T. Copeland & Sons Limited 1932-1969

The series of 2/ numbers for earthenware ended in July 1933, and was succeeded by the S and O numbers. The intention was for O to designate on-glaze decorations while S was for under-glaze patterns. However, in recent years the O prefix has been used very little.

S & O Earthenware numbers

1933	up to 0262	1951	up to s2668
1934	up to s814	1952	up to s2700
1935	up to s1280	1953	up to s2745
1936	up to s1688	1954	up to s2877
1937	up to s2007	1955	up to s3115
1938	up to s2197	1956	up to s3218
1939	up to s2408	1957	up to s3268
1940	up to s2480	1958	up to s3306
1941	up to s2532	1959	up to s3341
1942	up to s2558	1960	up to 03352
1943	up to s2572	1961	up to 03364
1944	up to s2584	1962	up to s3373
1945	up to s2601	1963	up to s3378
1946	up to s2608	1964	up to s3389
1947	up to s2619	1965	up to s3392
1948	up to s2628	1966	–
1949	up to s2638	1967	–
1950	up to s2646	1968	up to s3397
		1969	

On July 1st 1966, the Company was bought by the Carborundum Co. Ltd. but it retained the name of W. T. Copeland & Sons Ltd. However, in 1970 the name of the Company was changed to Spode Limited to mark the Bicentenary of the date accepted for the founding of the firm by Josiah Spode I in 1770, and also to take the opportunity to avoid the confusion in world markets of two famous names for one company.

(The name of W. T. Copeland & Sons Limited remains in the ownership of Spode Ltd.)

Spode Limited period

Spode Limited 1970-

The business remained with the Carborundum Co. Ltd. until July 1st 1976 when it joined with the Worcester Royal Porcelain Co. Ltd. to form Royal Worcester Spode Limited; Royal Worcester Ltd owned 55% of the shares to Carborundum's 45%. In 1978, on Carborundum being acquired by Kennicot, Royal Worcester bought Carborundum's 45%. In 1983, Royal Worcester was bought by Crystalate plc. who re-sold the porcelain divisions to The London Rubber Company in 1984. Derby International bought Royal Worcester Spode in 1988 and began the separation of the two firms so that the name of the new holding company became The Porcelain and Fine China Companies Limited in 1989. The manufacturing firms are now totally independent, but the retail division still operates jointly.

Y China numbers

1970	up to Y8168	1981	up to Y8377
1971	up to Y8192	1982	up to Y8409
1972	up to Y8205	1983	up to Y8430
1973	up to Y8221	1984	up to Y8489
1974	up to Y8239	1985	up to Y8518
1975	up to Y8248	1986	up to Y8539
1976	up to Y8278	1987	up to Y8547
1977	up to Y8292	1988	up to Y8554
1978	up to Y8313	1989	up to Y8555
1979	up to Y8333	1990	up to Y8570
1980	up to Y8357		

Most of the pattern numbers in these days are allocated to commemorative or decorative plates, and few to tableware designs.

S & O Earthenware numbers

1971	up to s3399	1982	up to s3413
1975	up to s3401	1983	up to s3415
1977	up to s3405	1985	up to s3416
1980	up to s3408	1988	up to s3418
1981	up to 03410	1990	up to s3424

Nearly all new introductions are decorated by the water slide-off transfer method (decalcomanias) and this means fewer new patterns. Some earthenware pattern numbers refer to specially commissioned badged ware.

Stone China and Fine Stone patterns
W numbers

In 1939, Stone China patterns were allocated their own numbers with the prefix letter W, instead of being included with bone china patterns.

In some years, no patterns were introduced, indeed none has been added since 1982. The formula was altered considerably in 1960 to one with a high alumina content; this increased its strength to make it the strongest domestic tableware in the trade, with a Modulus of Rupture test figure of 22,000 pounds per square inch. Its main purpose, however, was to reduce the incidence of 'spit out' during the decorating fire, which it achieved.

['Spit out' manifests itself as scores of minute air bubbles on the glaze surface which burst on being abraded yielding a result a bit like sand-paper. Its cause is thought to be small amounts of gas which erupt during the firing, but, due to the short time of the on-glaze decorating fire, the bubbles so formed do not have the chance nor high enough temperature to subside and become smooth again.]

The name of the body was changed to Fine Stone. Its properties were found to include excellent thermal properties so ware, designed for use in the oven, was named Alenite, to distinguish it from the high prestige character of the tableware.

W Stone China numbers

1939	up to w8	1960	up to w130
1940	up to w20	1961	up to w135
1941	up to w36	1962	up to w138
1944	up to w42	1964	up to w140
1947	up to w48	1965	up to w143
1948	up to w50	1966	up to w146
1949	up to w56	1970	up to w148
1953	up to w65	1971	up to w150
1954	up to w86	1972	up to w151
1955	up to w105	1977	up to w157
1958	up to w118	1980	up to w160
1959	up to w122	1982	up to w161

Miscellaneous pattern numbers

Ornament patterns O numbers

Three volumes of ornament patterns record the shapes and decorations on vases, centre-pieces, covered boxes and other objects, mostly in bone china. These are pre-fixed with the letter O.

Volume I

1867	D4937-D5056
1867 to Mar 20	01 to 028
1868 to May 9	to 053
1870 to Nov 5	to 0116
1873 to Nov 11	to 0189
1874 to Nov 24	to 0262
undated	to 0318

Volume II

1874 to Dec 12	0319 to 0354
1875 to Jan 30	to 0358
1876 to Oct 6	to 0443
1877 to July 23	to 0479
1878 to Oct 15	to 0497
undated	to 0578

Volume III

undated	0579 to
c1927	to 0657

The only dates available are those which note when pattern sheets were 'sent to London', and other occasional dates.

Toilet ware patterns T numbers

Six volumes of toilet ware patterns cover the period from January 1907 to about 1938. The numbers start at number 500, and are pre-fixed with the letter T.

Volume I Jan 1907	T500 to T678
Volume II	to T781
Volume III	to T878
Volume IV	to T975
Volume V 1919 [T980]	to T1096
Volume VI 1920 [T1100]	
to c1938	to T1169

Goode's patterns C & E numbers

Thomas Goode and Co. in London, founded in 1827, assumed considerable importance in the china and glass trade, becoming the world's leading dealer in the last part of the nineteenth century and retaining that position to the present time. In August 1880, Copelands started a new series of pattern numbers specifically for 'Goode's', and at one period a separate warehouse was set aside for the servicing of their orders.

The series started at number 200 with the prefix letter C for china patterns and E for earthenware patterns. C200 was chosen presumably to avoid confusion with the earlier series of C numbers. The series was most active up to 1925, and Goode's expected all of these patterns to be exclusive to themselves. The approximate dates of introduction are:–

1880 to 1885	C200 to C540
1885 to 1890	to C850
1890 to 1895	to C1000
1895 to 1900	to C1225
1900 to 1905	to C1540
1905 to 1910	to C1650
1910 to 1915	to C1760
1915 to 1920	to C1880
1920 to 1925	to C1980
1925 to 1930	to C2020
1930 to 1935	to C2070
1935 to 1940	to C2115
1940 to 1945	to C2150
1945 to 1950	to C2195
1950 to 1956	to C2240

The series ended with pattern C2240 in January 1956.

Acid etched patterns A numbers

Separate numbers were given to patterns which involved the acid etching of the glaze before being gilded. These patterns were allocated A numbers and ran from A1 in May 1911 to A502 in May 1941, when the process was discontinued on the Spode Works.

1911 to 1915	A1 to A110
1915 to 1920	to A200
1920 to 1925	to A300
1925 to 1930	to A405
1930 to 1935	to A455
1935 to 1940	to A495
1940 to 1941	to A502

American patterns SC, BD & CS numbers

There are three volumes purchased in 1910, 1913 and 1915 respectively, with a continuous series of numbers, but with different prefix letters.

It is thought that these patterns were prepared for retailers in the USA who required exclusive distribution rights for certain 'lines', that is lines, or ranges, of merchandise.

SC may stand for Spauldings of Chicago, who was an important retailer selling exclusive china. BD may stand for Bawo & Dotter of New York. In 1908, Copelands appointed Burley and Tyrell Company of Chicago as sole agent for the USA, but when the agreement came for renewal in 1913, Bawo & Dotter were granted the agency, because Burley evidently had not done sufficiently well in expanding the business. It is probable that this arrangement lasted for several years but details are missing. CS remains without a suggested explanation.

The earlier numbers embraced all bodies, but CS566-CS625 are bone china. The only dates are those when the volumes were supplied.

Book I Bought 1910	SC1 to SC8:
–	BD9 to BD269
Book II Bought 1913	to BD531
Book III Bought 1915	to BD565
	CS566 to CS625

In Book III there are a few P numbers: P1 to P10 are pencilled grounds of C1936 P11 to P40 are various china patterns.

Sample patterns X numbers

For many years samples and speculative patterns which were prepared to 'test the market' were allocated X numbers. If such a pattern was accepted as a production item, it was given a number in the appropriate series. These patterns were not illustrated until accepted, but there are manuscript notes stretching from the late nineteenth century to about the 1960s. This is included here in case examples are seen which have a paper label which includes an X number.

Sample pattern M numbers

Recently introduced to record sample designs.

March 1987 up to M2
1988 up to M8
1989 up to M60

Armorial, Badged and Specially Commissioned designs

Throughout the firm's history many designs have been produced to customers' own specifications, and most of these have not been allocated pattern numbers. This applied to many armorial designs and especially to bone china dessert services and to ornamental wares, including majolica.

Moreover, it was usual in earlier years to apply a pattern number to only a very few objects in a service of ware. Thus many pieces are not numbered, even if the pattern is recorded. It is not always possible to locate any reference to such designs, particularly those made before 1847, because the recording of armorial services only began in that year and does not seem to have been completely comprehensive until about 1880, when the regular *Arms Books* were started. Three volumes, starting in 1847, record many services up to about 1865. In general, if an heraldic device is applied to a pattern which is recorded elsewhere, only the device is entered, with a note of the pattern number on which it was to be applied.

Apart from the three early Arms Books mentioned above, there are 13 Books dating as follows:

Arms Book 1 1847 to c1865
2 c1860 to 1865
3 c1856 to 1864

These three seem to duplicate some of the records in the much neater books, above.

4 c1868 to 1869
5 c1864 to 1874
6 c1875 to 1879
7 1880 to 1887
8 1887 to 1891
9 1891 to 1895
10 1895 to 1905
11 1905 to 1930
12 1930 to 1967
13 1967 to 1980

From 1980 D pattern numbers have been allocated to specially commissioned services. See under that heading.

Specially Commissioned designs
D numbers (new series)

This is a new series begun in 1980 to record specially commissioned 'personalised' services with monograms and crests, but on regular merchandise. Provided that details of the manufacturer's mark is given, there is no risk of confusion with the earlier D series of numbers.

1980 up to D14	1985 up to D279
1981 up to D41	1986 up to D323
1982 up to D89	1987 up to D367
1983 up to D184	1988 up to D413
1984 up to D246	1989 up to D445
	1990 up to D447

Goode's Arms Books

In association with the introduction of C and E numbers for Thomas Goode & Co, there are four volumes of armorial devices applied to patterns to Goode's special orders. These are marked GA on the spine.

GA 1 1895 to 1899
GA 2 1899 to 1905
GA 3 1905 to 1912
GA 4 1912 to 1967

Scenic patterns N numbers

These numbers were introduced in 1936 specifically for Scene Plates, usually produced for institutions in the United States, especially for universities and for commemorative occasions.

1937 up to N107	1957 up to N315
1938 up to N197	1958 up to N325
1940 up to N209	1959 up to N356
1941 up to N217	1960 up to N373
1942 up to N218	1961 up to N378
1943 up to N227	1962 up to N380
1944 up to N232	1963 up to N382
1948 up to N284	1965 up to N386
1953 up to N286	1967 up to N390
1954 up to N298	1969 up to N391
1955 up to N300	1970 up to N400
1956 up to N308	

K Shape numbers

These numbers are allocated to shapes, that is, individual items usually of an ornamental or miscellaneous character. A full range of dinner, tea and coffee ware would not be given a K number. The series was begun in 1932 and runs to the present time; not all items were dated. There are three volumes.

Nov 1933 to K46	Apr 1963 to K1257
Oct 1934 to K310	Apr 1964 to K1282
Dec 1935 to K443	Jan 1965 to K1297
Nov 1936 to K538	Jan 1966 to K1307
Jan 1937 to K617	Jan 1967 to K1310
Nov 1938 to K685	Jan 1968 to K1317
Oct 1939 to K712	Jan 1969 to K1326
Oct 1941 to K778	Jan 1970 to K1337
Dec 1946 to K785	Jan 1971 to K1341
July 1947 to K789	Jan 1972 to K1369
Oct 1950 to K809	Sept 1973 to K1445
Aug 1951 to K822	Feb 1974 to K1458
Dec 1952 to K840	Jan 1975 to K1472
Dec 1953 to K863	Mar 1976 to K1484
Apr 1954 to K877	May 1977 to K1496
Feb 1955 to K908	June 1978 to K1503
Jan 1956 to K958	May 1979 to K1533
Jan 1957 to K1009	May 1980 to K1546
Feb 1958 to K1092	June 1981 to K1586
Jan 1959 to K1137	1982 to K1616
Jan 1960 to K1188	Sept 1983 to K1638
Apr 1961 to K1210	Nov 1989 to K1653
Apr 1962 to K1213	

Fancy Patterns and items
F numbers

A series of numbers was started in February 1934 to identify ornamental patterns on objects such as vases, lamp bases, figurines, ashtrays. &c.

June 1937 to F209	Nov 1974 to F1364
Mar 1941 to F420	Mar 1975 to F1368
Sept 1954 to F706	Dec 1976 to F1397
May 1957 to F945	Mar 1977 to F1399
Dec 1962 to F1152	June 1978 to F1413
Dec 1963 to F1180	Nov 1979 to F1426
Dec 1964 to F1212	Oct 1980 to F1468
Nov 1965 to F1224	Dec 1981 to F1500
Dec 1966 to F1226	Dec 1982 to F1571
Dec 1967 to F1249	Dec 1983 to F1629
Oct 1968 to F1253	Dec 1984 to F1638
Sept 1969 to F1256	Dec 1985 to F1649
Nov 1970 to F1285	Dec 1986 to F1650
Nov 1971 to F1302	Dec 1987 to F1653
Dec 1972 to F1337	Dec 1988 to F1655
Oct 1973 to F1354	Apr 1989 to F1664

A selection of patterns from the very early pattern book.

Appendix I
The families of Spode and Copeland

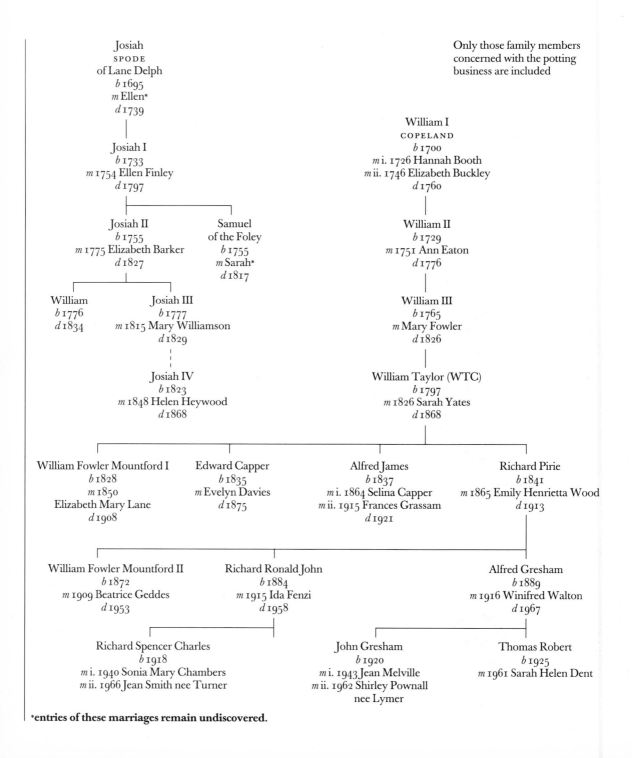

Josiah
SPODE
of Lane Delph
b 1695
m Ellen*
d 1739

Only those family members
concerned with the potting
business are included

William I
COPELAND
b 1700
m i. 1726 Hannah Booth
m ii. 1746 Elizabeth Buckley
d 1760

Josiah I
b 1733
m 1754 Ellen Finley
d 1797

Josiah II
b 1755
m 1775 Elizabeth Barker
d 1827

Samuel
of the Foley
b 1755
m Sarah*
d 1817

William II
b 1729
m 1751 Ann Eaton
d 1776

William
b 1776
d 1834

Josiah III
b 1777
m 1815 Mary Williamson
d 1829

William III
b 1765
m Mary Fowler
d 1826

Josiah IV
b 1823
m 1848 Helen Heywood
d 1868

William Taylor (WTC)
b 1797
m 1826 Sarah Yates
d 1868

William Fowler Mountford I
b 1828
m 1850
Elizabeth Mary Lane
d 1908

Edward Capper
b 1835
m Evelyn Davies
d 1875

Alfred James
b 1837
m i. 1864 Selina Capper
m ii. 1915 Frances Grassam
d 1921

Richard Pirie
b 1841
m 1865 Emily Henrietta Wood
d 1913

William Fowler Mountford II
b 1872
m 1909 Beatrice Geddes
d 1953

Richard Ronald John
b 1884
m 1915 Ida Fenzi
d 1958

Alfred Gresham
b 1889
m 1916 Winifred Walton
d 1967

Richard Spencer Charles
b 1918
m i. 1940 Sonia Mary Chambers
m ii. 1966 Jean Smith nee Turner

John Gresham
b 1920
m i. 1943 Jean Melville
m ii. 1962 Shirley Pownall
nee Lymer

Thomas Robert
b 1925
m 1961 Sarah Helen Dent

*entries of these marriages remain undiscovered.

Appendix II
The principal ceramic bodies:
bone china, stone china
earthenware and parian

Bone china

Josiah Spode is credited with the creation of Bone China in about 1800. What are the facts? Did Spode invent or merely perfect it? Was he the first potter to use bones in a porcelain body? And which Josiah Spode are we praising?

Bone China is a kind of porcelain, so first of all we should understand what porcelain is. Porcelain can be defined as a ceramic body which is completely vitrified, hard, impermeable, white or artificially coloured, translucent and resonant. From a materials point of view porcelain is basically an alumino-silicate fired to a temperature which renders it vitreous.

The earliest porcelain was made in China in the tenth century – about AD950. Essentially it was a mixture of equal parts of kao-lin (china clay) and pai-tun-tzu or petuntse (a feldspathic rock equivalent to Cornish, or china, stone). The Chinese deemed resonance as important as whiteness and translucence, but Europeans considered the latter features the more desirable. The Chinese were able to make pots of extreme thinness, and this might be explained by their practice of maturing the clay body mixture for up to one hundred years. The bacteria which developed within the mass may have had a beneficial effect on the physical characteristics of the body so that the 'green', unfired, strength was great enough to permit bowls and other objects to be potted thinly and to have an application of glaze.

The first Chinese porcelain objects reached Europe at least by the 14th century by coming overland by the 'Silk Road'. Vasco da Gama, who discovered the sea route to the East in 1497, brought back to Lisbon examples of porcelain amongst the other Chinese goods which he found at Calicut in India.

During the next two centuries attempts were made in Europe to reproduce this translucent ware which had been named porcelain. This name is derived from the Portugese 'porcella', a cowrie shell (which has an appearance somewhat like a pig's ear – hence porc..), because of the similarity of the inside of a shell to the Chinese ware. The potters invariably mixed with the clays some ground glass or glass-forming materials, believing the translucence of the porcelain to be due to glass. Because of this, the optimum temperature range in the firing was exceedingly narrow with the inevitable high kiln losses. But when the firing was successful the porcelain was very desirable.

The term artificial, or soft-paste, is applied to these early European porcelains. At first, when ground glass or a frit was added, the ware was called 'frit' porcelain, but when some English factories experimented with other substances, such as Worcester who used soapstone, or talc, this term was inaccurate, so whilst all frit porcelain is artificial, not all artificial porcelain is of the frit type. The term 'soft-paste' refers to the degree of fire applied to the clayware: a 'soft' fire being relatively low in temperature, whilst a 'hard' fire is at a high temperature. The

The centre depicts the Tower of Comares, the painting being attributed to Daniel Lucas Jnr. Exhibited at the 1851 Exhibition. Mark 238.

Teapot and sugar bowl in the style of Japanese porcelain, c.1874. Mark 269a.

dividing line seems to be 1350°C (2462°F), a soft-paste being fired to its highest temperature of about 1100-1150°C (2012-2102°F), and hard-paste, or 'true' porcelain being fired to 1400+°C (2552+°F).

A ceramic body consists of two elements: a refractory substance which remains stable when fired to a high temperature, and a flux which softens to form a molten or glassy substance which binds together the refractory particles. The firing temperature determines the type of ware produced. Put over-simply, a body mixture of earthenware is usually fired to about 1150°C; if this was to be fired at 1250°C, the result would be close to stoneware, while if it was to be fired at over 1350°C it might develop a degree of translucency and become vitreous. This makes it very difficult to decide exactly what porcelain is. Some white stonewares of the late 18th century are translucent, vitreous and resonant, and some examples of Spode's early Stone China have all these features.

Artificial porcelains were fired first at 1100-1150°C to the biscuit stage, glazed and re-fired at about 1050°C, much as fine earthenware is treated today. The biscuit state is vitreous and is enclosed in a skin of glass, or glaze.

True, or hard-paste, porcelains on the other hand were made in one of two ways:

1 Chinese porcelain, whose body enjoyed excellent 'green' strength, was once-fired, that is the clayware was dried, then painted with cobalt blue colour (if that was the decoration) before the glaze was applied either by dipping, or more probably by a floppy brush. The single firing reached a temperature between 1400-1500°C, when the molten flux permeated throughout the body to form a uniformly glassy mass.

2 European manufacturers of true porcelains adopted a different procedure. The clayware is dried and fired to about 900°C (1650°F), when it is very brittle and porous. The objects are glazed by immersion or other methods, so that the glaze permeates the open pore structure of the ware. The second firing is at about 1400°C. This effectively produces a glass-like material like that of the Chinese, where the biscuit serves as a matrix to support the glaze until at this high temperature both body and glaze are fused into one.

Bone china is a compromise between true and artificial porcelain. The ingredients are those of true porcelain (50% china clay and 50% china stone) to which is added its equal weight of calcined cattle bone. The 'standard' formula is, therefore, china clay 25%, china stone 25%, calcined bone 50%, although over the years there have been many variations from this. In these days the clayware is fired to about 1250°C (2280°F) peak temperature, glazed and re-fired at 1050°C (1922°F). The result is similar in appearance to artificial porcelain – a vitreous core enveloped in a skin of glaze. Bone china, with no glass-forming ingredients, has the advantage of a wider range of peak firing temperatures and the body is more stable at these high temperatures. This results in much less loss than was possible with the older artificial bodies and lower firing costs than for true porcelain. Fine bone china has greater strength than artificial porcelains, which were fragile, and permits a wider range of rich colours than is possible on true porcelain. This latter is because the high-fired glaze needs to be re-heated to a level at which some metallic colouring compounds are destroyed before the colours can be securely bonded to the surface satisfactorily.

The claim is made that English bone china is whiter than European porcelain. This is generally true, but it all depends on the examples used for comparison. Vista Allegre in Portugal made, and may still be making, a porcelain which was as white as Spode's bone china, but this is very unusual. In general, European porcelains are pale grey, while most English bone chinas are very pale ivory. (The only satisfactory way of comparing the colour of different bodies is to put the *backs* of

Vase hollandais, or jardinière eventail. The upper part has holes in the bottom to receive water from the lower vessel which has pierced holes in the shoulder for filling with water and inserting small flowers if desired. Pattern 1926. Mark 23 in black.

Unhandled cup, bone china, with portrait of Futteh Ali Shah, King of Persia. Mark 23a.

Reverse of the cup with portrait of Abbas Merra, Prince Royal of Persia.

Swan-handled comport and sugar tureen,
Dolphin embossed shape, pattern 1875. Three
white lilies compose the decoration: lily of the
valley, Lilium regale *and white water lily. No*
piece is known with a Spode mark: some dessert
plates have the pattern number 1875.

Bone China. The term seems to have been
used first in 1836 by Simeon Shaw, who is
thought to have written the Popular
Encyclopaedia, and certainly in his
Chemistry of Pottery (pp. 254 & 430)
published in 1837.

Tea cup and saucer with hand-painted floral
wreath. Mark 255 (below). c.1886.

Mark 255 showing the blurred image which
seems inappropriate for fine bone china.

the pieces together in order to avoid any effect caused by the decorations). The
ivory tint is caused by a variation in the formula by the addition of some plastic
'ball' clay which makes it possible to adopt the use of mechanical forming
machines for plates and cups. Ball clay also causes opacity, that is, a reduction in
translucence, so most bone china is potted fairly thinly so that the effective translucence remains good.

But these bone chinas do lose some strength because of this. It has been shown
by scientific tests that the whitest, strongest and most translucent bone china is
made by Spode Limited, but to achieve this the production methods are very
difficult to mechanise. (The fired strength of a test piece withstands a pressure of
18,000 pounds per square inch). Indeed, all the manufacturing processes prove
to be costly. Despite modern technology and the advantages of scientific
advance, it remains the case with bone china that if an eighteenth century
formula is retained to yield a twentieth century high quality product, the making
processes will remain less advanced and more costly than if a 'modern' formula is
used.

Until 1984, at Spode, china cups were thrown by hand on the thrower's wheel,
jolleyed by hand and turned by hand on a lathe, but in that year a mechanical
forming process was found to be sufficiently satisfactory. Scallops on cup rims
are still cut out manually, and handles are cut to shape and stuck on by hand.
Plates and saucers are jiggered, some by hand, and most dishes, salad bowls and
open vegetable dishes are either pressed by hand or cast. For the biscuit firing,
every item of 'flatware' needs to be supported individually on a firm 'bed'; this is
either of costly alumina powder, or on a refractory setter specially made to suit
each individual item.

THE HISTORY OF BONE CHINA

The Bow factory, near London, was probably the first manufacturer of porcelain
to use ground calcined bones in its formula. Thomas Frye and Edward Heylyn
patented a porcelain in 1744 (Patent 610) which proved unsuccessful, but which
led to Frye taking out a second patent in 1749 (Patent 649) to manufacture china
using calcareous matter. This time it contained a substance called Virgin Earth,
an eighteenth century term to describe 'the fixed indissoluble matter produced
by calcination of animal and vegetable substances and calcareous minerals such
as chalk and limestone'. Josiah Wedgwood, in his Experiment Book entry for
13th February 1759 notes the Bow recipe as '4 parts bone ash; 4 parts Lynn sand;
¼ part gypsum plaster or alabaster; ¼ part blue ball clay'. It seems likely that the
use of bone ash was the result of a search for a suitable refractory material, while
the Lynn sand is an established ingredient in glass-making.

By 1759, other porcelain manufacturers were using bone ashes in their
artificial bodies: Lowestoft, Chelsea, Derby, and both Chaffers and Pennington
in Liverpool, so it was more than probable that these developments were known
in Staffordshire. Indeed, Staffordshire workmen were employed at the Bow
factory as well as at Chelsea. It is known that John Baddeley of Shelton bought
large quantities of bone ashes between 1758 and 1761, and also that Josiah Spode
moved on to Baddeley's factory in 1761. It seems likely, then, that Spode was
aware of the possibilities of using bone, although opportunity and capital were
not present to enable him to develop a porcelain at the time. The other
Staffordshire potter who is known to have used bone in a porcelain body was
James Neale, who was making porcelain in the late 1780s. But there is more to
manufacturing than making a good quality product; the product needs to be
marketed successfully and a satisfactory profit ensured.

There is no evidence to show that Neale's bone porcelain penetrated the market to any degree. The credit for achievement is given to the person who does these things successfully, and not to the person who first thought of them. It is right, therefore, that Josiah Spode I has been given the credit for *perfecting* bone china, whilst his son, Josiah Spode II can claim the credit for marketing it superbly well. Spode's achievement was in taking the *true* porcelain mixture and adding a substantial quantity of calcined cattle bones, abandoning the method of using either a frit or other glassy substances. The success of this innovation caused his practice to be readily adaptable on earthenware factories.

In 1768, William Cookworthy of Plymouth patented a formula for hard paste, or true, porcelain using just the two materials china clay and Cornish, or china, stone. Although these substances had been known about before, it was Cookworthy who, in 1747, recognised their significance as ingredients for true porcelain. The terms of his patent, number 898, attempted to limit the use of the materials to the patentee only. This patent was assigned to Richard Champion who petitioned Parliament to grant an extension because of lack of success in solving the difficulties of manufacture. This move was opposed strenuously by Josiah Wedgwood, acting for the Staffordshire potters, and he succeeded in obtaining the important concession of the use of the raw materials providing that the formulae in which they were used did not contravene the limits of the recipe lodged with the patent. This effectively restricted their use to earthenwares and stonewares. The original patent, granted in 1768; was to run for 14 years, and the Act (15 Geo.III Cap.52) of 1775 extended the patent for a further term of 14 years (1768+14+14=1796). Potters could experiment with the materials in a porcelain body, but could not sell it without infringing the patent. This suggests that Spode would not have marketed his new ware until 1796 at the earliest, and an invoice from Spode to W Tatton dated July 9 1796 lists a wide range of objects and decorations in 'English China'. The composition of this is not known, but the prices are substantially higher than those for some Queensware listed on the same invoice; the least expensive English China being three times that of the creamware, so disposing of the suggestion that the English China was a euphemistic name for an earthenware. It is also possible that this could have been bone china because the first list starts with "18 dishes in sizes, 2 doz soups, 6 doz large plates . . ."; this suggests that dishes at least up to 16 inch in size were meant. Spode was, perhaps, the first Staffordshire potter to be successful in manufacturing porcelain dinnerware.†

This invoice also seems to justify the belief that it was Spode I, the master potter, who had experimented with new porcelain mixtures for some years and who had started to prepare models and stock perhaps as early as 1794. Certainly 'English China' was being sold before Spode I died in 1797. His son, Josiah Spode II, successfully marketing his father's products in London, had acquired larger premises in 1796 in readiness for the new china, and had moved to this new warehouse at No 5 Portugal Street. He must share the credit for the introduction of bone china – which he called 'Stoke China' – for without his marketing skill the popularity of bone china might never have been achieved.

There are two reasons for the Spodes' success. First, they had brought to perfection the formula and making methods for 'a china as near as possible in appearance to Sèvres soft paste', and secondly, it had been marketed at the right time. Imports of Chinese porcelain by the East India Company had ceased in 1799, and the war with Napolean's Europe had stopped supplies from there. Although cream coloured earthenware was popular with the wealthy classes in their Neo-classical and Georgian houses, there was still a demand for the greater elegance and style of porcelain.†

Two figures made from Derby moulds. Top, Air. Lower, Miss Philpotts. c. 1925. Several versions followed, the last in 1972.

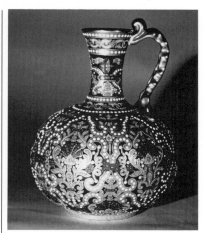

Handled flask, with exquisite enamelled jewelling of many colours upon a cobalt blue ground. Exhibited at the Great Exhibition of 1851.

Display of bone china objects finely painted and jewelled. Exhibited at The International Exhibition of 1862.

1948. One of the dessert plates with painted studies of New Zealand ferns. Made for the projected visit of King George VI and Queen Elizabeth.

Bone china is a hard, vitreous ceramic renowned for its strength (Spode bone china withstands 18,000 pounds per square inch pressure on the modulus of rupture test), whiteness, translucence, resonance, and for the richness of enamel colours and gilding used in decoration.

The term 'bone china' may be used only to describe a translucent whiteware made from a body containing not less than 25% (USA) or 30% (UK) of calcium phosphate derived from cattle bone. The usual composition is: calcined cattle bone 45-50%, china clay 20-25%, Cornish or china stone 25-30%. It is fired to 1100-1260°C (biscuit), glazed and re-fired to 1050-1100°C (glost).

The bone varies according to the quality. The very best is from oxen and is derived from carcasses imported from South America and Australia as well as United Kingdom beasts. Lower grades of bone china may use all or some bones from sheep and goats. Only knuckles and shins from leg bones are suitable for use. The bones are calcined at 900-1000°C before being ground to a fine powder.

Cornish stone is partly decomposed granite and consists of feldspathic minerals and quartz (silica). The best stone is that which has decomposed least and is called 'hard purple' and this has the maximum fluxing properties; the next stages are 'mild purple' and 'dry white', which is one stage away from china clay.

Stone also contains fluorspar which on being heated evolves fluorine. To minimise the effect on the etching of glass windows, de-fluorinated stone, or DFS, is now used widely.

China clay is nearly pure kaolinite. In South West England the deposits were formed by the decomposition of granite in situ by superheated gases from the earth's interior resulting in clays of a high degree of purity, uncontaminated with other minerals and organic matter. The process is called pneumatolysis, and clay so formed is called a primary clay. China clay may be formed by being the product of erosion; clays of this sort are called secondary, and such china clays are found in Brittany and in Virginia.

In SW England, the clay is washed from the sides of the quarries by powerful water jets, the sand is removed and clay slurry has the mica removed before being allowed to settle to thicken before being dried. The quality and characteristics of a clay from one pit vary from those of clay from another face of the same pit, so several clays are blended to produce one of standard characteristics.

The glaze is a mixture of ingredients, ground to a fine powder and mixed with water. One formula is: Lead Bisilicate frit 40%, Borax frit 40%, Quartz 10%, Clay 10%.

† A paper, *Closer to the Bone: the Development of Bone China,* was read by the author to the Ceramics of the Nineties Summer School at the University of Keele on 12th August 1991. This was published in the *Journal of the Northern Ceramics Society* Vol. 9, 1992 pp. 1-24. This deals comprehensively with the subject, but I mistakenly stated that 'the English porcelain manufacturers did not sell dinnerware'. In fact, several manufacturers, notably Bow, Chelsea, Caughley, Derby and Worcester, and later Coalport, did make table services which included dinner plates of 9 inch diameter and large meat dishes, some even up to 20 inches. While Chinese porcelain was available it was less expensive and better, but English porcelain table services were made in the late eighteenth century before Spode.

Stone china

Pottery bodies, now called 'stonewares', have been made for many hundreds of years. Stonewares are dense, impermeable, and hard enough to resist scratching by a steel point, but differ from porcelain in being more opaque. They are usually coloured due to the use of naturally stained clays, and early stonewares were often unglazed, the vitrification achieved rendering this unnessary. There are many exceptions, however, of which these are some: dry stonewares, white salt-glazed stoneware, stone china and ironstone china.

Stoneware was introduced into England in the late 17th century by John Dwight of Fulham, who took out two patents, No. 164 in 1671, and the second, No. 234 in 1684, which related to improvements to the Cologne wares from Germany, from which this type of ware originated. Dwight was probably the first English potter to introduce flint into a pottery body. He recorded in his notebook of 1698, when giving the ingredients for a white body, "calcined beaten and sifted flints will doe instead of white sand and rather whiter but ye charge and trouble are more". The earliest record of flints being used in North Staffordshire is in 1718.

In 1690 the Elers brothers from Amsterdam settled at Bradwell, just north of Newcastle-under-Lyme, and commenced to make an exceedingly fine-grained dry red stoneware in imitation of the Yi-Hsing wares of China and of those by Arij de Milde in Holland (1677-8). They had left Staffordshire by 1700.

The next important development took place in about 1720 when, in North Staffordshire, potters succeeded in making a white ware of ball clay (from Devon) and calcined flints, which they glazed with salt (from Cheshire) by introducing it into the kiln when the temperature had reached about 1200°C (2192°F). The heat caused the sodium of the salt to combine with the silica of the red hot body to form a sodium silicate glaze, the chlorine gas merging with the smoke to intensify its denseness. This ware, known as white salt-glazed stoneware, came close in appearance to some white Chinese porcelain and was sometimes used for providing replacements for Chinese services. White salt-glazed stoneware continued to be manufactured until late in the 18th century, Samuel Spode of the Foley, second son of Josiah Spode I, still making it around 1800.

In the late 1700s, a new form of white stoneware appeared which was not glazed with salt, but relied for its vitrification on a high proportion of feldspathic material, probably Cornish stone. The surface of the ware was smooth and usually matt; it is common to find examples which display large areas which are translucent. Two of the prominent manufacturers were John Turner of Lane End, and Josiah Spode, the former having been the partner until 1762 with R Banks in Stoke at the time when Spode went there to work in 1754. The restrictions placed by the Act of Parliament on the use of Cornish stone and china clay may be the reason for these two potters developing this type of stoneware, but the body was used mainly for pitchers, or jugs, and drinking vessels. The knowledge and experience gained in its production led each potter to new ventures.

Spode turned his attention to developing a practical porcelain, bone china, in which dinnerware could be made. Turner produced some of the finest Jasper ware of all time, but died in 1787; his sons, William and John, continued their business successfully for twenty years. In January 1800, they patented, No. 2367, a fine stoneware using a white argillaceous (or claylike) rock which they discovered in Tabberner's Mine in the neighbourhood. This ware became known as 'Turners' Patent' and some pieces are so marked. It is grey in colour, dense, and strong, and is the first of the class of wares to be called Stone China.

The Turner manufactory closed in 1806 and their stock was sold. The truth of

Vase shape coffee pot, pattern 2061 Cabbage, but copying a Chinese tobacco leaf design. This is the only coffee pot in stone china known to the author. Mark 7b and 2061, c.1822.

what happened to the formula for Turners' Patent remains obscure. Writing in 1829, Simeon Shaw states: "The stone is very different from the Iron Stone; and therefore the present Patent Ironstone China must not be confounded with the other Patent Porcelains, Champion's and Turner's. The late J Spode Esq., (the Second) purchased the right to manufacture this patent Stone Porcelain". Subsequent authors have assumed that Spode acquired this right in 1805, but Shaw does not specify the date. Jewitt did. Leonard Whiter, in his study of Spodes' wares suggests that it was not until about 1813 that Spode actually began to manufacture the ware which he called 'Stone China'.

The choice of this date is based on the pattern numbers for designs *known* to have been produced first on stone china and which did not appear before then. Certainly, a few patterns, notably 282 and 1407, do occur on stone china, but they were introduced first on bone china; both are patterns in the style of the Japanese and were probably made as replacements.

Although Turners' Patent stresses the inclusion of Tabberner's Mine Rock as a major constituent, no other recipe mentions it, and it is clear that a similar product could be made by using alternative materials.

It seems likely that Miles Mason, in Lane Delph, Fenton, was next to produce stone china, even though he did not call it by that name, and may have used a formula of his own. It does seem that he bought some of the Turners' copper engravings when their business was sold, but there is no way of proving whether Miles Mason purchased the right to the Patent. One theory is that he did acquire it and, just before it expired in 1814, his son, Charles James Mason, took out a related patent in July 1813, No. 3724, to continue their advantage, even though the recipe is spurious. Another theory is that Shaw might have been right, but that Spode, having bought the right, did not choose to use the body until Mason's new patent and success obliged him to enter the field to offer strong competition and to protect his own strong presence in the market for replacement Chinese-type designs. At all events, Spode's first stone china was often translucent and more like porcelain than any stoneware that Mason made.

Moreover, his quality continued at a very high level. The more elaborate Chinese patterns which required much enamelling and gilding could not sensibly be decorated on pearlware, and bone china was too white to match the grey of Chinese porcelain, so a grey-tinted vitreous body like stone china was ideal for this purpose. One more theory is that one of the Turners retained the patent until about 1813, when he sold it to Spode, and this provoked Mason to invent his spurious formula to be significantly different that it could be justified as a patent; Spode's earliest pattern which is known to have been produced first on

Peacock was one of the most popular Chinese patterns exported to Europe. Spode's earliest number 2083 was followed by 2118 and very many other versions since c.1814.

Pheasant, in the Chinese style, pattern 3438, c.1822.

Pattern 3858, later called Currants, of which many versions were produced on bone china and earthenware. c.1824.

Footed comport. Bang Up border in blue and red with the badge of the Kings Royal Irish Hussars. Pattern 3504, Mark 7b, c.1825.

stone china is number 2053, whose recording in the pattern book may have been in May 1814, although Spode might have been producing this and other designs earlier – including replacements for Chinese services. This theory would fit with Shaw's statement, yet does not contradict the statement in the obituary notice for Miles Mason in 1822 which says that 'he had brought the manufactory of the *ironstone china* to the highest perfection…in the nature of its fabrick…for which he held an exclusive patent.' Neither Turner nor Spode ever called their products '*ironstone* china', and although this might be thought to be splitting hairs over one word, Leonard Whiter and others have found, after careful study and interpretation, that Shaw's statements can very often be shown to be correct after all. We may never know, and Mason's patent did not secure for him the protection that perhaps he sought. What he did succeed in doing was to establish a name that any advertising agent would be proud of: Patent (exclusive), Ironstone (strong), China (quality and delicacy). Some of the early ware did support this claim, but within a few years the production became coarsely and heavily potted, while the decorations lacked delicacy of execution. Nevertheless the wares sold widely – mostly at special auction sales which antagonised the retailers – and these wares were strong enough to appeal to the Federal Army in the United States (or, at the time, dis-united states) during the Civil War, when they would survive falling off the back of a waggon!

Several manufacturers made stone china including Minton, Davenport, Wedgwood, Hicks and Meigh, the Ridgways, H. & R. Daniel, Clews, Alcock, and others.

In the mid-nineteenth century, the term 'earthenware' became synonymous with crude pottery like flower pots. Indeed, manufacturers did not apply the name 'earthenware' to their wares: Spode went so far as to name two of his earthenware bodies 'New Fayence' and 'New Blanche', but by the 1850s, manufacturers were adopting the term 'ironstone' to describe what was only medium quality earthenware with none of the special attributes claimed for Mason's original formula. Other manufacturers called their earthenwares by many fancy-sounding names like 'Opaque China'.

In 1820, Spode changed the formula of his stone china, which he re-named 'New Stone'. It was stronger than previously, often potted a little heavier, and lacked any translucency. Spode's successors, Copeland and Garrett, continued to manufacture this body without applying the name to the ware. In the early years of the partnership, however, they decorated ware which had been made previous to 1833 and which was impressed SPODE'S NEW STONE, but printed marks show that it was decorated after March 1833. The product continued to be made throughout the Copeland period, and in 1925 the New Stone printed mark was introduced, using the pseudo-Chinese seal. Its re-emergence then was due mainly to Sydney Thompson, Copeland's agent in New York, who recognised a growing interest in what was known in antique circles as 'Oriental Lowestoft', the term used in those days to describe what is now recognised as Chinese Export Porcelain, or 'China Trade Porcelain'. Originally, Spode had made little teaware, but now it was essential. Mr Thompson had the designers reproduce Chinese shapes of teapot, teacups, and saucers without 'wells', and the 'helmet' shape cream jug; also matching covered sugar box, which, like the teapot, had nicely twisted handles with sprig-style finials, and ly-chee knob. The covered vegetable dish was based on a Chinese design – rectangular to suit the American market – to augment the square Pine knob shape of Spode's original copy of the Chinese, which continued to be made until about 1960.

The Spode pattern books were studied and old designs like Fitzhugh, Gloucester, Peacock and others were re-introduced. Patterns which reproduced

Plate, printed in Royal Blue, pattern 1/3822, c. 1893. New Bridge pattern. Mark 254. This pattern has been wrongly called Queen Charlotte, due to a misunderstanding in 1933. In Copelands (Late Spode) China, 1902, an account was reprinted of Queen Charlotte's visit to Spode's London showroom in 1817 which stated that the Queen had ordered a set of "the newly-invented China, called Stone China …" An illustration at the head of the page showed items in New Bridge. On the 150th anniversary in 1933 of the birth of Josiah Spode I, a plate of this pattern was used as a commemorative with an inscription alleging it to have been the service ordered by the Queen. There is no evidence to support that claim, nor that the pattern was named after her.

Replica plate copying exactly an original Chinese porcelain plate including the raised ridges at the edge (shape K951) and every minute imperfection of the hand painted original. Border printed in blue, badge printed in pale brown and hand coloured and gilded. Ermine head printed in gold, and raised ridges at edge gilded. Mark 258 with inscription:

REPLICA OF GEORGE WASHINGTON CHINA (1785)
MASSACHUSETTS SOCIETY OF THE CINCINNATI (1955)

Pattern W103. 200 plates were supplied in 1955, and a few more were ordered in 1964. Also in 1964 a small bowl (K1216 shape) was made and supplied through Shreve, Crump & Low, Boston. This carried the inscription on the side:

The Society of the Cincinnati
Triennial Meeting
Boston
May 1965

SHREVE, CRUMP & LOW
BOSTON

Spode
FINE STONE
ENGLAND

This bowl is backstamped with mark 296.

Selection of items in Trade Winds pattern, available in red, pattern W128 (1960) or in blue W146 (1970), both with gold edge.

Chinese designs which had been popular in the young United States in the 1790s were newly engraved and given appropriate names as Newburyport, Amherst, Heritage, Plymouth, Independence and Cape Cod. This range was called 'Spode's Lowestoft' and a small booklet was published in about 1929 in New York. It was a great success.

In 1960, a new formula was devised to overcome some of the production difficulties, in particular the serious fault called 'spit-out', and, to distinguish this from earlier bodies, it was re-named 'Fine Stone', in allusion to Turner's name and for its high quality.

Earthenware

Earthenwares of various sorts have been made since man first realised that a piece of clay could be shaped into a vessel and hardened by fire. This essay, however, concerns only those types of earthenware which are relevant to the industrial development of pottery making in North Staffordshire in the eighteenth century and to the Spode factory in particular.

It was not until about 1720 that it became possible for North Staffordshire potters to start trying to produce a white-burning ceramic body. Their first attempts were to apply a thin clay slip of locally mined 'pipe' clay to a red clay pot. The local deposits of white-burning clay, however, were exhausted quite soon, and were not extensive anyway. In 1720, supplies of similar clay from Devon became available. At first, these were known as 'Chester' clays after the name of the port of Chester where they were unloaded from the coastal sailing ships, but later they were called by their present name, Ball Clays. This term is in allusion to the balls, or lumps, of clay weighing about 35 pounds, which were dug from the clay mines. Devon has two main areas of ball clay deposits: in the North around Torrington, being shipped from Bideford and Barnstable, and the larger area of Newton Abbot, which had Teignmouth and Exmouth as ports. Dorset also has an important deposit around Wareham.

Supplies of flint and ball clays gradually increased, but the cost of transport was high. Flints, picked from the beaches of south-east and eastern England, were shipped to the mouth of the River Humber and then transferred to barges which brought them to Willington, near Repton, on the River Trent. From here they were taken by pack horse or horse-drawn waggons through Uttoxeter to Burslem, and later to the other Potteries towns. Ball clays were shipped either to Chester, or to the mouth of the River Weaver (on the River Mersey), when they, too, came to North Staffordshire by similar means. Another route was up the River Severn to Bewdley or Bridgnorth, from where only pack horse trains could carry them across the hills.

Such difficulties did not concern pottery manufacturers who were established near the sea or a navigable river, such as Liverpool or Nottingham. North Staffordshire is land-locked, and one might wonder why the principal centre of pottery manufacture is located here. It is because of the readily available supply of high bituminous coal, the seams of which 'outcrop' from Tunstall in the north-west to Fenton in the south-east; coal has been mined here since AD1312, and it is of the sort which is ideal for firing pottery ovens, with its high gas content which yields long flames. It is heavy and up to 15 or so tons were needed to fire one ton of clayware; it was less costly to import the new white-burning clays than to try to disrupt an established industry and transport all the heavy fuel and fireclays to the south-west.

As supplies of clays and flints increased, potters were able to experiment with solid white bodies. The earliest type was the white salt-glazed stoneware, which was suitable for dinnerware, and moulded shapes became popular. In 1740, Ralph Daniel, on his return from a visit to France, introduced plaster of Paris as a mould material: up to that time, moulds had been made of alabaster, fired earthenware or other hard wearing substances. Plaster made it much easier to reproduce working moulds in quantity for the production of objects like plates and cups, as well as complicated pieces like teapots and tureens with embossments.

In the mid-eighteenth century, most objects continued to be hand thrown on the potter's wheel and turned on a treadle-operated lathe. Oval and embossed items were press-moulded with plastic clay. But changes were taking place

c.1827. Plate, earthenware, Botanical pattern. Supplied to the Persian market. Pattern 4565. Marks 43 & 67.

Dessert dish, earthenware. Border of Union Wreath I with the centre of Union Wreath III. Mark 49a.

Model of Shakespeare's birthplace, 1847, Mark 234.

Soup tureen and stand, Fern pattern. From a service bought in Russia c.1852. Marks 202a and 304.

Willow pattern border to a plate depicting a portrait of Albert Smith. 1858. Mark 243.

Queen Charlotte's bed bath 1890. Mark 245.

slowly. By 1750, the process of slip-casting was in use for making small objects of hollow-ware like cream jugs and small teapots.

This slip was just clay in the fluid state, called 'water slip', and the clay:water ratio was low. A larger article, being thicker, would not be firm enough before the mould was sodden with water, so when the mould was tipped up to pour out the surplus slip, the cast would flop out also. Such large objects continued to be pressed until the 1920s, when the so-called 'patent slip' was in use. This had sodium compounds added in small quantities which had the effect of deflocculating the slip ie. increasing the clay:water ratio. For earthenware, soda ash (sodium carbonate) is used, whilst this with sodium silicate is used for bone china slip.

From medieval times to the middle of the 18th century, a clear shiny glaze was achieved by dusting on to the damp surface of the clayware finely powdered galena (lead sulphide) which melted during the firing to form a glaze in association with the silica of the clay.

The dipping process of applying a glaze is said to have been introduced by Enoch Booth in about 1740, but it was ten years later when the practice became adopted more generally. Instead of the lead being applied to the clayware before the firing (Once-fired ware), the clayware was fired first to the 'biscuit' stage, and the glaze applied to this biscuit ware and re-fired at a lower temperature to yield a 'glost' piece. This glaze was 'raw', or un-fritted, consisting of lead carbonate or lead oxide suspended in water with the help of some ball clay to assist in preventing the heavy lead compounds from sinking to the bottom of the dipping tub. This was a big step forward and paved the way for various developments which became the mainstay of the earthenware industry: creamware, pearlware, and under-glaze decorations.

The lead and some iron in the glaze stained it to a pale yellow, so that this class of pottery is called cream-coloured earthenware, or Creamware. By 1762, Josiah Wedgwood had perfected formulae and firing techniques so that a consistently good quality could be maintained; in 1765 he supplied a 'set of tea things' to Her Majesty Queen Charlotte who was kind enought to permit Wedgwood to call the ware Queensware.

Now it was possible to paint on the smooth glaze and re-fire the colours at a lower temperature. At first, the quality of the painting lacked the refinement associated with porcelain, but perhaps this was appropriate. Earthenware was and is less expensive and intended for daily use, whereas porcelain was very costly and kept for special occasions.

Soon transfer prints were applied to white salt-glazed stoneware and creamware in the mid-1750s following the successful application of the method by Sadler and Green to tin-glazed tiles, in 1756.

Wedgwood's success was partly due to his recognition of a new market need, tableware to compliment the Neo-classical style of architecture and interior decoration which was coming into fashion. Chinese porcelain with blue and white designs did not sit well with Adam designs and the new furniture of Chippendale, Hepplewhite and Sheraton. Wedgwood's neo-classical shapes and neat patterns did look marvellous on the dark mahogany, and these facts led to a rapid decline in the sales of Chinese porcelain. The East India Company began to reduce their orders so that by about 1790 very little Chinese porcelain was entering the United Kingdom market.

A very important event took place in 1777. The canal was completed which was designed to link the River Trent with the River Mersey. Clays and flints and Cornish stone now could be brought direct to the wharves in the Potteries in very much larger quantities and at a fraction of the cost. The industry burgeoned forth. A safer means of transport was also now at the disposal of the manufacturers, and the export trade now began to grow substantially.

The 1780s and 1790s saw tremendous growth in the industry. Up until then the wealthy classes had used Chinese porcelain for their dinnerware; the English porcelain houses could not fire the larger plates straight enough to be saleable, so, with the change of fashion, Queensware took over in this market. Also at this time impetus was given to tea drinking. In 1784 the Commutation Act reduced the tax on tea from 119% to effectively only 12½%, so eliminating smuggling and the adulteration of tea with other leaf substitutes. In addition, a tax was imposed on silver, making it more costly to buy a silver teapot, sugar box and cream jug. Apart from stimulating the trade in pottery in general, it also led to a demand for matchings of Chinese porcelain services now that it had become almost impossible to obtain them from Canton. To match the Chinese ware, a cobalt stain was introduced into the glaze, and this removed the creamy tone of the creamware to yield a pale grey tone which matched the chinaware closely. It became known as pearlware, and was used for non oriental wares too.

Transfer-printing in blue under the glaze was developed in England, first by Worcester in about 1761, and later by Caughley, in Shropshire. In both cases this was on porcelain. The printing onto biscuit earthenware proved more difficult to achieve successfully, but by 1784, Josiah Spode had perfected the process and initiated the production of objects made to appeal to persons owning Chinese blue and white porcelain, and requiring matching pieces. The early engravings on copper were coarse, but soon the techniques of the complete process were mastered and established Spode as the manufacturer of the finest wares.

Blue was the best colour which would withstand the high temperature of being fired underglaze; indeed, its richness was only obtained by the reaction of the cobalt oxide with the silica in the glaze to produce the blue cobalt silicate. Refining of the metallic ores and preparation of the colour led to the early dark blue yielding to a brighter, paler blue. Later, other colours were discovered which could be printed underglaze. Black, manganese purple, and brown were sometimes used as plain print colours, but more often as outline prints which were later filled in with hand applied colours. Called 'print and paint', this became the established process of producing large amounts of polychrome designs, especially on earthenware.

Green prints became possible in about 1822 to 1825, and pink in about 1832, when chromium was added to the ceramicist's list of suitable elements.

The body formulae for both creamware and pearlware seem to have been very similar, the differences in appearance being due to the tinting of the glaze. In about 1820 Spode attempted to reverse this by creating a clear, colourless glaze for application to a tinted body. The result was the introduction of two new formulae, one for an ivory tinted body which he called 'Spode's Imperial', and the other for a white body which was impressed with a crown mark and became known as 'Crown' body. Various other bodies were introduced during the company's history and these are included in the Catalogue of Marks.

A hideous example of commemorative ware. A triumvirate of bald eagles formed into a three handled vase for J. M. Shaw & Co., New York. 1876. Mark 308.

Mask jug, depicting Bacchus with lurid pink nose and cheeks and lecherous, steel-blue eyes. Mark 103. Underglaze painted.

Coffee cup and saucer. Willow Pattern centre, grasshopper border. Very thinly potted which seems unusual for ware made in Y body. Marks 206 and 231. c.1890.

Plate in white earthenware with the arms of James Craggs. Mark 9. 1889.

One of several decanters made for James Hawker & Co. of Plymouth.

Tazza, diameter 41.8cm, made to mark the contributions made by Prince Albert to the Arts, Education and Science.

Parian

Figurines have been made in ceramic material since the dawn of history. Primitive peoples made small figures which are presumed to be some sort of household gods; more sophisticated societies like the Greeks and the Romans certainly had these and other images which they worshipped and venerated. In Europe in the eighteenth century, great banquets had the tables embellished with sculptured decorations in sugar which included figurines, also of sugar, which were all destroyed after the event. To avoid this waste and to save the expense of the sugar-modellers' talents when porcelain became available in the second decade of the eighteenth century at Meissen, porcelain figurines were used as decoration instead of sugar ones. Later, 'biscuit' porcelain figurines were popular: Sèvres started the vogue and was followed by Derby. The fineness of detail was wholly apparent and the figures were carefully tooled to sharpen up the detail which would have been obscured had the piece been glazed. At the end of that century, John Turner of Lane End – and probably others – made a fine portrait bust in unglazed stoneware of Matthew Prior; this vitreous material was easier to clean than biscuit porcelain, yet it did not need a glaze. In the 1830s, Copeland & Garrett also made some portrait busts of notable personalities, of which those of the Duke of Wellington and Milton are known so far; these were in Felspar Porcelain, either unglazed or 'smear-glazed'.

Soon after the accession of Queen Victoria it seems that a vogue for marble statuary became popular amongst the wealthy and this inspired Copeland's Thomas Battam, the art director, to investigate the possibility of producing smaller portrait busts and figures in a porcelain which would simulate marble.

Battam's first essay in 'statuary porcelain' was to reproduce the statue of "Apollo, as the shepherd boy of Admetus" in a reduced size. This statue was in the possession of His Grace the Duke of Sutherland at Trentham Hall near Stoke-upon-Trent. The figure was probably made in an unstained version of Spode's stone china, which, after the biscuit fire, could be smoothed to a fine surface. Battam showed the resulting figure to the Duke – apparently on 3rd August 1842 – when the Duke bought it.

In 1844, Battam showed it, or one like it, to the committee of the Art Union of London as a suggestion for one of the prizes in their lottery. The advice of the renowned sculptor, John Gibson RA, was sought and he pronounced it "the next best material to marble", and offered his prize sculpture of "Narcissus" to be copied in Stone china as a prize. The modeller E. H. Stephens re-modelled it in a reduced size and fifty of these were offered by the Art Union in 1846. Meanwhile, John Mountford had left Derby to come to work for Copeland & Garrett, bringing with him skills and knowledge of modelling and figure-making. It seems that he revised the formula completely, and, with the support of Spencer Garrett, changed the firing sequence; this resulted in a fine porcelain which matured in the second, higher, fire to yield a smooth, sensuous surface. By December 1845, the firm was able to display a range of objects at the First National Exhibition of British Industrial Art held in Manchester. The report in the *Art Journal* of 1846 was highly complimentary and enthusiastic about the display of Copeland & Garrett, and this undoubtedly helped to promote statuary porcelain in general and Copeland's productions in particular.

There were other claims to being the first with this product but only Minton was a serious contender, and recent opinion believes that what their protagonists were claiming were really their china biscuit figures and that Minton did not start to make parian until 1847.

Example of a handled jug, with convolvulus design. Size 30s. Registered 4 November 1848 Mark 227.

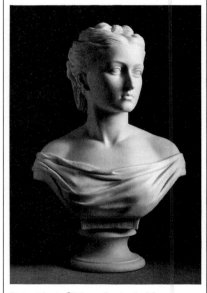

Portrait bust of Princess Louise, by Mary Thorneycroft. 1871. Above, the inscription moulded into the back.

Mary Thorneycroft's model of Edward Prince of Wales as Winter. 1848.

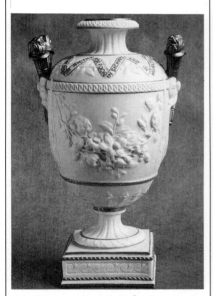

Handled vase, embossed with floral swags and ribbons, bearing the words of the marriage vows.

The flying figure of Morning, by Raffaele Monti. 1862.

The name 'Parian' was coined by Minton, after the island of Paros, whence the Greek sculptors obtained their marble. 'Carrara', the name adopted by Wedgwood, is the district in Italy whence the Romans got their marble.

It is hoped that a fuller account will appear in a book on Copeland Parian, which is in the course of preparation.

Appendix III

Pottery trade sizes

If anyone could be said to be 'down to earth' it is the potter, who, working with raw materials dug from the ground, learnt to be intensely practical. Even holes in the road are called 'pot-holes' after the sinful practice of some Burslem potters in the seventeenth century who, when they ran short of clay, dug some from the road!

In the early days of the Staffordshire pottery industry, when most journeymen and journeywomen, as well as some master potters, were illiterate, it was necessary to establish a system for settling wages which was easily understood. The method adopted was based on the 'dozen', for which one price was fixed for each object, so that a maker to obtain that price needed to make twelve articles. That 'price per dozen' held for all the other sizes made of the same design, but, in order to obtain that price either more smaller articles or less larger ones had to be made. The 'count to the dozen' was determined by the number of a given size that would fit on a standard size of work-board, in the case of clay articles, or which would fit into a warehouse basket, in the case of fired ware. These trade sizes were applied particularly to hollow-ware objects; it was the number and not the capacity that decided the count to the dozen. So a Barrel Jug, 12s, (ie 12 to the board), held 2 pints, a Churn Jug 12s held 1¾ pints, and a Dutch Jug 12s held 2½ pints. The standard size of work-board was 6 feet by 9 inches.

The trade sizes were mostly multiples of 6 or 12, with the largest trade size holding the smallest volume. Thus, a 2s Barrel Jug could hold 11 pints and a 36s held only ¾ pint. The full range of trade sizes was:

2s, 3s, 4s, 6s, 9s, 12s, 18s, 24s, 30s, 36s, 42s, 48s, 54s, 60s, 72s. Sizes above 42s were seldom made, and then usually for the catering trade, when, for example, a cream 'tot' would be a 72s. Articles which were larger than 2s were generally called 4, 6, 8 Quarts according to their approximate capacity.

CLAY DEPARTMENTS

Items such as cups, mugs and eggcups which were thrown and turned were counted by the 'long-dozen', that is of 36 cups to count as a 'dozen'.

Plates were measured in inches and counted by the 'short dozen' of twelve. In general, the trade sizes were 10″, 9″, 8″, 7″, 6″, 5″, 4″, but manufacturers often increased the actual diameter of the plates but charged them to the customer, and paid the maker, at the lower price; so, often a trade 10″ plate might measure 10½″, and other trade sizes larger in actual measurements in proportion. In times of fierce competition some manufacturers stooped to selling a 9½″ actual as a trade 8″! Over the years such practices led to utter confusion within the trade itself, and particularly among retailers, many of whom experienced the receipt of a

An impressed mark to be seen on tankard shape jugs. A variation of Mark 212, with the actual capacity of 1 PINT or 1QT (QUART) added.

Pad mark 227 as applied to early parian ornamental objects and agate ware.

Marks on stoneware jug, including 36, stating the size.

different size of plate to that which they believed they had ordered.

Saucers were counted 15 to the dozen.

Sometimes the trade size, like 24 or 36, is marked in the mould of a hollow-ware article such as jugs and teapots.

Meat dishes, or platters, or achettes in Scotland, were measured in inches, and generally were within about an inch of the trade size; they were counted as a dozen of twelve.

Sometimes, impressed numbers are seen on the backs of meat dishes like 16, or 18, or 22IN, and these refer to the trade size, and not to the exact length.

Whisky decanter made for Ushers to commemorate the coronation of King George V and Queen Mary, 1911. Mark 202.

PRINTING SHOP

A similar system was operated in the under-glaze printing department, but the counts were not necessarily the same. For instance, in 1833-4, plates of regular patterns all counted 15 to the dozen, 'Twiflers' (8″ plates) counted 18s, 'Muffins' (7″ & 6″ plates) counted 24s, and 3″, 4″, and 5″ counted 36 to the dozen. Dishes up to 14 inches, 12s, and all above that size counted 6s.

WAREHOUSES

The warehouses had different counts for the payment to the 'sorters', the women who chipped off the bits of glaze which were stuck to the places where the object had been supported, and to the selectors, who separated the good ware from the seconds and those pieces which needed to be ground, polished or re-glazed. It was here that some of the counts depended on the number of articles of the same sort which could be held in a standard warehouse basket.

PAYMENT TO THE WORKERS

The payment to most clay makers, printers and decorators was by the system known as 'good from oven'. It was an unfair one because each worker was not completely responsible for the handling of the ware he had worked on. A plate-maker's work was scalloped or fettled by a woman, and placed in the saggar by a placer, either one of whom could spoil the plate; unless it emerged from the kiln, or oven, as a 'best' piece no-one got paid. In some badly managed manufactories, a foreman might deem ware not good for payment, yet allow it to pass on to the next processes, so robbing the workers while enabling the master to sell a product for which he had not paid a proper price. The practice of 'good from hand' did not replace it until about 1872, and then only in a few first class firms like Mintons and Copelands. It was only abolished completely in 1964.

SELLING PRICES

Pricing of articles for sale was according to the individual size and complexity of shape and decoration. Usually these prices were obtained from 'Scales' which were published by the industry or, sometimes, by an individual manufacturer.

Each pattern was allocated a 'Rate', which was based on the cost of a dinner plate and a teacup and saucer. All the other items were related, and a set of Scales was established which listed in the left column all the objects available, and across the top of the pages a series of Rates of steadily increasing value. In the Fine Bone China scales, for example, the 6/4 rate would start with a plate 10″ priced at 6/4d, and the teacup and saucer would also be 6/4d. In the earthenware scales, plates, cups and saucers, etc. were usually priced per dozen, but the principle was the same. The selling price of any item could be discovered by following down the appropriate column until the line opposite the desired article was reached. There were many adjustments made to accommodate varying circumstances. Plates, cups and saucers were often priced low to encourage buyers in believing that the

The Columbus pitcher, 1892. Dark blue dip or engobe on grey stoneware, with scene of Columbus landing sprigged in white clay. Mark 349.

patterns were good value, but in the days when hollow-ware and meat dishes were essential elements in a 'closed' set, the prices of those items were enhanced so that on average the correct level of profit was achieved. When the North American market adopted the 'place setting' as the basic unit of sale, the firm was in dire danger of losing a lot of money, so the Rates for those patterns were increased to compensate for the lower sales of the serving pieces. Rates were also different for different markets to take account of local composition of sets, whether commission had to be paid to an agent, or whether the market expected the firm to untertake advertising expenses, etc. It was, therefore, impossible to publish a price list for universal use; this was only achieved in 1961, after every item had been more carefully costed, and a satisfactory level of profit placed on every item. At the same time actual measurements were given alongside the trade sizes, and the 'dozen counts' of 18s, 24s, 30s, etc. were gradually replaced by large, middle and small, or No. 2, No. 3 etc. The transition was made possible by the markets not requiring the huge range of sizes, usually being content with no more than three sizes of any one hollow-ware item.

One small variation which obtained until 1939 was the gilding of knobs and handles of hollow-ware articles of dinnerware in certain earthenware patterns; the pattern itself might not have a gilded edge, but there was often a choice available for a customer to have the extra gilding to enhance the appearance of the items on the dinner table. Of course, this cost extra.

Appendix IV

The McKinley Tariff Act, 1890

This Act is often mentioned in connection with the dating of ceramics, because in 1891 all articles imported into the United States of America were required to carry the name of their country of origin. I am indebted to Geoffrey Godden for pointing out that some manufacturers included ENGLAND in their marks before 1891.

William McKinley was the chairman of the Ways and Means Committee of the Congress of 1889-90, and was the champion of trade protection. In the election of 1888, the country had declared itself in favour of a policy of protection. In the fifty-first Congress, Session I, Chapter 1244 was 'An Act to reduce the revenue and equalize duties on imports, and for other purposes'. It was enacted by the Senate and House of Representatives of the United States of America in Congress on October 1st 1890.

The section relating to imports, Section 6, states:
"That on and after the first day of March, eighteen hundred and ninety-one, all articles of foreign manufacture, such as are usually or ordinarily marked, stamped, branded, or labeled, and all packages containing such or other imported articles, shall, respectively, be plainly marked, stamped, branded, or labeled in legible English words, so as to indicate the country of their origin: and unless so marked, stamped, branded, or labeled they shall not be admitted to entry".

Furthermore, Section 7 states:
"That on and after March first, eighteen hundred and ninety-one, no article of imported merchandise which shall copy or simulate the name or trade-mark of any domestic manufacture or manufacturer, shall be admitted to entry at any custom-house of the United States . . . .".

Although the terms of this part of the Act were adopted by countries who exported to the United States, the McKinley Tariff Act, as it became known, was in existence for little more than a month before the Fall (autumn) elections of 1890 gave it its death blow. A Democratic Congress alarmed those whose businesss the tariff would have benefitted.

The origins of the clauses concerning marking lay in the practice of some exporters to the USA of manufacturing goods which were calculated to mislead people into believing that those goods were of domestic American origin, even to simulating American-style markings.

The need to mark the name of the country of origin was only necessary if the goods were intended for export; often Copeland wares are to be found without the word ENGLAND even though it is clear that they were made later than 1891. This sometimes happened when a mark was engraved on the copper plate of a pattern which had been introduced, say, in the 1870s, and had not been revised even as late as the 1920s if the pattern was destined for the home market.

REFERENCES

McLure, A K & Morris, C (1901) The Authentic Life of President McKinley. pp150-7

Leech, M (1959) In the Days of McKinley. New York: Harper & Brothers, pp43-9

Godden, G A (1988) Encyclopaedia of British Porcelain Manufacturers. London: Barrie & Jenkins, p34

Appendix V

Pattern numbers missing or incomplete in early pattern books (Spode period)

Compiled by Dr. Angus Johnston II, to whom I give grateful thanks.

Pattern numbers					
1-132	435	1153	1675	2080 D.O.	2656 B.
134	436	1154	1686 D.O.	2090 D.O.	2657 B.
137-145	473 D.O.	1155	1687	2103 D.O.	2658 B.
160-217	484	1190 D.O.	1692 D.O.	2104 D.O.	2661 D.O.
219-235	500	1222 D.O.	1694	2112 D.O.	2662 D.O.
237	501	1223	1701 D.O.	2118 D.O.	2663 D.O.
238	502	1226	1702 D.O.	2148	2664 D.O.
239	503	1227 †	1727 D.O.	2150 D.O.	2665 D.O.
240	506 D.O.	1231	1728	2151	2666 B.
242	507 D.O.	1313	1736 B.	2160 D.O.	2667 B.
243	518 †	1314	1744 D.O.	2175 B.	2668 B.
244	519	1329	1750	2193	2669 B.
245	520	1360	1751	2208 D.O.	2670 B.
246	521	1380 D.O.	1752	2209 D.O.	2673 B.
247	522	1381 D.O.	1753	2210 D.O.	2683 D.O.
248	523	1392 D.O.	1766 D.O.	2211 D.O.	2684 D.O.
249	539	1403 D.O.	1767 D.O.	2212 D.O.	2685 D.O.
250	673	1417	1772 M.	2242 D.O.	2686 D.O.
255	709	1418	1773 M.	2259	2687 D.O.
272	774 B.	1419	1774 M.	2264 D.O.	2688 D.O.
274	776	1420	1775 M.	2288	2689 D.O.
275	777	1421	1787 M.	2355 D.O.	2690 D.O.
277	798 B.	1422	1801 M.	2362 D.O.	2691 B.
288	803	1423	1824 B.	2393 D.O.	2692 B.
290	808	1424	1834 B.	2403 D.O.	*End of Book 2*
291	809	1425	1889 B.	2404 D.O.	
292	876	1426	1890 B.	2417 D.O.	2709 D.O.
293	904	1434	1929 M.	2450 D.O.	2710 D.O.
294	905	1497	1930 M. †	2456 D.O.	2711 D.O.
295	942	1498	1942 M.	2457 D.O.	2712 D.O.
296	943	1499	1961	2471 D.O.	2713 D.O.
297	977	1508	1964 D.O.	2483	2714 D.O.
298	981 D.O.	1509	1989	2488 D.O.	2725 D.O.
299	983 D.O.	1510	1994	2496	2726 D.O.
313 B.	984 B. †	1513 D.O.	1995	2499 D.O.	2727 D.O.
371	1000	1516 D.O.	1999 D.O.	2500 B.	2728 D.O.
373 †	1001	1545 D.O.	2000 D.O.	2501 B.	2729 D.O.
374	1014	1546 D.O.	2004	2502 B.	2731 D.O.
388	1019	1547 D.O.	2042 *	2503 B.	2732 D.O.
398	*End of Book 1*	1577 D.O.	2043 *	2565 B.	2733 D.O.
399		1582	2044 *	2648 D.O.	2734 D.O.
400	1028	1625	2045 *	2649 D.O.	2735 D.O.
401	1125 B.	1639	2046 *	2650 D.O.	2737 D.O.
402	1132 D.O.	1648	2057 D.O.	2651 D.O.	2738 D.O.
434	1134	1674	2059 D.O.	2652 D.O.	2739 D.O.
			2067 B.	2653 D.O.	2740 D.O.
			2079 D.O.	2655 B.	2741 D.O.

Vase on ball and claw feet. Imari-style decoration. Bone china, pattern 1227.

Pattern 373. Hand painted sprigs, brown edge. Thinly potted pearlware.

2761 D.O.	2896 **	2931 D.O.	3155 ***	3383 D.O.	3712 D.O.
2762 D.O.	2898 **	2940 **	3184 D.O.	3384 D.O.	3714 D.O.
2763 B.	2900 **	2991 D.O.	3200	3385 D.O.	3716 D.O.
2764 B.	2910 D.O.	3031 **	3201	3386 D.O.	3777 D.O.
2771 D.O.	2912 **	3032 **	3251 D.O.	3387 D.O.	3778 D.O.
2772 D.O.	2913 **	3050 D.O.	3252 D.O.	3388	3779 D.O.
2773 D.O.	2914 **	3098 B.	3264	3389	3811 D.O.
2774 D.O.	2915 **†	3118 **	3286 D.O.	3406 D.O.	3814 D.O.
2775 D.O.	2916 **	3119 **	3289 D.O.	3431 D.O.	3815 D.O.
2788	2917 **	3134 D.O.	3296	3468 D.O.	
2791 D.O.	2918 **	3144 D.O.	3305 D.O.	3579 B.	
2892 **	2919 **	3145 B. M.	3340 D.O.	3632 P.L.	
2893 D.O.	2920 **	3150 D.O.	3342 D.O.	3633 P.L.	

There are no missing patterns after Pattern 3815 (late 1822 or early 1823) to the end of the Spode period on March 1, 1833. As of that date Spode pattern numbers had reached 5350.

If it is assumed that Henry Daniel's connection with Spode began at the beginning of 1805 and terminated at the end of 1822, it will be found that 277 Spode patterns are missing or incomplete to 1805 and that 280 patterns are missing or incomplete in the Daniel period.

The 557 missing or incomplete patterns in a total of 5350 amounts to 10.8 per cent.

From 300.
136 missing or blank, or pattern lost.
9 missing, gained details from Mr. Daniels working copy.
158 Directions only.

D.O. Directions only.
B. Blank.
P.L. Pattern lost.
M. Missing from Spode copy, but details obtained from Mr. Daniel's Working Copy, in 1989.
† Actual items found & authenticated.
* "Refer to Mr. Daniels pattern book".
** Shape shown with incomplete pattern and directions for the missing pattern.
All patterns so marked between 2892 and 2920 were to have "Blue printed Broseley" on gold decorated teacups.
*** "Look at the Large Cannister in the Daniel's Book".

Pattern 518. Old Oval & Bute shapes. Brown vine border and gilded lines and bands.

Pattern 984. Onglaze iron-red pluck and dust print, with rich gilding. New Oval shape.

Bone china coffee cup and saucer, pattern 1930. Richly gilded design with touches of red, and yellow bands.

Appendix VI

A suggested scale of rarity and authenticity

Rarity

Unique	1	(nearly unique, fairly unique, these terms should NOT be used; unique is unique, i.e. one only)
Extremely rare	2 or 3	
Very rare	4-6	
Rare	7-10	
Scarce	11-20	
Uncommon	21-40	
Fairly common	41-60	
Common	61-100	
Plentiful	101+	

Tray for hairbrushes, from the dressing table set made for use by Princess Alexandra in the boudoir set aside for her during the Banquet given by the Corporation of the City of London on the occasion of the presentation of Freedom of the City to the Prince of Wales, 8th June 1863. This tray is unique! For a full account of the service, refer to Spode Society Recorder, *pp12-14.*

Authenticity

Possibly	one or two features suggesting a certain maker
Probably	three or four features suggesting a distinct likelihood that the maker can be identified
Attributed	enough characteristics which are identical to, or sufficiently close to a known piece to leave no doubt
Documented	the object is marked or signed

For those of us who take a light hearted view of rarity, I suggest:

Scarcely credible	probably a fake or a forgery
Unbelievable	Just the other fellow's luck!

Incidentally, the difference between a fake and a forgery is:

Fake	an object seeming to be genuine, a sham, made in the style of but not a copy
Forgery	a copy of an original, fraudulently made

This matter was highlighted by Bill Coles in the *Spode Review,* page 124, after a misunderstanding of the term 'rare' by a correspondent. He and I devised this scale, and I am grateful to Arlene Palmer Schwind, one time Keeper of Glass and Ceramics at Winterthur, for checking the above list and recommending some improvements.

Appendix VII

The identification of ceramic objects facilitated by clear description, drawing or photography

Museum curators and auctioneers receive many requests to identify, or give information about, ceramic items. Such items may have been inherited, bought at a church sale, found in the attic, or acquired at a flea market or 'won' in some other way. Often there is a request for a valuation, but museums do not give valuations, and for this you should ask an auctioneer or antique dealer of upright reputation.

Valuations

Valuations may be for different purposes, and the valuation will be different for each one.

1. Valuation for 'insurance purposes' will be the highest, and the premium will vary depending on what 'cover' is required. Replacement value will cost the most, especially if the object is regarded as irreplaceable!

2. Valuation for sale will depend on where and how it is sold. Sold at an internationally known auction with several rich dealers and collectors all bidding for your treasure, the value may be beyond your wildest dreams! Sold to the antique shop on the corner, the same object may not yield enough to repay the bus fare into town!

3. Valuation for probate is usually the lowest of all, and may represent the nearest to its true value. If it is liable to be taxed, you want this value to be as low as possible.

Identification

A. "I am enclosing a snap which is not very good I'm afraid of an ornament I found in someone's waste-paper basket . . ." (A somewhat embellished remark!). This snap was so enveloped in greenery that I could not distinguish any details. I had to ask for another photograph before attempting an identification.

B. Plates are sometimes held by hand. Against a wall or chair may be all right, but held in front of the face or the body might give enough information about the object, and might be even more revealing about the 'support'.

C. At a meeting at which I lectured, one nice lady gave me a photograph of her ballet-dancing daughter. She really wanted me to identify and tell her something about the vase on the mantelpiece!!

D. My favourite picture, however, is of a step-ladder in a garden. (The illustration here is a reconstruction to avoid embarrassment). "Please will you identify the pattern, &c. . ." Apart from being extremely small, the cups were also out of focus, so blurred. All I could do was to say what the name of the shape might be. In her letter, the lady vouchsafed that she had a complete teaset and she gave the pattern number. I wrote to ask for better photographs of some of the other pieces as well as of the teacups. Two months later, a package arrived with a broken slop bowl and several much better pictures. (The cat had got into the cupboard and knocked

The object for identification is the vase to the left of the girl's right arm.

off the bowl so she sent it if it would be of any help). The shape of the teapot looked like New Hall, so I sent everything to David Holgate who specialises in the wares of that factory. He confirmed that the ware was of New Hall bone china after 1815, but that the pattern was of the earlier true porcelain period. All very interesting, and the enquirer was delighted.

Many of the objects enquired about are of very considerable interest and merit, but often people fail to appreciate the importance of sending good quality, clearly defined, photographs or drawings, and giving *full* details of marks, &c...

"Please will you identify the pattern on the two teacups..."

Seeking help in indentifying a problem piece of pottery

Although your piece of pottery is not marked with the name of the manufacturer, it may still be possible for it to be identified. If you write to a museum or other source of information, like an antique dealer or auctioneer, try to follow these general rules.

1. Send a good, clear photograph, showing the pattern, and, if it is an item of hollow-ware, a side view to show the characteristic shape. Most cameras do not focus sharply any nearer than 36 inches (91.5 cms), so ensure that the pattern detail is sharply defined in the viewfinder and in the range-finder (if the camera has one). It is better to have a small, sharply defined image than a large hopelessly blurred one. You can ask the film processor to enlarge just the object so it is easy to see. Notes on photographing pottery objects are at the end of these notes.

2. Measure the object: diameter, length, width, height. State the units you have used, either inches or centimetres. Metric measures tend to be easier for accurate measurement.

3. Describe **every** mark which you can find on the back/base of the object. Look especially for impressed, or indented, marks made in the clay. Try to reproduce the way in which the mark is applied – painted, printed or impressed. Are letters capitals (upper case), little letters (lower case), or italic or some other form? Non-glossy, translucent self-adhesive tape can be applied over the mark, when you may be able to trace the mark onto its matt surface. When complete and dry, cover it with another piece of the same tape before removing, so it will not smudge. Then re-lay it onto a white card or paper. Be sure to give *every* mark, whether you understand it or not.

4. Note any 'process' marks, like placing marks caused by stilts which were used to separate the pieces during the glost fire. What sort of footring does it have, if any? Is there any colouring to the glaze? This might be seen if the glaze has collected in a corner.

Is the piece translucent or opaque when it is held in front of a light?

5. If the piece is a blue transfer-printed pattern, try to describe the tone of blue. There is a guide to blue colours in *Spode's Willow Pattern and Other Designs after the Chinese* (facing page 79). If this book is not available to you from your library, use a description like dark, medium or light-blue; if it has a distinctive shade, state it as, for example: "medium grey-blue, dark violet-blue, &c.".

6. If it is not possible to obtain a good photograph, try to draw it if you can, and if you can't, describe it as fully as possible. Shape, colour, any moulding and what sort and where on the object. Describe the pattern. Centre or main central decoration. Rim and border. Identify any special objects like particular flowers, insects, abstract motifs, and so on.

7. Try to keep a record of these marks for security purposes. If the object is stolen, such identification may prove to be very useful in recovering your property, by authenticating your ownership.

Sections of plates and saucers to show type of foot ring used.

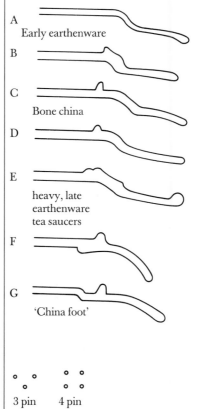

A — Early earthenware

B —

C — Bone china

D —

E — heavy, late earthenware tea saucers

F —

G — 'China foot'

3 pin   4 pin

STILT MARKS

Photographing Pottery and Porcelain

Definition of subject – clarity and sharpness

The first point to remember is that the object must be clearly defined. Many cameras will not focus to a sharp image any nearer than 36 inches (91.5 cms): small objects, like a teacup or teapot, therefore, will need to be photographed with a camera able to focus close enough to render the object clearly. The use of close-focussing extension rings or supplementary lenses with certain cameras will achieve this. Another solution is to use a macro lens, but for recording *very* small subjects the former scheme works well. Sets of supplementary lenses usually comprise three lenses, of + 1, +2, and +4 diopters. By combining these all strengths from +1 to +7 diopters can be chosen. This range is especially useful when photographing marks, signatures and other very small details. Close-focussing rings, or extension tubes, can be used instead of or with supplementary lenses.

Background

The second point is to place the object against a plain background so that maximum attention may be directed towards the pot, with no distraction caused by such things as patterned cloth, other items on a shelf, etc.

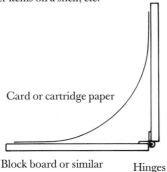

Card or cartridge paper

Block board or similar   Hinges

The best background is plain, matt, thin card, such as Colorama, or thick paper of neutral tint such as grey, fawn, or pale brown. Blue and white pieces look very well on deep red art cartridge paper, but if you are using black and white film this background tends to be overpowering, and if reproduced in a publication may prove less satisfactory than a medium tone of background. Suitable paper may be obtained at any good art materials shop; the paper should always be kept rolled

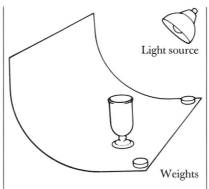

Light source

Weights

and, if possible, protected in a wide cardboard cylinder. Folds and creases should be avoided. This paper may be arranged as shown so that no lines or joins between surfaces are visible. A folding board is ideal for supporting the paper; when in use it might measure about 2 feet high by 2ft 6ins wide to give ample room for arranging small groups of objects. A plain cloth without pattern is the next most satisfactory background; it should be arranged without folds, and, like the paper, should be stored on a roller to keep it free from creases.

Check that the base of every object is clean before it is placed on the background; this includes plate stands and supports. Dirty marks may spoil a photograph, and once on the background material may prove difficult to remove without being noticeable.

Exposure

Most people use Single Lens Reflex cameras, often with Through the Lens metering, and this enables very accurate exposures to be made. All close up photographs should always be taken at an aperture of not less than f8; preferably at f11 or f16. I use as high an aperture number as possible to ensure clarity and maximum depth of focus of hollow-ware objects. The depth of field is very restricted at close quarters, and the further rim of a teacup may be blurred when the nearer rim is sharp if a high enough stop, or aperture, is not used. When using range-finder cameras, or cameras that have neither range-finder nor meter, the distance from the object to the film plane needs to be measured very carefully, and a good exposure meter used, taking into account the longer exposure needed as the distance decreases. Unless the camera has TTL or automatic exposure, extension tubes and supplementary lenses for close-up photographs will require at least another

stop, i.e. a longer exposure or more open aperture.

The use of a KODAK grey card is recommended for perfect exposures.

Arrangement of objects

A single object presents little problem. A bowl, cup or open object is often seen best if at least a little of the inside can be observed. (Fig B), but where the *exact* shape needs to be illustrated then a side elevation (Fig A) may be preferred.

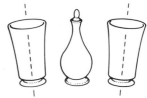

A   B

The handle may be turned to be slightly towards the camera so that the point of fixing may be seen.

When two or more objects need to be shown side by side some distortion may become evident. With close-up photography all objects appear to lean outwards: the more items in a group the worse the effect on those items further from the centre.

In order to counteract this effect, the outer items must be tilted inwards until they appear vertical when seen through the view-finder. A small piece of folded paper or card slid beneath the outer edge is usually sufficient and can be placed so that it is not visible in the picture. A gap may be apparent, but this is preferable to something which looks as if it might topple over. One other way to avoid this form of distortion is to use a long-focus, or zoom, lens which means placing the camera some distance away from the object.

A group of pieces of hollow-ware may be arranged more compactly by placing one or two items so that they are partly in front of others; this also looks more natural and interesting.

Fig C is rather dull, Fig D is better.

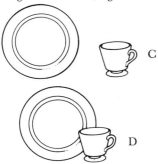

But don't obscure some interesting detail on the saucer or item behind. The arranging of objects to present an attractive, yet instructive, picture that illustrates the features one wishes to stress, takes much time and is very tiring, but is rewarding eventually.

Plates, saucers and other flatware may be supported on a conventional plate stand which will show a small amount of the stand at the lower side of the plate. (Fig E). This may be avoided by using a heavy block of wood, or metal, with a lump of Blu-Tack, or other suction type of soft material to which the plate may be pressed. (Ensure that the bases of these supports are clean). (Fig F).

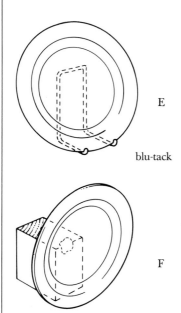

blu-tack

Lighting

The more even the lighting, the better the result, and daylight is to be preferred whenever possible. Bright sunshine is *very* intense and casts black shadows as well as making the lit areas too pale. A bright, slightly overcast sky yields a clear, soft and even light. Side lit objects show their shape better, but a shadow will occur on the side of the item further from the light source. This may be moderated by holding a white card or sheet of expanded polystyrene to reflect some light onto the darker side. (The matt surface of polystyrene reduces the chance of creating an extra highlight). This method yields a good appearance of three-dimensional shape, and the side lighting will distinguish any modelled features, like flutes or moulding.

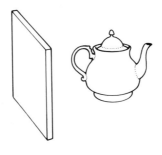

Professional photographers with expensive equipment should have special overhead lighting of a soft and even kind, which may tend to diminish the three-dimensional effect, but the quality of result is often better for reproduction in books and journals.

If photographs, especially black and white ones, are wanted for printed illustrations, it is best to use a medium tone of background because the printing processs tends to darken dark backgrounds yielding a very dull effect.

Using flash

Many cameras have built-in flash or have a 'hot shoe' to accept a flash unit. When used to illuminate shiny objects this direct flash yields disappointing results; the flash usually obliterates all detail immediately in front of it by causing a large area of highlight. Some cameras have sockets for an extension cable so that a flash unit may be held away from the camera, at 45° angle is best. The light striking the object is reflected away at the same angle, instead of reflecting back to the camera lens.

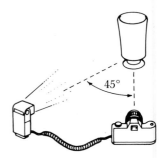

The same principle applies when photographing objects behind glass in a display cabinet. Flash is intense, like sunlight, and will cast strong shadows; photoflood lights are intense also. When it is not possible to use a white reflector card, the flash unit should be held high *above* the camera (a). If the object being photographed is bulbous, then the flash unit should be held high and *behind* the camera (b) to provide as much light as posssble to the lower parts.

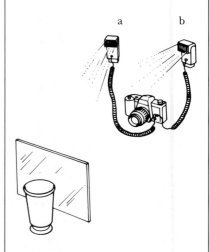

Lens hoods

It is advisable to use a lens hood at all times, but especially when using flash and photographing objects in illuminated display cases where the case lighting may shine into the lens to spoil the picture.

Display case lighting

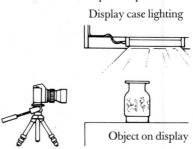

Object on display

Support for the camera

Maximum quality may be obtained best by the camera being supported rigidly and the shutter operated by means of a cable release. A tripod may prove to be the best support, but if a table-top layout is adopted, a mono-pod with suction pad is ideal. (They are not easy to find, however). The use of a cable release removes the risk of shaking the camera. In museums, the authorities seldom permit the use of tripods because of the risk of one falling over and smashing a display case or exhibit. Single leg, telescopic legs may be found to help to steady the camera.

Copying

The photographing of documents, book illustrations, marks, etc. is best done using a copying stand: for taking pictures of small subjects extension tubes or supplementary lenses are essential; a wide angle lens is also useful for the larger subjects. Daylight may be satisfactory, but for some large sizes of subjects the light might lessen noticeably on the side further from the light source; a white card reflector may overcome this. If photoflood lights are used, two, each at 45° angle to the subject, should be ideal. Watch for reflections of light on shiny surfaces like glossy paper, and check through the viewfinder at each exposure for this defect. Also, check the exposure each time. A grey card is very useful when copying; the intensity of daylight can vary greatly from one moment to another.

When copying a page in a book, the leaves may be held in place by tying a fine thread around them: this should not cause any damage to the book and will not be offensive in the picture.

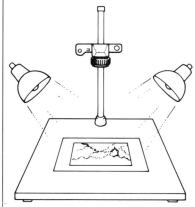

The author more than usually immersed in his subject. See also page 53.

Appendix VIII

Some popular patterns

Spode's Tower Pattern

The pattern is believed to have been introduced first in 1814: although Jewitt, writing in 1866, suggests 1815, he also includes the Milkmaid pattern which shares the identical border pattern and this he dates to 1814. Jewitt consulted persons working on the Spode factory about the dates when popular patterns were first produced so his well-quoted list depends for its accuracy on the memories of long-serving employees of the firm.

It was not the practice to record on paper those patterns which were transfer-printed in an underglaze colour on earthenware. The existence of the engravings coupled with the memories of printing-shop employees in those days must have been considered sufficient to ensure accuracy when orders came to be executed. However, when some additional decoration was added on-glaze, such as a coloured edge or filling in of part of the pattern, which required an 'enamel' or decorating firing, then a record was entered in the pattern book. Pattern number 3166 of 1821 records the border of Tower pattern being enamelled.

The scene depicts the Bridge of Salaro, near Porta Salara in Rome. It was derived from the printed illustration appearing in Merigot's *Views of Rome and its Vicinity,* published 1796-98.

Spode produced the Tower pattern on pearlware – the name given to earthenware having a glaze 'whitened' by the addition of a cobalt blue stain – printing it in a medium Ultramarine blue of clarity and brilliance.

The print in Merigot's Views of Rome and its Vicinity *of the Bridge of Salaro.*

3a   **Spode**

Impressed 1814-1833.

4   **SPODE**

Impressed 1814-1833 sometimes with a number beneath which is the clay-makers mark. The higher the number the later the piece.

31   **Spode**

33   **SPODE**

Printed in blue, or the same colour as the pattern. 1814-1833.

101   **COPELAND & GARRETT**

Impressed 1833-1847.

135   **COPELAND & GARRETT LATE SPODE**

Printed 1833-1847.

204   **COPELAND**

Impressed 1869-c1880 – indicates white earthenware.
The mark continued to 1970, but not for Tower.

Impressed 1890 onwards indicates ivory "Imperial" earthenware.

231 Copeland

Printed 1847-c1855.

232 **Copeland Late Spode.**

Printed in blue 1847-1890.

419

Printed in blue, it is not known when the mark was used first but it may have been about 1902 or later. It was discontinued in 1970.

501a **Spode**
ENGLAND
BLUE TOWER
SPODE DESIGN
C.1814 G

Printed. This mark was adopted in 1970 to coincide with the Bicentenary of the firm's foundation in 1770. Earthenware marks were and are printed in black, usually with the name of the pattern and date where of historical interest. The letter after the date is an internal factory code to indicate the year of production.

Cup and saucer, Tower pattern. Note that the cup is decorated inside and outside and down the back of the handle. 1991.

Like Blue Italian, introduced in 1816, Tower has been one of the most popular patterns in Spode's wide range of transfer-prints. Also, like Italian, it was used to decorate a huge variety of objects besides tablewares of every description and size. Hospital and toilet wares from invalid feeding cups to plumbed bidets were available before 1833. Later in the nineteenth century conservatory requisites like garden seats, stools and lily pans were made. In the twentieth century, catering ware was produced, in one instance being specially modified, for the Hamburg-Amerika-Lloyd shipping line, with a picnic scene and HAPAG in the foreground.

In about 1860 the pattern was printed in a darker blue and one with 'flowing' properties, that is, the blue colour diffused slightly beyond the limit of the engraved line or dot. The result appears blurred but at that period 'flow blue' was popular and in great demand. Soon after this the pattern was produced on ivory-coloured earthenware and changed to the Gadroon shape. This was copied from Georgian silver and first produced by Spode in the early 1820s.

The engraving for this darker blue needed to be coarser so that the pattern did not clog and lose the definition. 'Tower Zaffres' blue which is bright, dark royal blue, was used from about 1880 onwards superseding the royal saxon flowing blue of the previous era.

The pattern has also been printed in other colours including brown which was sometimes coloured, but the most popular alternative is Pink Tower. Its date of introduction is not known but it was in production in the 1920s, being widely distributed in North America and Western Europe, especially Germany. Unlike the range of blue and green underglaze colours which were all compounded personally by the proprietors of the Spode factory until 1960, the pink was made by commercial colour makers, but calcined in the Spode kilns as it is today. The underglaze colours of Spode have always been regarded as the brightest and most luminous available, avoiding the muddy appearance of many competitors' products.

In the 1960s, a Light Blue Tower was produced for the European market to meet a request from certain retail shops, but it did not enjoy sustained success and was withdrawn about 1973.

The decoration of Tower follows the high standards set by Josiah Spode. The decoration of the cups, for example, still has the border inside with the scene outside and this continues behind the handles, no concession being made to short cuts in the transferring process. All the objects are printed from hand-engraved copper plates or rollers.

It is this sort of attention to detail which distinguishes Spode.

Spode's Blue Italian

Josiah Spode in developing the underglaze transfer-printing process brought it to perfection when he produced the world-famous Blue Italian pattern in 1816. He introduced 'blue printing into Stoke in 1784'.[1] The early prints were reproductions of landscapes on Chinese blue and white porcelain. Spode's engravers steadily improved their technique to enable light and shade to be represented, the very early engravings being more like wood cuts 'in which the specimens have scarcely anything deserving the name of a fine part'![1] While the copper plates were engraved with lines only to begin with, by about 1795 stipple punching with dots became more widely used. This made shading easier to achieve. The darkness or lightness of tone depends on the depth of the engraved line or dot: soon the engravers learnt to exercise great delicacy of touch which resulted in the quality seen in Blue Italian.

Very few of Spode's original engravings survive in any condition to be used. The popularity of the pattern made heavy demands on their use which required them to be repaired frequently until they were replaced. Over the hundred or so years since then many engravers worked on the coppers and the high quality of the originals was not always repeated. By the late 1940s the coarseness of the engravings was such that in 1948 Gresham Copeland instituted a plan to engrave new copper plates to a standard comparable to the very best example of Spode's earliest production. The comparison between the new and old was striking, and quickly more new engravings were prepared for all tableware items to provide a display of uniform high quality. Once again the fine gradations of tone impart a sense of distance and atmosphere to a scene of haunting interest.

The Blue Italian pattern has decorated almost every domestic object which can be imagined. When toughened glass and plastics were unknown, glazed earthenware was the material for utensils requiring to be cleaned to a high standard of hygiene. Tableware items are the predominant objects found today, but examples of other household wares include toilet wares in great variety, cheese dishes of many different sorts, hospital wares like invalid feeding cups, as well as ornamental and decorative vases, fern pots and candlesticks.

As early as 1935 the Company supplied famous firms with Blue Italian wares as incentive gifts for sending in coupons cut from the cartons of their products.

A fruit set consisting of a fruit bowl and six 'stone rim' fruit saucers was a reward for sending in coupons from a quantity of packets of Lever's Lifebuoy or Sunlight soap: many thousands of these sets were manufactured. In 1937, Angus Watson offered a Spode sandwich dish or three sandwich plates free for only 10 top labels from the 9d. size Skipper sardine tin. This scheme was so successful that it ran for two years with Blue Italian and another Spode pattern, Byron. The sandwich dish was octagonal with a raised cross in the middle.

Spode derived several of his pictorial patterns from scenes which appeared as prints: two famous ones are his Tower pattern, based on a view of the Bridge of Salaro, near Rome, and the Castle pattern, taken from a print of the Gate of San Sabastian on the Appian Way in Rome, also from Merigot's *Views of Rome and its Vicinity*. Castle is supposed by Llewellynn Jewitt to have been introduced in 1806, and Tower in 1814.[2]

Blue Italian has fascinated people for many years, and the origin of the scene continues to puzzle collectors and researchers. It seems likely that the ruin on the left of the scene was a famous Roman building which is still unidentified. S. B. Williams suggested that the ruined arch may be one of a series which formed an aquaduct. Fourteen aquaducts, having an aggregate length of over 359 miles, brought water to Rome: 304 miles of these ran underground, but 55

3a Spode

4 SPODE

Impressed. 1816-1833.

31 Spode

33 SPODE

Impressed or printed in blue 1816-1833.

37 SPODE

Printed in blue – on a few early engravings c.1816-c.1820.

Melba shape fruit bowl. 1935.

Sandwich plate. 1937-8.

Tea cup and saucer, Princess shape (modified London shape – see page 16).

101 COPELAND & GARRETT

Impressed. 1833-1847.

135

Impressed, or printed in some form 1833-1847.

231 Copeland

232 Copeland Late Spode.

Printed in blue 1847-1890s.

204

Impressed. This mark is found from 1869 onwards, and identifies the white earthenware on which Italian has always been produced. The mark was discontinued only in 1970.

miles ran above ground, some lengths being carried on great multi-arched bridges.[3] It features on a round plaque of Italian maiolica in the Collection of Dr. Gianni Leopardi, Penne (a town 40km west of Pescara). This plaque is attributed to Nicola Cappelletti (1691-1767) who worked in the village of Castelli d'Abruzzo in the province of Teramo.[4]

Another example of the scene is on a large rectangular plaque of Castelli maiolica attributed to Francesco Antonio Saverio Grue (1686-1746), son of Carlo Antonio Grue (1655-1723). The Grue family was one of the most famous maiolica manufacturers in Italy.

In 1989, a friend observed in the Louvre, Paris, a drawing by Casper van Wittel (died in Rome, 1736) of the Colosseum in Rome. The Colosseum had suffered from earthquakes since the fifth century and also in the 13th, 14th and 18th centuries. In addition to the steps of the amphitheatre, the southern wall was severely damaged. My friend considers that Wittel's drawing represents this southern wall as seen from the interior. The right side of the drawing shows three arches, one above the other on the broken-off end of the ruined wall.[8] This structure may well have provided the inspiration for the maiolica painters of Castelli, especially those by Cappelletti and Grue, both of whom were contemporary with Casper van Wittel.

In 1974, a pen and wash drawing of the late seventeenth century came to our notice. The rendering of the scene is so close to that of Blue Italian that it seems certain to have been the origin, although Spode usually used prints not paintings. In a collector's feature in *Country Life* of May 9th, 1974, it was suggested that this landscape drawing might be by the Dutch artist Frederik de Moucheron (1633-86). The writer stated that Moucheron "was a facile painter who produced a large number of pleasing, essentially decorative landscapes, usually embodying some quasi-Italian piece of scenery ..... No engraving after this design has been traced; but large numbers of artists, both French and Flemish, imitated its components." However, this work is not in his style, neither is it in the style of his son Isaac de Moucheron (1667-1744).[8]

Maiolica plaque attributed to Nicola Cappelletti.

Maiolica plaque attributed to Francesco Antonio Saverio Grue.

One wonders if the Italian maiolica artists used this drawing or a similar one. The scene depicts a river, whereas the Castelli plaques show this area as a sward on which people are walking. The lady by the river is cutting reeds. On longer scenes, such as those on Spode meat dishes, three more figures are seen in the field at the right. Altogether there may be about 13 persons in the picture, most of them being on the riverside in the centre of the scene. In the old drawing two people are shown on the extreme left of the scene but these are replaced by two posts on early platters long enough to include this section. The other difference is that the person in white sitting by the rock and the sheep shown in the ceramic ware are absent from the drawing.

In 1989, the pen and wash drawing – which is not now thought to be by de Moucheron – was purchased at auction by Paul Wood, managing director of Spode Limited, for the Spode Museum Trust Collection.

A few pieces of the earliest production have an inscription "This BLUE WARE is printed from the CALX of British COBALT, produced from Wheal Sparnon Mine in the County of Cornwall. August 1816". Some examples omit 'Wheal' because this word is Cornish for mine.

The border is a direct copy of an Imari design on Chinese export porcelain of the Yung Chen period (circa 1736). It is remarkable how successfully this oriental design frames a scene in western style.[5]

The dating of objects in Blue Italian pattern is helped by the use of different marks.

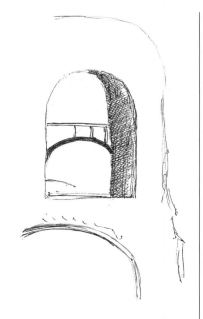

Sketch after a drawing by Casper Van Wittel of the inside structure of the Colosseum in Rome.

Pen and wash drawing by an unknown artist. Purchased in 1989 for the Spode Museum Trust.

418

5

Printed, it was in regular use from about 1891, the year in which the name of the country of origin had to be applied to wares exported. The name of the pattern has not been found so far applied to wares made earlier than this. It was discontinued in 1970.

501a

Spode
ENGLAND
ITALIAN
SPODE DESIGN
C.1816 E

To mark the bicentenary of the firm's foundation in 1770 all backstamps and marks were redesigned to present a uniform image. Earthenware marks are usually printed in black. 1970 – the present.

REFERENCES:
1 Shaw, S (1829) History of the Staffordshire Potteries, p.213.
2 Whiter, L (1970) Spode. A History of the Family, Factory and Wares from 1733-1833. London: Barrie & Jenkins.
3 Williams, S. B. (1949) Antique Blue and White Spode, pp118-9, p12. London: Batsford.
   Little, W. L. (1969) Staffordshire Blue, Fig.13.
4 Polidori, G. C. (1949) La Maiolica Antica Abrussese, Pl.51 Milan: Luigi Alfreri.
   Rebuffat, O. (1929) The Majolicas of Castelli (Abruzzi) Trans. Ceramic Society. Vol.XXIX pp.111-7.
5 Copeland, R. (1980) Spode's Willow Pattern & Other Designs After the Chinese. London: Studio Vista.
6 Coysh, A. W. (1970) Blue and White Transfer Ware pp76-7. Newton Abbott: David & Charles.
7 Pulver, R. (1987). Spode's 'Blue Italian' pattern. Antique Collecting: the Journal of The Antique Collectors' Club. (5 Church Street, Woodbridge, Suffolk) Vol.22 No.4 September 1987. pp30-33.
8 An Zwollo (1989) – personal correspondence.

In 1870 the practice was adopted of impressing the date of manufacture in the clay. This usually occurs on flat objects made of plastic clay; cast ware and thrown or jolleyed wares are not so stamped.

The mark consists of a capital (upper case) letter above two numerals.

The letter denotes the month:

J	January	A	April	L	July	O	October
F	February	Y	May	T	August	N	November
M	March	U	June	S	September	D	December

The numerals represent the last two numbers of the year: thus

An impressed mark $\frac{N}{37}$ shows the object was made in November 1937.

The practice was discontinued in 1957.

Spode was not the *only* manufacturer to produce the Italian pattern in blue. Others who copied the design include:

JOHN MARE of Hanley (c.1800-30)
POUNTNEY & ALLIES of Bristol (1816-35) } Coysh[6], Pulver[7]
POUNTNEY & GOLDNEY of Bristol (1836-49)

EDWARD & CHALLINOR of Tunstall (1842-67) } Correspondence
WOOD & CHALLINOR, Tunstall (1828-43) & Pulver[7]

JOSEPH STUBBS, but with border of 'Wild Rose' pattern, Burslem (1822-36)
ZACHARIAH BOYLE of Hanley (1823-30) } Pulver[7]
                  of Stoke (c.1828-50)
WARREN, possibly a retailer
BRISTOL

(Dates are of the factories span of business *not* when Blue Italian was in production)

Byron Pattern s518

The pattern first appears as Patent No. 79300, registered on June 19, 1851. This shows the trellis border with a view of a girl giving a drink to a boy. Although this scene does not appear to have been used in the Byron pattern tableware, it does record the first use of the trellis border. The scene was used later and reference will be made in the next paragraph. The pattern was last produced in about 1968 and was first produced in this form in 1933.

In 1937 the Spode company produced a series of plates for the firm of Angus Watson, proprietors of Skipper sardines; they offered sandwich sets as premium gifts in connection with a sales promotion. It seems that they had two different promotions each one offering the same object but with a different scene printed upon it. This object was a sandwich plate with a raised cross in the centre and most of these plates are impressed with the date 37 with a letter above it which indicates the month of the year in which the clay article was manufactured.

Series No. 1 depicts a scene of two girls in peasant costume talking to one another beside a wall in front of a house. The girl on the left carries two baskets containing provisions, the one on the right is leaning on the wall with her right hand supporting her cheek and with a dog at her feet. The source for this design is not discovered.

Series No. 2 shows a woman giving a drink to a young boy and it is this scene which first appeared in 1851, but was not used again except for this particular series 2.

The 4 ridges are to suggest the use of the object as a sandwich plate.

The name of the pattern so far as I know has no connection at all with the poet Lord Byron, but was probably named after him as being appropriate to the romantic feel of the design.

Earlier in the 19th century another pattern, called Byron Views, was produced by Copeland & Garrett (1833-1847) from views by Edward & William Finden and published by John Murray in *Finden's Landscape & Portrait Illustrations to the Life and Works of Lord Byron*. The first volume appeared in 1832. This pattern is totally different from the one under discussion.

The Byron tableware pattern of the 1930's employed a different scene on each different object, and a list of these is given here. Most of the pictures were derived from illustrations in the *Art Journals* published between 1849 and 1865.

Sandwich plates, Series No. 1 and 2.

		Art *Journal-*	*Page*	*Printed on*
1. Passing the Brook	E. Verboeckhoven 1845	1854	224	7″ Zeigler bowl.
2. Crossing the Stream	Sir A. W. Callcott R.A. 1830	1850	190	12″ dish.
3. The Rustic Bridge	Jacob Ruysdeal or Ruisdael as he sometimes signed 1645	1852	143	Boat & stand.
4. The Cow Doctor	C. Tscheggeny	1860	88	14″ & 16″ dish.
5. From the Moors	Park	1859	348	Cream soup & stand.
6. The Harvest Field	C. Tscheggeny 1831	1857	120	9″ dish.
7. Preparing for the Chase	J. Mourenhout 1830	1857	278	Large teapot.
8. The Farm at Lacken	Rubens	1858	272	Small teapot.
9. Crossing the Ford	N. Berghem 1650	1858	336	Coverdish bottom.
10. The Waterfall	F. Zuccherelli 1760	1858	364	Coverdish cover.
11. The Crown of Hops	W. J. Witherington, R.A. 1840	1851	8	Coffee pot.
12. Rest	John Linnell	1862	216	7″ plate.
13. A Dream of the Future	Frith (Figure) Creswick (Landscape) Ansdell (dog) 1830	1865	360	Boat and stand.
14. Market Morning	J. W. Whymper 1846 (engraved)	1856	41	B'fast saucer.
15. The Pet of the Common	J. C. Horsley A.R.A.	1863	196	9″ Card bowl.
16. Hadrian's Villa	R. Wilson, R.A.	1850	356	Teacup.
17.		1857	–	10″ plate.
18.		–	–	Teacup & saucer.
19. Monmouth Castle from the Monmow	Article by Mr. & Mrs. S. C. Hall *Excursion in South Wales*	1849	159	Cream jug.
20. The Valley Farm	J. Constable ,, ,,	1849	159	Sauce tureen, middle.
21.	J. Micklewright (Copeland artist)	–	–	8″ plate
22. Garameen Bridge, Killarney	Article by Mr. & Mrs. S. C. Hall *A Week in Killarney*	1865	120	Coffee saucer.
23. Glene Bay	,, ,,	1865	149	Sauce tureen, cover.
24.		1855	256	Sauce tureen, stand,
25. The Bell Inn	J. F. Herring, senior	1844	–	Square bread & butter, or cake plate.

Scenes used on the 6″ & 7″ plates have not been traced.

Chinese Rose

This most popular of Spode earthenware coloured designs was introduced as pattern 2/9253 in 1931. Its origins, however, are very much older. The design is based on, rather than copies, a Chinese pattern of the K'ang Hsi period around 1720. This was hand painted in cobalt blue on true porcelain. Examples of this pattern are seen occasionally and will be survivors from services imported by the Honourable East India Company.

Josiah Spode II (1755-1827) copied this pattern initially to meet a market need for replacements. This was in 1813. The earliest record is in the pattern book under number 2489 which is coloured by hand over the printed pattern. Spode's pattern is usually seen as a plain blue underglaze print and is known as India pattern.

In 1911, this old pattern provided the inspiration for a new pattern for bone china, No. R5008, and two years later it was registered on 13th December 1913 as number 629599, and known as Waring's Rock when it was stocked by Waring & Gillow. This version, 2/6576, was known also as Rockery (but not backstamped as such), until the present colouring 2/9253 on Spode's Imperial earthenware was adopted in 1931.

In 1939 tea and coffee ware made in fine bone china was produced as pattern number Y5926, with an ivory groundlay beneath to match the earthenware: it was withdrawn in about 1962.

The design represents the Chinese artists' interpretation of a rock with flowers growing from its holes. Rocks like this do exist – (they are like tufa – a porous limestone in which plants grow). The flowers, although a bit fanciful, probably are meant to represent single and double peonies.

The pattern was reproduced by transfer-printing from hand-engraved copper plates and rollers, the print being 'hardened-on' in a kiln at about 680-700° Centigrade before being dipped in glaze and re-fired at 1070°C. Skilled paintresses applied the colours over the glaze and the green edge, too, was applied with a brush. It was re-fired at about 760°C.

Today, most items are decorated with one application of a pre-printed slide-off transfer which is loosened in water from its backing paper then slid into position on the glost (glazed) piece. Spode have not compromised their standards in this exchange of a traditional for a modern method: borders and beads remain continuous even behind cup handles, while a few items are hand-painted still.

The most common marks are:

Chinese Rose pattern.

Spode's India pattern.

256   COPELAND
       Late
       SPODE
       Rd No. 629599
       "CHINESE ROSE"

c.1935-c.1969.

257   COPELAND
       Late
       SPODE
       ENGLAND
       Rd No. 629599.

'Spode Imperial'. Ivory earthenware 1931-c.1969. The pattern number was often painted by hand.

259   2/9253
       COPELAND
       SPODE
       ENGLAND
       Rd No 629599
       "CHINESE ROSE"

c.1937-c.1969.

       SPODE
       ENGLAND
       CHINESE ROSE
       2/9253

On small items the COPELAND was omitted.

242   SPODE
       COPELAND'S CHINA
       ENGLAND

       Y5926

Fine Bone China 1939-c.1963. The pattern number was painted by hand.

501a   Spode
       ENGLAND
       2/9253 I
       CHINESE ROSE
       FROM A
       SPODE DESIGN
       C.1815

1970 to the present.

The Hunt

The kill, one of the subjects depicted on dinner plates.

421

" THE LAST DRAW "

421a

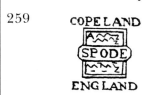

" THE HUNTSMAN "
6

Used on the base of coffee cups.

259

The modified gridiron mark incorporating the date letter. 1964-

The pattern which has proved most popular was introduced in 1931 as number 2/9265 on ivory coloured earthenware with a green band at edge. Many of the larger items of flatware enjoyed twelve different scenes, while other items of smaller size had six scenes. The decoration is transfer-printed from flat copper plates engraved by hand. The print colour is brown and applied under the glaze on biscuit; it is glazed and fired, then painted by hand in proper colours, banded in colour, and fired again. The result is reminiscent of the hand coloured sporting prints which have remained popular for over two hundred years.

The difficulty of maintaining proper stocks of such a wide choice of centres on so many items led to the restriction of the selection in 1973 when the present scenes on flatware and cups were adopted. The process of decoration remains the same and the scenes on the meat dishes are unchanged. There are six different scenes on the 10½ inch dinner plates.

In addition to this full range of tableware, a set of six plates in Fine Bone China is also available in 1991 on a coupe shape.

Dating pieces of The Hunt. The principal earthenware patterns, 2/9265 (green band) and 2/9344 (crimson band), were introduced in 1931. A special mark, or backstamp, was used from then until 1970 when the name of the Company was changed from W. T. Copeland & Sons Limited to Spode Limited on the occasion of the Bicentenary of the founding of the firm by Josiah Spode I in 1770.

The other mark often found on pieces is the 'gridiron' which was also printed in brown and was superseded in 1970 by the present mark. This 'gridiron' mark was used on many other patterns on earthenware.

During the period 1870-1957, a date stamp was impressed into the clay on most items of flatware like plates, saucers and meat dishes. This stamp consisted of a letter for the month and two figures below it for the year. The example would be November 1938.

From 1958-1963, a letter was introduced into the upper left corner of the gridiron mark A = 1958 – F, F = 1963.

In 1964 this was replaced by a code letter and number printed separately. The letter represented the year A = 1964, M = 1975 (letter I was omitted), and the figure represented the printing team who decorated it. In 1976, the year letter was added to the pattern number 2/9265-A = 1976, and in this mark was incorporated in the hunting cap design. F = 1981.

History of the pattern. One or two hunting scenes were included in a pattern called Field Sports which was patented on September 14 1846 as number 37254, when the firm was run by the partnership Copeland and Garrett. Scene No 12 Drawing the Dingle was the particular one used. This, like most of the other scenes, was engraved after a painting by J. F. Herring. The pattern Field Sports was used for a South American Steamship Company and some engravings have their name on the copper plates.

Later, a number of other fox hunting scenes were added so that a comprehensive collection of views showing different incidents in the field could be used for all manner of pieces of table services.

In 1930, when the full pattern was introduced, the original drawings and paintings were still in the possession of the Copeland family at Kibblestone Hall, Stone, Staffordshire. Some of them are no longer in their possession and the Hall has been pulled down. Moreover, some of the designs are derived from the works of other sporting artists especially Ben Marshall and Henry Alken.

In 1938, a booklet was produced which tells some of the story about J. F. Herring, and in particular it relates how his paintings came to be in the possession of the Copeland family.

John Frederick Herring, Senior, was born in 1795 in Surrey, the son of an American of Dutch extraction. In 1814, after working for his father in London, he moved to Doncaster and became the driver of the Wakefield and Lincoln 'Nelson' coach, painting inn signs and coach panels in his spare time. He changed coaches several times and undertook commissions to paint horses for titled owners. In 1818 he began to paint pictures of the St. Leger winners, starting with Filho da Puta, 1815 and continuing without a break until Van Tromp in 1847. Herring moved to Fulbourne near Newmarket in 1830, and to Camberwell and Cottage Green three years later, during which time he took lessons from Abraham Cooper, R.A. About this time he incurred a debt of £500 for which he had given bills he could not honour. William Taylor Copeland, learning of this, took up the bills and offered the artist a house on his estate at Leyton in Essex. He also commissioned Herring to paint his own racehorses, to do pictures of fox hunting and scenes of rural life incorporating horses. It is from these paintings that most of the subjects of The Hunt are derived.

This act of generosity by Copeland seems to have been the turning point in Herring's career. In 1841 he was elected a member of the Society of British Artists, becoming Vice-President in the following year. In 1844 he painted 'The Start of the 1844 Derby' – the dirtiest Derby in history – in which all the principal horses in the scandal can be seen clearly. Herring purchased the lease of Meopham Park near Tonbridge in 1853 and lived there, painting rural subjects and horses sent to him until his death on September 23 1865.

Bibliography

Anon (1965) Catalogue of a Loan Collection of Oil Paintings by John Frederick Herring, Snr. (1795-1865) 28 April-15 May 1965. London: Arthur Ackermann & Son, Limited.

Anon (1938) The Hunt portrayed by J. F. Herring Sen. Famous Hunting Scenes on Spode China. Stoke-on-Trent: W. T. Copeland & Sons.

Anon (1865) The Late Mr. J. F. Herring. Obituary notice in The Illustrated London News. Oct 14 1865.

Anon (1848) Memoir of J. F. Herring, Esq. Sheffield: James Culbert.

Beckett, O (1981) J. F. Herring & Sons. London: J. A. Allen & Co. Ltd.

Chester, A (1912) The Art of J. F. Herring. The Windsor Magazine Vol. 36 No. 210 June 1912 pp3-18.

Connor, P. & Lambourne, L. (1979) Derby Day 200: Catalogue to an Exhibition held at the Royal Academy of Arts, London 5 April-1 July 1979. pp 63 and 73.

Details of scenes used before 1981

Plate 10 in trade   Series One

Plate 8 in trade
Soup plate 8 in trade

1	Full cry	7	The meet
2	The find	8	The death
3	Throwing off	9	Going to halloa
4	Off to draw	10	Drawing the dingle
5	Gone away	11	The kill
6	The huntsman	12	The last draw

Plate 7 in trade   Series Two

Soup plate 7 in trade
Breakfast saucer
Fruit saucer 6 in trade
Oatmeal saucer 6 in trade
Cream soup stand

1	First over	7	Homeward
2	Gone away	8	The meet
3	A check	9	Going to halloa
4	The find	10	In the spinney
5	The last draw	11	Full cry
6	The huntsman	12	Drawing the dingle

Teacup   Series Three

1	Leaping the brook
2	Taking the lead
3	The death
4	A check
5	The chase
6	The first over

Tea saucer   Series Four

Plate 6 in trade
Fruit saucer 5 in trade
Cream soup cup

1	The find
2	The last draw
3	Gone away
4	First over
5	Well cleared
6	Full cry

Teacup and saucer, New Bute shape.

The scenes used for the Fine Bone China plates are from series one.

510

THE HUNT

Spode
ENGLAND
2/9265 ⊢
FROM ORIGINAL DRAWINGS
BY J. F. HERRING SEN.

"FIRST OVER"

The revised mark, 1976-present.

Breakfast cup Series Five	1 Full cry
	2 Off to draw
	3 The huntsman
	4 First over
	5 Leaping the brook
	6 The meet
Coffee cup Series Six	1 Full cry
	2 The last draw
	3 Off to draw
	4 Well cleared
	5 Leaping the brook
	6 The huntsman
Coffee saucer Series Seven	1 Homeward
Individual butter dish	2 The hounds
Ash tray	3 Full cry
	4 First over
	5 The huntsman
	6 The find

Scenes in use on 2/9265 pattern, from 1981.

	from Series One
Plate 10½ in 27 cm	1 Full cry
	2 The find
	7 The meet
	8 The death
	9 Going to halloa
	10 Drawing the dingle
	from Series Two
Plate 7½ in 19 cm	1 First over
Soup plate 7¾	9 Going to halloa
Oatmeal saucer	1 First over
Cream soup saucer	1 First over
	from Series Three
Teacup	1 Leaping the brook
	from Series Four
Tea saucer	3 Gone away
Plate 6¼ cm	
Cream soup cup	
	from Series Six
Coffee cup	3 Off to draw
	from Series Seven
Coffee saucer	1 Homeward
Individual butter dish	4 First over

Billingsley Rose

This pattern on the Jewel shape has done much to popularise the name of William Billingsley among non-collectors and specialists of historical ceramics. William Billingsley never worked on the Spode factory, but it was his technique of painting roses which established the practice of 'taking' out the highlights and mixing the rose colour with tar that led to this particular style becoming known as Billingsley Rose.

William Billingsley was born in Derby in 1758. His father, William, had been a flower painter at the Chelsea factory in London and was recorded as still working there in 1756. William, senior, came to Derby and may have been a freelance painter of porcelain. When he died in March 1770, he left the Nottingham Arms alehouse to his widow and son.

William, junior, was one of six children of the marriage. He was apprenticed to William Duesbury I, the proprietor of the Nottingham Road works at Derby, on 20 September 1774 at the age of sixteen, for a period of five years at the weekly wage of five shillings. In 1780 he married Sarah Rigley.

Billingsley left the Derby works in April 1796 to work with Mr. John Coke in whose partnership he established the Pinxton China Works. He left in April 1799, to move to Mansfield in Derbyshire and from thence to Torksey in Lincolnshire.

By October 1808, Billingsley had arrived at Worcester, and was engaged by Martin Barr. It was reported that Billingsley and his future son-in-law Samuel Walker were responsible for a marked improvement in the Worcester body. These two, leaving Worcester, started the manufacture of porcelain at Nantgarw in South Wales in mid-November 1813. Here they began to produce a beautiful porcelain, but the losses were colossal. The partners petitioned the Board of Trade for help, which came in the form of support from Lewis Dillwyn, proprietor of the Cambrian Pottery at Swansea. After disagreements, the partners accepted an offer from John Rose to move to Coalport where they worked. Billingsley died on 16 January 1828, and was buried in the churchyard at Kemberton, near Coalport.

Plate, Jewel shape, in Spode Imperial (ivory) earthenware, with the printed and hand painted Billingsley Rose pattern 2/8867. The pattern was produced with a slide-off transfer, or decalcomania, in about 1972, and discontinued with the withdrawal of the Jewel shape in 1989.

423   SPODES JEWEL
COPELAND
SPODE
ENGLAND
REG Nº 70392
U.S. PATT. JUNE 15ᵗʰ 1926
SPODE'S BILLINGSLEY ROSE

Teapot in Jewel shape.

One of the grand comports made in 1857. This one bears the portraits of Queen Victoria and Prince Albert, with the Coat of Arms of the British Royal Family.

Spode's Jewel Shape

First, it must be stated that much of the production called Spode's refers to wares made on the Spode factory and not necessarily during the personal direction of those works by Josiah Spode.

In the 1850s, W. H. Goss was the Art Director at the Spode factory of W. T. Copeland. A dessert service of unparalleled splendour in bone china was required for presentation in 1857 and Copeland's had been commissioned to design and manufacture it. In 1856, Goss devised a shape which incorporated embossed rings into which mirror-backed simulated rubies, emeralds and topaz gemstones were later inserted.

A mystery exists concerning the original dessert set. The two magnificent comports have on one portrait medallions of Queen Victoria and Prince Albert with the Royal Arms of Great Britain, and on the other, portrait medallions of Emperor Napoleon III and Empress Eugenie with the Napoleonic Arms of France. Every object has a scene of a popular European beauty spot painted by Dan Lucas. The mystery is in its presence in the Golestan Palace, Tehran. For what occasion was it ordered? At about the time of its manufacture, Britain and France were trying to renew a friendship which had been seriously strained. In 1855 Emperor Napoleon III and Empress Eugenie came to England on a State Visit which was followed by a visit to France by Queen Victoria and Prince Albert in the same year. The Third Treaty of Paris marking the end of the Crimean War was signed in 1856. In 1857, shortly after Prince Albert had been created Prince Consort, Napoleon III and Eugenie were received by Queen Victoria in Osborne – her home on the Isle of Wight. This was followed by a short visit to Cherbourg by Queen Victoria and Prince Albert. A likely occasion for the presentation of this service was the State visit to Paris in 1855, but the date seems to be too early. It seems probable that it could have been for the second visit to England of Napoleon and Eugenie in August 1857, to act as a reminder of the Treaty of Paris and of the good relationship between Great Britain and France. The mystery of its original purpose is only exceeded by the lack of information concerning its presence in Tehran and the circumstances by which it got there.

The range of general tableware items was modelled in the mid 1920's; they were based on the design of the dessert plate, moulds of which had survived. Knowledge of the magnificent dessert service does not seem to have been suspected as the idea, for the shape was ascribed to a painting of a halo around a saint in the medieval painting! The name Jewel, however, must have been marked on the mould. Since then, Jewel shape has been made only in ivory Imperial Earthenware.

Despite the considerable attempts to widen the range of patterns, and evident failure, the acceptance of plain Jewel Imperial and Billingsley Rose has been so successful that they are now over fifty years in continuous production. Unfortunately, due to economic pressure, the Jewel Shape, along with Billingsley Rose, was withdrawn from production in 1989. The tableware range was registered at the Patent Office in London in 1924 – No. 70392, and Patented in the United States on June 15 1926.

Spode's Stone Hunting
and other sprigged wares

Late in the nineteenth century Copeland's (W. T. Copeland & Sons, the successors to Spode and proprietors of the Spode Factory) introduced a range of ware with raised, or 'sprigged', ornaments on a blue or green ground on stoneware. This ware continued in production from about 1890-1910: the versions on blue were re-introduced in the late 1920s-1938. It seems that substantial quantities were made as today it is not rare.

The first use of ornaments applied in clay in North Staffordshire is credited to John Philip Elers, a Dutch silversmith and potter who settled in Bradwell, near Newcastle-under-Lyme, in 1693. Throughout the eighteenth century this type of decoration was used until Josiah Wedgwood exploited its potential as sophisticated adornments in jasper and basalt. He introduced figures from Greek mythology as decorative features, and a few similar figures were used on Copeland's stoneware, especially the so-called dancing hours, or houris (a dozen dancing damsels in diaphanous dresses). These applied features are called 'sprigs' and are made by pressing clay into shallow 'sprig' moulds made of a special fine-textured earthenware. The surplus clay is scraped off to leave a flat back to the sprig, which is gently coaxed away from the mould with a special flattish tool that is pressed gently onto the clay and levered upwards: the slight suction effect eventually releases the clay sprig, which is placed flat side down on a damp plaster slab. When all the sprigs have been made and assembled on the slab, the ornamenter moistens with water the surface of the clay pot and lifts the first sprig with a damp 'pencil' (in the pottery industry a 'pencil' is an artist's pointed paintbrush) and, placing it into the correct position, gently presses it down with a finger. The same procedure is followed until all the subjects and border ornaments are in place and secure. One gentle brush over is all that is needed. Too much brushing or pressure blurs the sharpness of the image.

The Copeland stonewares were made usually of either brown or grey clay in the 1890s, or in a buff coloured clay in both 1890s and 1930s. The basic shapes were 'thrown' on the potter's wheel in the traditional way and when made the objects were allowed to stiffen (not become absolutely dry) to a 'leather hard' condition. Then each item was placed in the chock of a turner's lathe. The turner with his steel tools shaped the foot and turned off the clay at top and sides to the correct dimensions. Then, with the coloured clay slip (liquid clay) in a 'blow-bottle' he applied the coloured slip to the pot as it revolved on the lathe. This stiffened quickly enough for him to turn it smooth and then apply the ornamented beads by pressing into the clay a small embossed wheel which formed the design: this was called 'running a bead', and the tool was a 'roulette'.

Green clay was added onto brown, dark blue onto grey, and medium blue onto buff coloured clay, with the latter being unglazed on the outside but the two former being glazed all over.

This ware, which was a speciality of the Spode Factory, derived its designs from the late eighteenth and early nineteenth centuries when Spode, Adams, Turner and their contemporaries were producing white stoneware with 'sprigged' decoration. While sporting and drinking subjects were popular, by far the most common was the hunting scene which was adopted by most manufacturers of white stoneware.

Copelands also produced commemorative objects. Several items were made to mark the occasion of Queen Victoria's Diamond Jubilee in 1897. The Great Fire of Chicago of 1871 was included on a large jug, with 'sprigged' scenes of the

The well-known fox hunting scene, of which many colour variations were made. This has a blackish-brown dip with ivory coloured sprigs on a buff stoneware body. Mark 259.

202

212

Most wares of this type are marked with the name COPELAND, either in a straight line or curved, and ENGLAND: both impressed in the clay.

266

This unusual mark, of an Egyptian felucca, was registered as No. 180288 on 11th September 1894. It was used on earthenware and stonewares.

259

When the sprigged stoneware was re-introduced in the 1920s, this mark with the pseudo-Chinese seal had been adopted.

24
30
36

Impressed numbers are sometimes seen on objects of hollow ware. These are the sizes, based on the number of objects which could be carried on a 6 foot workboard. The higher the number, the smaller the article. See Appendix III.

The numbers 202, 212 etc. refer to the central catalogue of Marks.

raging fire as well as others recalling events in the history of the city. The special mark on the base was engraved on May 18th 1906 and the Chicago Pitcher was produced exclusively for Burley & Co., Chicago. Another item – the Columbus Pitcher – was produced in 1892, also for Burley & Co.

Whisky decanters were made for Ushers and Buchanan before and during the first World War, and tankards were made depicting scenes of rugby football and cricket.

Jugs were made to mark the centenary of the death of George Washington in 1799, being decorated with the head of George Washington born Feb 22nd 1732, the badge of the United States of America with motto, and crossed flags of the original Union – Independence 1776 – of thirteen states. These jugs were blue on grey, and green on brown clay.

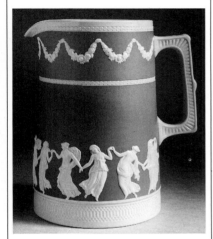

Tankard shape jug, or pitcher. Medium blue dip over buff stoneware. Twelve damsels dressed in diaphanous draping. Generally known as the dancing hours, they may represent twelve houris, the beautiful virgins of the Koranic paradise.

The Chicago pitcher, 1906. Medium blue dip on buff stoneware. Mark 354.

Stag hunting scene.

Appendix IX The purchasing power of the Pound since 1700

	1700	1710	1720	1730	1740	1750	1760	1770	1780	1790	1800	1810	1820	1830	1840	1850	1860	1870	1880	1890	1900	1910	1920	1930
1700	100																							
1710	83	100																						
1720	104	125	100																					
1730	110	133	106	100																				
1740	103	124	99	93	100																			
1750	112	135	108	102	109	100																		
1760	104	125	100	94	101	93	100																	
1770	94	113	90	83	91	84	90	100																
1780	91	110	88	83	89	81	88	98	100															
1790	76	92	73	69	74	68	73	81	84	100														
1800	43	51	41	39	41	38	41	45	47	56	100													
1810	40	48	38	36	39	36	38	43	44	52	94	100												
1820	49	59	47	45	48	44	47	53	54	65	116	123	100											
1830	58	70	56	53	57	52	56	62	64	76	137	146	118	100										
1840	52	62	50	47	50	46	50	55	57	68	122	129	105	89	100									
1850	69	82	66	62	67	61	66	73	75	90	161	171	139	118	132	100								
1860	51	61	49	46	49	45	49	54	55	66	119	127	103	87	98	74	100							
1870	54	64	51	49	52	48	51	57	59	70	126	134	109	92	104	78	106	100						
1880	57	68	55	52	55	51	55	61	62	75	134	142	115	98	110	83	112	106	100					
1890	70	85	65	64	69	63	68	75	77	92	166	176	143	121	136	103	139	131	124	100				
1900	67	81	65	61	65	60	65	72	74	88	158	168	136	115	130	98	133	125	118	95	100			
1910	67	81	65	61	65	60	65	72	74	88	158	168	136	115	130	98	133	125	118	95	100	100		
1920	27	32	26	24	26	24	26	29	29	35	63	67	54	46	52	39	53	50	47	38	40	40	100	
1930	42	51	40	38	41	38	40	45	46	55	99	105	85	72	81	61	83	78	74	60	63	63	157	100
1940	30	36	29	27	30	27	29	32	33	40	71	76	61	52	59	44	60	57	53	43	45	45	114	72
1950	21	25	20	19	20	19	20	22	23	27	49	52	42	36	40	30	41	39	37	29	31	31	78	49
1960	15	18	14	14	15	13	14	16	16	20	35	37	30	26	29	22	29	28	26	21	22	22	56	35
1970	10	12	10	9	10	9	10	11	11	13	24	25	21	17	20	15	20	19	18	14	15	15	38	24
1971	9	11	9	8	9	8	9	10	10	12	22	23	19	16	18	14	18	17	16	13	14	14	35	22
1972	9	10	8	8	8	8	8	9	9	11	20	22	18	15	17	13	17	16	15	12	13	13	32	21
1973	8	10	8	7	8	7	8	8	9	10	19	20	16	14	15	12	16	15	14	11	12	12	30	19
1974	7	5	7	6	7	6	7	7	7	9	16	17	14	12	13	10	13	13	12	10	10	10	26	16
1975	5	7	5	5	5	5	5	6	6	7	13	14	11	9	11	8	11	10	10	8	8	8	21	13
1976	5	6	5	4	5	4	5	5	5	6	11	12	10	8	9	7	9	9	8	7	7	7	18	11
1977	4	5	4	4	4	4	4	4	4	5	10	10	8	7	8	6	8	8	7	6	6	6	15	10
1978	4	5	4	3	4	3	4	4	4	5	9	9	8	6	7	5	7	7	7	5	6	6	14	9
1979	3	4	3	3	3	3	3	4	4	4	8	8	7	6	6	5	7	6	6	5	5	5	12	8
1980	3	3	3	3	3	3	3	3	3	4	7	7	6	5	5	4	6	5	5	4	4	4	11	7
1981	3	3	2	2	2	2	2	3	3	3	6	6	5	4	5	4	5	5	4	4	4	4	9	6
1982	2	3	2	2	2	2	2	2	3	3	5	6	5	4	4	3	5	4	4	3	3	3	9	5
1983	2	3	2	2	2	2	2	2	2	3	5	6	4	4	4	3	4	4	4	3	3	3	8	5
1984	2	3	2	2	2	2	2	2	2	3	5	5	4	4	4	3	4	4	4	3	3	3	8	5
1985	2	3	2	2	2	2	2	2	2	3	5	5	4	4	4	3	4	4	4	3	3	3	8	5
1986	2	3	2	2	2	2	2	2	2	3	4	4	4	4	4	3	4	4	4	3	3	3	7	4
1987	2	3	2	2	2	2	2	2	2	3	4	4	3	3	3	3	3	3	3	3	3	3	7	4
1988	2	2	2	2	2	2	2	2	2	2	4	4	3	3	3	2	3	3	3	2	2	2	7	4
1989	2	2	2	2	2	2	2	2	2	2	4	4	3	3	3	2	3	3	3	2	2	2	6	4
1990	2	2	2	2	2	2	2	2	2	2	4	4	3	3	3	2	3	3	3	2	2	2	6	4
1991	1	2	1	1	1	1	1	1	1	2	3	3	3	3	3	2	3	3	3	2	2	2	5	3

THESE FIGURES ARE ROUNDED UP OR DOWN TO THE NEAREST WHOLE NUMBER

To estimate the approximate price of an object made years ago, divide the value of the pound in the later year into 100 to yield the factor by which to multiply the original price.

EXAMPLE 1. A teaset invoiced at £20 in 1820; the price in 1991 would be $\dfrac{100}{3} = 33 \times £20 = £660.$

EXAMPLE 2. A dinnerset sold in 1910 for £6; the price in 1974 would be $\dfrac{100}{10} = 10 \times £6 = £60.$

whilst in 1991 it would be £300.

Year	1940	1950	1960	1970	1971	1972	1973	1974	1975	1976	1977	1978	1979	1980	1981	1982	1983	1984	1985	1986	1987	1988	1989	1990	1991
1940	100																								
1950	69	100																							
1960	49	72	100																						
1970	33	49	68	100																					
1971	31	45	62	91	100																				
1972	28	42	58	85	93	100																			
1973	26	38	53	78	86	92	100																		
1974	22	33	46	67	74	79	86	100																	
1975	18	26	37	54	59	64	69	80	100																
1976	16	23	32	47	51	55	60	69	86	100															
1977	13	20	27	40	44	47	51	60	74	86	100														
1978	12	18	25	37	41	43	47	55	68	80	92	100													
1979	11	16	22	33	36	38	42	49	60	70	81	88	100												
1980	9	14	19	28	30	32	35	41	51	60	69	75	85	100											
1981	8	12	17	25	27	29	32	37	46	53	62	67	76	89	100										
1982	8	11	15	23	25	27	29	34	42	49	57	62	70	82	92	100									
1983	7	11	15	22	24	26	28	32	40	47	54	59	67	79	88	96	100								
1984	7	10	14	21	23	24	27	31	38	45	52	56	64	75	84	91	95	100							
1985	7	9	13	20	22	23	25	29	36	43	49	53	60	71	80	86	90	95	100						
1986	6	9	12	19	21	21	24	28	34	40	46	50	57	67	75	81	85	89	94	100					
1987	6	9	12	18	20	21	23	27	33	39	45	48	55	65	72	78	82	86	91	97	100				
1988	6	8	12	17	19	20	22	26	31	37	43	46	53	62	69	75	78	82	87	93	96	100			
1989	6	8	11	16	18	19	21	24	31	35	41	44	50	59	66	71	75	78	83	88	91	95	100		
1990	5	7	10	15	17	17	19	22	28	33	38	40	46	54	61	66	69	72	76	81	84	88	92	100	
1991	5	6	9	14	15	16	17	20	25	29	34	36	41	49	54	59	62	65	68	73	75	78	82	89	100

Appendix X

Additional marks of Spode and Copeland

SPODE PERIOD 1770 to 1833

19

Large impressed mark on a double-walled vessel made of stoneware, of uncertain date but probably 1806–1812.

COPELAND AND GARRETT PERIOD 1833 to 1847

113

1846. The Beauvais Jug. Embossed parian jug. Different numbers may refer to individual makers.

143a

1837. Similar to Mark 143 but larger and more detailed. Example printed in pink on pattern 5771.

149a

c1840. Similar to Mark 149 but omitting the frame and engraved specially for ware for the ship Precursor.

COPELAND PERIOD 1847 to 1969

207a

Variation of Mark 207 using the St. Edward's crown. Impressed.

224

1885. Mark seen on Walpole shape tableware. Registered 1 May 1885. Impressed.

225

c1946. Seen on early Flemish Green. Impressed.

226

c1847. Seen on an item of Berlin shape. Compare to Mark 236. Impressed.

227

c1868. Impressed version of Mark 248, seen on a plate with a printed script WR (?Ward Room) on reverse.

234c

1860–70. Printed crown and COPELAND, similar to Mark 207a but printed instead of impressed.

243aa

COPELAND
LATE SPODE

Same words as 243 but smaller, with lettering in Roman rather than italic style.

243bb

W.T. COPELAND
NEW BOND S^T

Very rare mark, seen once printed in orange on Honeysuckle Empire pattern.

257c

Another variation of Mark 257, see page 70, with ENGLAND in a straight, not curved, line. Seen on Heron pattern, also printed on sprigged stoneware.

278a

As Mark 278, see page 73, but with S added to COPELAND. Seen on a model of a small greyhound in bone china, possibly because the regular backstamp was too large for the available space.

288a

The mark used for the Ministry of Works in 1966. The year date changed according to the date of delivery.

293a

A variation of the Alenite mark, probably pre-dated Mark 293.

294a

SPODE *Meadow Glory*
ENGLAND

Similar to 294, this is the mark for Meadow Glory, which was Spode ivory (Imperial) body back and rim with yellow centre.

317

c1860. A mark recorded in the Engravers' Book.

318

c1860. A mark of a retailer in Paris.

341a

As Mark 341, see page 77, but omitting ENGLAND.

This invalid feeding cup was made in 1899 for Princess Christian's Hospital Train. Mark 342.

371a

As Mark 371 but with LEADLESS GLAZE added. Recorded in July 1922.

372

FOOTBALL
Copyright
1895
J. Mc D & S

Mark seen on a tankard jug with a sprigged football subject.

378

COPELAND'S
GROSVENOR CHINA
ENGLAND
Tudor Rose

c1940. Another mark used by Jackson & Gosling, probably before the manufactory was commandeered for war work.

379

c1930. Mark used on ware exclusive to Plummers of New York. Seen on white Crown earthenware.

410

Another variation of this mark.

421a

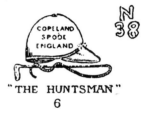

1938. The Hunting Cap mark, but with only COPELAND SPODE ENGLAND, used on small items like coffee cups. (See page 163).

433

MEADOW
R^d N° 142594

c1890. A simple mark for MEADOW on Charlotte shape tableware.

434

R^d No. 553455

1909. A mark sometimes used on china pattern R3827. No link with pattern B233 is known. See pages 108/9.

435

c1933. Seen on an item with the sheet pattern 'Spode's Moss Sprigs' printed in blue.

SPODE LIMITED 1970 to the present

501

Note: This mark has been seen with FLEMISH GREEN printed beneath. It had been thought that this coloured body had been withdrawn before 1970. Refer to Mark 290.

516

1992. A fruit and flowers pattern was introduced as an in-glaze transfer on the Marlborough shape on ivory earthenware, and called 'Victoria'. It is inspired by Spode's pattern 4485.

517

1993. The Mansard shape was re-introduced, but in fine bone china. Pattern Y8588, with white flowers based on Spode's pattern 1875, it is called 'Virginia'.

518

A variation on Mark 506.

519

1995. The Royal Coat of Arms was introduced into a special mark for use on gifts. The gift, in this instance, was of the President of The Royal China and Porcelain Company, an associate US company of Spode (Refer to Mark 271a).

519a

1996. A variation on Mark 519, the gift this time of the Managing Director of Spode.

520

1995. Used on a set of dessert plates of St.George Shape, with copies of flower and fruit subjects painted in 1916 by James Worrall (pattern R5768) based on Spode's pattern 4485 of 1828. (Patterns F1789 – F1794.)

Appendix XI

New information on the early years of the Spode business

Since 1991, when the text of the first edition of *Spode and Copeland Marks and other relevant intelligence* was passed to the publisher, much new information has been revealed by Peter Roden's diligent research, especially his study of the Court Rolls of the Manor of Newcastle-under-Lyme. Peter Roden is a direct descendant of Samuel Spode, the younger son of Josiah Spode I, and he has unravelled much of the early years of the Spode story.

Instead of revising the original text of this book, I chose to write a brief account of Peter Roden's research – with his full consent – so that readers may compare the new information with the previously 'accepted' account.

Spode I had three elder sisters: Anne, the eldest, was married at Stoke on 31 December 1745 to Ambrose Gallimore, and Mary was married on 14 August 1749 at Wolstanton to Joseph Mountford. It is not yet known if or how Joseph Mountford might be connected to Spode's later partner Thomas Mountford.

Ambrose Gallimore, however, besides being a partner with Thomas Turner in the Salopian porcelain manufactory at Caughley, had a brother, John Gallimore, who was a blacksmith, and who owned property which subsequently became part of the present Spode Works. Ambrose Gallimore was granted the lease of the Caughley Works in 1754 and may have been involved in the pottery industry in Staffordshire before that. If so, he would have been well placed to help his young brother-in-law, Josiah Spode, from 1745 – four years *before* Spode went to work for Thomas Whieldon.

Roden has pointed out the importance of one of Spode's other talents – other than his potting ones – namely his reputation as an accomplished violinist, which he seems to have earned *before* he achieved fame as a potter. Learning to play the violin with competence is not easily achieved and is not associated with sons of eighteenth century paupers! It was probably some cultured person who taught him, and his musical abilities may have provided his introduction to influential potters in the district. However it came about, it seem likely that young Josiah Spode I had a more fortunate start in life than has been realised up to now. It was probably someone of influence who introduced him, with a strong recommendation, to Thomas Whieldon in 1749. This may explain the remark in Whieldon's notebook for 9 April that year ..if he deserves it. That is, that his sponsor was suggesting that Spode would be worth *more* than the 2/3d which Whieldon expected to pay him initially. It has always been assumed that Spode was an *apprentice*, but the entry does not state that, and at 16 years old it seems more likely that he was employed as a workman. Spode probably left Whieldon's employment in 1754, having been paid at the rate of 7/6d a week.

The site of the present Spode Works was owned by a yeoman named Benjamin Lewis from 1725, and in 1751 he was selling a 'newly erected' potworks. (This term 'newly erected' implies that it was newly erected since the land was last described in 1731, so it is not possible to date its erection precisely.) This potworks passed through several hands until William Banks and John Turner bought it on 17 October 1759, two days after Turner's marriage, and shortly after he had reached the age of 21. It is quite likely that they had been leasing this works for some years earlier.

Josiah Spode married Ellen Finlay on 8 September 1754. He was 21 and described as 'Earth Potter', and Ellen, aged 28, had her own haberdashery business. Roden has discovered that in 1756 they were living in a cottage, rented from Thomas Lovatt, on the south side of Church Street in Stoke-upon-Trent on a site which later became the Market Hall. In 1758, Spode, or Ellen, bought a place of their own on the north side of Church Street.

At present we do not know what Spode was doing from the time he left Whieldon to his partnership with Tomlinson. There is no doubt that he was a competent potter, and he *may* have worked for Banks and Turner, but *exactly* where he worked and earned his money is still a mystery.

It now seems clear that Spode did not take over the Baddeley manufactory in Shelton in 1761 upon John Baddeley's bankruptcy, because Baddeley was permitted

View of Church Street, Stoke-upon-Trent looking south east with Spode & Tomlinson's potworks on the right foreground, c1767.

by the Court to continue to manufacture, and on 31 July 1761 his new partnership with Thomas Fletcher commenced.

It is possible that Spode was working for Banks and Turner from some date in the mid-1750s when they might have leased the site which they purchased in October 1759. Turner had left Banks by 1763, and Banks had to sell the potworks and Madeley's Meadow to Jeremiah Smith on 29 February 1764, though he may have continued in occupation as a tenant. The mention of Banks as the previous occupier of the site in 1776 when Spode bought it from Jeremiah Smith suggests that this might have been so. Spode might have been working with Banks then, or it may be that Spode could have run this potworks for Smith until 1767 when he took over a different potworks further down the road in partnership with Tomlinson. That potworks was part of a property owned by Michael Ward, but rented to George Harrison for seven years. It was Harrison who sub-let that potworks to Spode for the same seven year term. By 1781 Michael Ward, after various arbitrations, rented the property to Thomas Wolfe junior and George Bell for seven years. Subsequently, the site passed into the ownership of John Davenport's wife, and became known as the Bridge, or Bridge Bank, Works because it was next to the bridge which carried Church Street over the Newcastle Branch of the Trent and Mersey Canal; the site was between the present Campbell Place and South Wolfe Street. The site is only about 150 yards from the entrance to the present Spode Works.

Spode rented this potworks from 27 October 1767 until 25 March 1775. Roden believes that this was the site intended for the partnership between Spode and Tomlinson which, being due to end at Martinmas, 17 November 1774, might be expected to have begun at Martinmas 1767 to run for the conventional period of seven years.

The agreement with Thomas Mountford of 11 November 1772 was for seven years and prevented both parties from trading outside their partnership as potters or in the wares of a potter, with two exceptions. These were: Spode's partnership with Tomlinson, and his wife's haberdashery business. This effectively tied up Spode until the end of 1779.

But Josiah Spode bought the Spode potworks (the present one) from Jeremiah Smith on 29 February 1776. The agreement with Mountford did *not* exclude Spode from investing in property, and it is probable that this is what happened. Spode I was training his two sons on the Church Street Works during the Tomlinson partnership, and may have continued the lease after Lady Day, 25 March 1775, until 29 February 1776, when young Josiah II (nearly 21) and his brother Samuel (18) moved across the road to run the family's newly bought site. Spode I, legally, was only the owner of the property as an investor, but obviously had considerable influence on how the potworks was run by his sons until the end of the Mountford agreement in 1779 when he would take it over.

The agreement with Mountford stated that the partnership was to be carried out on the Mountford potworks in Shelton which they rented from Thomas Mountford's mother. Mountford would live in the house on the site while Spode would continue to live in Stoke. The site of the potworks is at the bottom of Snow Hill on the land occupied now by a building of the Stoke-on-Trent College, called 'Howard Place', (once it was called 'The Elms'). Mountford subsequently gave up potting, joined the army, and leased the potworks to a series of different tenants including William Shirley. After the

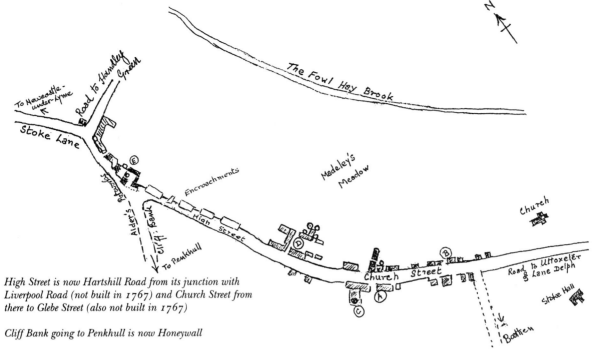

High Street is now Hartshill Road from its junction with Liverpool Road (not built in 1767) and Church Street from there to Glebe Street (also not built in 1767)

Cliff Bank going to Penkhull is now Honeywall

The Village of Stoke-upon-Trent c.1767
A *Likely site of Spode's Cottage, with 'cowhouse and garden' 1756*
B *Possible site of Spode's 'dwelling house and shop' in 1758*
C *Probable location of Spode & Tomlinson's potworks 1767-74*
D *Site of William Banks & John Turner's potworks 1759 and manufactory bought by Spode in 1776*
E *Hugh Booth's pottery, houses and gardens*

Encroachments are where owners or tenants have extended their holdings into the road

Map based on the research of Peter Roden. 1996

Mountford estate was split up the site was bought by Charles Meigh in 1839.

Josiah Spode II, who wanted to set up a retail business in London, delayed his departure until 1778 by which date Samuel would be nearly 21 and considered capable of running the works on his own, with father's guidance. Spode II rented a house at No.29 Fore Street, Cripplegate in the City of London.

These researches by Peter Roden show that a pottery manufactory on the present Spode site dates from at least 1751, that Spode I established a business in Stoke-upon-Trent in 1767, and that his ownership of the present Spode Works dates from 1776. The 'adopted' date of 1770 is shown to be incorrect.

Spode II's London business prospered. In 1780 he rented a warehouse at No.17 London Wall, and in 1782 moved from No.29 to a larger house at No.46 Fore Street, where the Land Tax Records show that he lived for the next twelve years. By 1790, he was renting another warehouse in Moor Lane; an invoice dated Nov.1st 1790 and headed 'at his Warehouse No.45 Fore Street, Moor Fields' suggests also that he was occupying at least some of the premises adjoining his house at No.46.

These several premises must have been awkward, so in June 1794 he moved to Portugal Street to take over the Salopian Warehouse with living accommodation at 37 Lincoln's Inn Fields.

It is now realised that the site of the Foley potworks in Lane Delph, on the south side of the road, passed into the ownership of Josiah Spode II, probably in 1782 on the death of his wife, Elizabeth (daughter of Thomas Barker). The works was probably built by Josiah Spode II, and it may be that Samuel Spode managed it for his brother who was in London. On the death of Josiah Spode I in 1797, by his will, Josiah Spode II, in choosing to accept the Stoke-upon-Trent manufactory, granted the 'request' in his father's will to sell the Foley Works to his brother Samuel in 1797. What was made there during Spode's ownership and what, if any, were the marks applied to the wares, has not been discovered.

There is more to be found out, but Roden's research is really useful in helping us to understand more of the early years of the Spodes.

I am extremely grateful to Peter Roden for correcting this short account of his researches so that it presents an accurate picture.

Appendix XII
Spode's blue printed Chinese landscapes

Pattern name	Page no.*	Suggested dates of introduction	Cat. No.**
Bridge I	92–96	c1808	P612–2
Bridge II	92–96		P612–1
New Bridge (Queen Charlotte)	92–96	1884	P612
Broseley [Two Temples II]	53–66	c1817	P614
Buddleia			
(Temple-Landscape, first)	80–82	c1792	P601
Buffalo	100–116	c1789	P616
Bungalow	80	c1818	P617
Flying Pennant	91	c1805	P610
Forest-Landscape I	83–84	c1795	P607
Forest-Landscape II	83–84	c1805	P607
Lake			
(Dagger-Landscape, second)	99	c1825	P604
(Long Bridge)	117–124	c1800	P619
Mandarin			
(Dagger-Landscape, third)	45–48	c1788	P605
Net	91	c1800	P620
Pearl River House			
(Trench Mortar)	72–77	c1800	P618
Rock	50–52	c1790	P608
Spode's Landscape	125,128–129	c1825	
Tall Door	89	c1818	P615
Temple [Two Temples I]	53–66	c1815	P613
Temple-Landscape I			
(Temple-Landscape, second)	96–99	c1813	P611–2
Temple-Landscape II	96–99	c1814	P611–1
Temple-Landscape, var. Parasol			
(Parasol)	96–99	c1808	P606
Temple with Panel			
(Dagger-Landscape, first)	83–85	c1798	P603
Two Figures I	67–69	c1784	
Two Figures II	67–69	c1786	P602
Two Temples I [Temple]	53–66	c1815	P613
Two Temples II [Broseley]	53–66	c1817	P614
Willow I	33–44	c1790	P609
Willow II	33–44	c1795	
Willow III	33–44	c1810	

* *Spode's Willow Pattern and Other Designs after the Chinese*
** *Spode Printed Ware* The pattern names in brackets (..) refer to those names adopted by Drakard & Holdway, following Leonard Whiter. The names in square brackets [...] are alternatives.

Appendix XIII
Spode's Chinese non-landscapes designs

Pattern name Page no.	Page No. *	Suggested dates of introduction	Cat. No. **
Aspidistra (Chinese Gardens)		c1822	P613
Bamboo [Bamboo and Rock]	150	c1806	
Bowpot	136	c1812	P813
Bude	136	c1814	
Chinese Flowers	145	c1815	P816
Chinese Plants [Aster]	154	c1834	
Chinese of Rank	154	c1805	P632
Cracked Ice and Prunus (Marble)	136–141	c1821	P807
Dragons, first	145–146	c1815	P626
Dragons, second	145–146	c1828	P627
Fence	136	1800–1805	P809
Filigre	167	c1823	P818
Fitzhugh (Trophies-Dagger)	92,95–97	c1800	P630
Gloucester	96,148	c1800	P811
Grasshopper	85,125,142	c1812	P621
Group	136,144	c1809	P814
House and Fence, painted	14	c1780	
India	144–145	c1815	P623
Japan	148	c1815	P625
Jar and Scroll	150	c1825	
Lange Lijsen [Long Eliza]	143	c1815–1825	P622
Lattice Scroll	136	c1810	P803
Lily	148	c1803	P801
Lyre	150	1800–1805	P802
Marble (Mosiac)	136	c1821	P807
New Japan	148		
Old Peacock (Oriental Birds)	154	1800–1805	P633
Peplow	148	c1819	P812
Peony		c1814	P808
Ship and Star	150	c1823	
Spode's Phoenix (Old Peacock)	154	c1820	P624
Spotted Deer	136,138		
Trophies-Dagger, see Fitzhugh	92,95–97		P630
Trophies-Etruscan	130–131	c1825	P629
Trophies-Marble	130–132	1825–1826	
Trophies-Nankin	130–131	1800–1805	P628
Tumbledown Dick	136	1823	

* *Spode's Willow Pattern and Other Designs after the Chinese*
** *Spode Printed Ware*

Appendix XIV
Other Spode plain printed designs

Pattern Name	Earliest Pattern No.	Date	Page No. *	Cat. No. **
Rotunda		c1790		P707
Flower Cross (Persian Quatrefoil)		c1800	156–157	P804
Daisy		c1800	156–157	P805
Leaf		c1800	156–157	P806
Chantilly Sprig		c1801	158–159	P810
Greek	1111	1806	170–171	P906
Castle		c1806	168–169	P711
Indian Sporting (now thought to be later, c1815)		c1807	170–171	P904
Caramanian		c1809	170–171	P905
The Turk		c1809		P715
Turkish Castle		c1809		P716
Love Chase		c1810		P717
Rome [Tiber]		1811	168–169	P713
Sunflower and Convolvulus	1864	1813	168–169	P819
Tower	3166 [border]	1814	168–169	P714
Milkmaid		c1814	166–167	P702
Blossom		c1814		
Gothic Castle	1966	c1814	166–167	P708
Shepherdess		c1815		P705
Italian	2614	1816	168–169	P710
Woodman		c1816	166–167	P703
Lucano		c1819	168–169	P712
Daisy and Bead		c1820		P827
Geranium	3037	c1821	162–163	P821
Honeysuckle and Parsley	3244	c1821		P829
Dresden Border	3499	1822	168–169	P719
Waterloo [Italian Church]	3395 [border]	c1822	166–167	P709
Vandyke		c1822		P828
Nettle		c1623		P826
Girl at the Well	3661	1823	164–165	P701
Union Wreath, third (Girl at Well border, Union sheaf centre)	3813	1824	164–165	P825
Country Scene		c1825	166–167	P704
Union Wreath, first	4158	1826	164–165	P823
Blue Rose	4162	1826	164–165	P822
Union Wreath, second (Blue Rose centre)	4158	1826	164–165	P824
Musicians [Village Scene]	4207	1826	166–167	P706
Jasmine (Jessamine)	B118	1826	162–163	P820
Fruit and Flowers [May]	B139	1826	160–161	P817
Botanical	B146	1826	162–163	P903
Dresden Sprays (English Sprays in reverse)	4615	1830		
English Sprays	4697	1830	160–161	P815
British Flowers	4794	1831	162–163	P902
Floral 4977	4977	1831	160–161	P901
Aesop's Fables		1831	170–171	P907
French Birds		c1831		P718
Portland Vase	5057	1832	170–171	P720

* *Spode*, Leonard Whiter
** *Spode Printed Ware*

Appendix XV
Spode's sheet patterns

What is a 'sheet' pattern? It is one that is not engraved specially to fit the different objects that are decorated; perhaps only three of four engravings are needed for the decoration of a whole range of tableware and toilet ware.

There are two basic types of sheet patterns. The more common is one in which a uniform appearance is given. Examples of this type include among others Marble, Star sheet, Fibre sheet, Thyme sheet, Parsley sheet, Broth or Shagreen, Moss Sprigs. These may be used on their own or to cover other sprays of flowers, birds, etc., in the manner described below.

To illustrate this method we will consider the pattern 'Tumble down Dick' – the version with the Marble background as shown as Pattern 2/6445. First, the principal pattern is printed and then transferred into position on the pot. The transfer-paper is removed, either by peeling or washing it off to leave the printed outline of the pattern. The flowers, leaves, branches and birds are painted with a water-soluble resist called 'ackey', a mixture of flour and water, which is allowed to dry. Then the Marble sheet is printed, probably in a different colour to that of the pattern, and transferred over the whole surface. When the paper of this is washed off the 'ackey' is washed off too, leaving the main pattern visible and available to be coloured by hand. Other well-known patterns produced in this way include Peacock and Parsley, King's Sheet, Currants, George III or Raleigh, and Primular or Wildflower (with Angus sheet).

The second type of Sheet pattern is that which is a complete design in itself, and where it is not used as a background to another pattern. Examples include Sunflower and Convolvulus, Grapes, Valencia or Vine sheet, Patricia, Rosebud Chintz, etc. Primular was later fully engraved to include the pattern and the sheet background.

The eight great Torchères in the Banqueting Hall of Brighton Pavilion are printed in Cobalt Blue using a sheet pattern of thousands of small dots which, during firing, merge together to yield an even surface of deep blue, an effect which could not have been achieved so successfully by any other method. In fact, two applications of blue were made to ensure perfect evenness. These 'Jars for the King' are three feet high, presenting an enormous challenge to Spode in 1819.

Appendix XVI
Copeland Manufactory plain printed patterns, in any colour

	DESIGN REGD.	SPODE −1833	C & G 1833–1847	COPELAND 1847–1867	COPELAND & SONS 1867–1932	COPELAND & SONS LTD 1932–1970	SPODE 1970–
Aden					X		
Aesop's Fables		X	X	X			
Albion	30 June 1848				X		
Alhambra				X	X		
Antique Vase (Mimosa)			X	X	X		
Antionette			X	X			
Aquatic			X	X			
Arabesque			X	X	X		
Athenian			X				
Bang Up		X	X	X			
Bedford			X				
Beverly (Grecian)			X	X	X	X	
Blue Rose		X	X				
Botanical		X	X				
Bramble				X			
British Flowers		X	X	X	X	X	
Broseley		X	X	X	X	X	
B700			X	X			
B772			X	X			
B773			X	X			
Byron Groups			X	X			
Byron Views			X	X			
Byron	19 June 1851			X		X	
Cairo					X		
Camilla			X	X	X	X	X
Castle		X	X				
Ceylon			X	X	X		
Chatsworth			X	X	X		
China Rose			X	X			
Chinese Flowers		X	X	X			
Chinese Gardens			X	X			
Chinese Plants (Later called Aster)			X	X		[X]	
Congress					X		
Connaught					X		
Continental Views	21 Oct 1845		X	X			
Convolvulus				X			
Coral			X	X			
Corinthian			X	X	X		
Corn & Poppy				X	X		

	DESIGN REGD.	SPODE –1833	C & G 1833–1847	COPELAND 1847–1867	COPELAND & SONS 1867–1932	COPELAND & SONS LTD 1932–1970	SPODE 1970–
Coronal	22 May 1863			X	X		
Coventry	11 June 1861			X	X		
Cracked & Prunus		X	X	X	X		
Crete	4 April 1892				X		
Cyril					X		
Daisy Grass					X		
Delhi				X	X		
Denmark				X	X		
Duncan Scenes				X	X		
Elcho	24 July 1863				X		
Etna	10 Jan 1860			X	X		
Etruscan (Trophies–Etruscan)		X	X	X	X		
Fables	28 Jan/12 Mar 1879				X		
Fern				X	X		
Field Sports	14 Sept 1846		X	X	X		
Filligree		X	X				
Floral		X					
Flower Vase		X	X				
Fleur de Lys	16 May 1862			X	X	X	X
French Radiating Sprigs			X	X			
Fruit & Flowers (May)		X	X	X			
Game Birds (various borders)					X	X	X
Garland	17 Aug 1849			X	X	X	
Geranium		X	X	X	X		X
Granada	19 June 1856			X	X		
Grecian (Beverly)			X	X	X	X	
Harlean				X			
Hawthorn					X		
Honeycomb				X			
Honeysuckle Empire	7 April 1855			X	X		
Honeysuckle (italic)					X		
Ilium					X		
Indian Tree					X	X	
Ionian	11 June 1851			X	X		
Italian		X	X	X	X	X	X
Ivy			X				
Japonica	9 March 1850			X	X		
Jasmine		X	X				
Kew (Chinese Bouquet)					X		
Lake		X	X				
Landscape		X			X	X	

	DESIGN REGD.	SPODE -1833	C & G 1833-1847	COPELAND 1847-1867	COPELAND & SONS 1867-1932	COPELAND & SONS LTD	SPODE 1970 -
Lily			X	X	X		
Lobelia	19 June 1845		X	X			
Lotus	20 Dec 1850			X			
Louis Quatorze	2 Dec 1844		X	X			
Macaw			X	X	X		
Madarin		X	X	X	X	X	
Marble sheet pattern		X					
Meander					X		
Melrose (Ruins)	15 Sept 1848			X	X		
Milkmaid		X	X	X			
Mock Orange (Syringa)	22 Nov 1849			X	X		
Morocco					X		
Nineveh					X		
Nymphea	13 March 1862				X		
Old Salem						X	
Onyx (Sphinx)					X		
Open Ivy				X	X		
Osborne					X		
Pagoda			X	X	X		
Parthenon	19 March 1861			X	X		
Passion Flower					X		
Pearls				X	X		
'Pergola'					X		
Pekin	6 Sept 1864			X	X		
Persian	14 Oct 1859			X	X		
Persian Bird (ex Davenport)					X		
Persian Rabbits					X		
Piccadilly (Rose Wreath)	9 Sept 1847			X	X		
Portland Vase			X	X	X		
Primrose	28 April 1881				X	X	
Rafaelesque	25 April 1845		X	X			
Rhine (Severn) (ex Davenport)					X	X	X
Ribbon				X			
Richmond	29 April 1856			X	X		
Roma				X	X		
Roman Beads				X			
Rose & Sprigs				X			
Rose Wreath (Piccadilly)	9 Sept 1847			X	X		
Ruins (Melrose)	15 Sept 1848			X	X		
Rural Scenes	19 Sept 1850			X	X	X	
Sardinia	17 Dec 1858			X	X	X	
Seasons			X	X	X		
Seasons Star			X	X			
Seaweed			X	X			
Severn (Rhine)					X	X	X

	DESIGN REGD.	SPODE –1833	C & G 1833–1847	COPELAND 1847–1867	COPELAND & SONS 1867–1932	COPELAND & SONS LTD 1932–1970	SPODE 1970–
Sevres			X	X			
Shagreen (Broth)			X				X
Shamrock	17 Sept 1861		X	X	X		
Ship Border		X	X	X	X		
Siam (ex Enoch Wood)				X	X	X	X
Silvester					X		
Souvenir	18 Oct 1861			X	X		
Star				X	X		
Statice			X	X			
Stella					X		
Stork					X		
Strawberry	1 Oct 1852			X	X		
Suez Key				X	X		
Sunflower & Convolvulus		X					X
Syringa	22 Nov 1849			X	X		
Temple		X	X		X		
Thistle					X	X	
Tower		X	X	X	X	X	X
Tulip			X		X		
Turco					X		
Tuscan	14 June 1852				X		
Union		X	X	X			
'Vase & Peony'			?				
Venetia					X		
Violet				X	X		
Warwick Groups			X	X			
Warwick Vase			X				
Waterloo		X					
Watteau				X	X		
Weeping Willow		X	X				
Wellington			X				
Willow		X	X	X	X		

Appendix XVII
Spode and Copeland designs that bear several different names

Alden • Fruit & Flowers (S2280)
Ancre • Estoril
Antique Vase • Mimosa
Antoine • Yellow Rose • Billingsley Rose
Arcadia • Convolvulus and Sunflower • Sunflower
Aspidistra • Chinese Garden
Aster • Chinese Plants
Audubon Birds • Plummer's Birds

Bamboo and Rock • Weeping Willow
Berkeley • Lotus
Beverley • Grecian Scroll
Billingsley Rose • Yellow Rose • Antoine
Bird and Grasshopper • Grasshopper
Black Sprigs • Windermere
Blue Bird • Cherry Picker
Blue Flowers • Rembrandt
Bouquet • British Flowers • Mayflower
Bridal Rose • Savoy Rose
Bridal Veil • Eden • Gorringe • New Eden
Bridge • New Bridge • Queen Charlotte
Brighton • Charlie Mason
British Flowers • Bouquet • Mayflower
Buchart • Hollyhock
Buddleia • Temple-Landscape, first

Caracas • Kingston • Lash leaf border • Valentine
Charlie Mason • Brighton
Cherry Picker • Blue Bird
Chelsea Bird • Rock Bird
Chinese Blossom (1/9720) • Ting
Chinese Blossom • Shanghai (R5321 type)
Chinese Garden • Aspidistra
Chinese Plants • Aster
Chinese Rose • Rockery • Rock Garden • Waring's Rock
Convolvulus and Sunflower • Sunflower • Arcadia
Cracked Ice & Prunus (only when the sprays are absent) • Marble
Currants • Mulberry

Dagger-Landscape, first • Temple with Panel
Dagger-Landscape, second • Lake

Dagger-Landscape, third • Mandarin
Delft • Tower Border
Duncan Scenes • Rural Scenes • Priscilla Alden

Eden • Bridal Veil • Gorringe • New Eden
Estoril • Ancre

Fitzhugh • Trophies-Dagger
Florida • Onion (old Meissen pattern)
Flower Cross • Persian Quatrefoil
Font • Girl at the Well
Fontaine • Marlborough Sprays • Luneville
Frascati • Vine Border
Fruit and Blossom • Glendale
Fruit and Flowers • May
Fruit and Flowers (S2280) • Alden

George III • Raleigh
Girl at the Well • Font
Glendale • Fruit and Blossom
Gorringe • Bridal Veil • Eden • New Eden
Grasshopper • Bird and Grasshopper
Grecian Scroll • Beverley

HB Border • Wicker Dale
Hollyhock • Buchart

Irene • Sydney
Italian Church • Waterloo

Jumping Boy • Long Eliza • Lange Lijsen

Kent • Oak & Vine Border
Kingston (Y7326) • Lash Leaf Border • Caracas • Valentine

Lace • Richmond
Lake • Dagger-Landscape, second
Lange Lijsen • Long Eliza • Jumping Boy
Lash leaf border • Caracas • Kingston • Valentine
Lotus • Berkeley
Long Eliza • Lange Lijsen • Jumping Boy
Luneville • Marlborough Sprays • Fontaine

Madeira • Valencia
Madrid • Trophies-Marble
Majestic • Royal Bracelet
Malayan Village • Trench Mortar • Pearl River House
Mandarin • Dagger-Landscape, third
Marble • Cracked Ice & Prunus (only when the sprays are absent)
Marlborough Sprays • Fontaine • Luneville
May • Fruit and Flowers
Mayflower • British Flowers • Bouquet
Melrose • Ruins
Mimosa • Antique Vase
Mulberry • Currants
Musicians • Village Scene

Naran • Nigel
New Bridge • Bridge • Queen Charlotte
New Eden • Eden • Bridal Veil • Gorringe
Nigel • Naran

Oak & Vine Border • Kent
Old Peacock (on one leg) • Oriental Birds
Old Peacock (flying) • Spode's Phoenix
Onion (old Meissen pattern • Florida)
Onyx • Sphinx
Oriental Birds • Old Peacock (on one leg)

Parasol • Temple-Landscape, var. Parasol
Parrot • Shagreen (sheet)
Pearl River House • Trench Mortar • Malayan Village
Persian Quatrefoil • Flower Cross
Plummer's Birds • Audubon Birds
Primular • Wildflower
Priscilla Alden • Duncan Scenes • Rural Scenes

Queen Charlotte • Bridge • New Bridge
Queen Mary • Watteau

Raleigh • George III
Rembrandt • Blue Flowers
Rhine • Severn
Richmond • Lace

Rock Bird • Chelsea Bird
Rock Garden • Chinese Rose • Rockery •
Waring's Rock
Rockery • Chinese Rose • Rock Garden •
Waring's Rock
Romany (S3157, Y7932) • Vine Bead
Rome • Tiber
Royal Bracelet • Majestic
Ruins • Melrose
Rural Scenes • Duncan Scenes • Priscilla
Alden

Savoy Rose • Bridal Rose
Severn • Rhine
Shagreen (sheet) • Parrot
Shanghai (R5321 type) • Chinese
Blossom
Silver Mist • Thistledown
Sphinx • Onyx
Spode's Phoenix • Old Peacock (flying)
Sunflower • Convolvulus and Sunflower
• Arcadia
Sydney • Irene

Temple-Landscape, I • Temple-
Landscape, second
Temple-Landscape, first • Buddleia
Temple-Landscape, second •Temple-
Landscape, I
Temple-Landscape, var.Parasol • Parasol
Temple with Panel • Dagger-Landscape,
first
Thistledown • Silver Mist
Tiber • Rome
Ting • Chinese Blossom (1/9720)
Tower Border • Delft
Trench Mortar • Pearl River House •
Malayan Village
Trophies-Dagger • Fitzhugh
Trophies-Marble • Madrid

Valencia • Madeira
Valentine • Caracas • Kingston • Lash
leaf border
Village Scene • Musicians
Vine Bead • Romany (S3157, Y7932)
Vine Border • Frascati

Waring's Rock • Chinese Rose • Rockery
• Rock Garden
Waterloo • Italian Church
Watteau • Queen Mary
Weeping Willow • Bamboo and Rock
Wicker Dale • HB Border
Wildflower • Primular
Windermere • Black Sprigs

Yellow Rose • Antoine • Billingsley Rose

There are several other patterns to
which various authors have given other
names and some more of these were

listed on page 159 of my book *Spode's
Willow Pattern and other Designs after the
Chinese.* There may be other patterns to
which more than one name has been
given. Whilst the names of the patterns
listed above refer to the same basic
designs but in different versions, in
recent years names which have been
used for earlier patterns have been re-
used for entirely different ones. As this
might cause confusion in the future I list
some of them here.

Delphi (old) Y8022; (new) Delphi Y8575
Regency (old) as Y6170, Y5799; (new)
Regency as Spode's 1166
Romany (old) as S3310, S3157, Y7932;
(new) Romany S3420
Hallmark (old) 1/4223; (new) Hallmark
Y8557 as the Old Regency
Victoria (old) S2922; (new) Victoria
S3425 on Marlborough
Virginia (old) Y4787 on Stone China;
(new) Virginia Y8601 on Mansard
Green Garland (old) Y8054; (new)
Green Garland S3432
Garland (old) Y8054; (new) Garland
S3424
Provence (old) Y7843 on RCA; (new)
Provence Y8599
Park Lane (old) Y7487; (new) Park Lane
Y8587
Kingston (old) Y7326; (new) Kingston
Y8573
Lauriston (old) S2248, Y5954; (new)
Lauriston Y8595
Mimosa (old) Antique Vase; (new)
Mimosa S2822
Pearl (old) Y5137; (new) Pearl Y8593
Lotus (old) 8627; (new) Lotus
[Berkeley] S1765
Savoy shape (old); (new) Savoy pattern
Y8563
Roma (old) D7747; (new) Roma Y8607
Chatsworth (old) 5889 [1834]; the
design was given the name Chatsworth
in 1894, 1/1490, 2/9043; (new)
Chatsworth Y8571

There may be more!

It is very important when enquiring
about any old pattern to quote all the
marks on the base of the items, especially the pattern number if one is present.
Sometimes the same design has been
produced in more than a dozen different ways but the mark still uses the same
name.

Appendix XVIII
Medals awarded to W.T. Copeland and the firm at international fairs

1851 LONDON
Exhibition of the Works of Industry of All Nations
Bronze medal to Alderman Copeland 'For Services'

1853 NEW YORK
Exhibition of the Industry of All Nations *Bronze medal*

1854 LONDON
The Universal Society for the Encouragement of Arts
and Industry – Founded in London A.D.1851
Bronze medal presented to Mr Alderman Copeland MP
Jan 31 1854

1855 PARIS
Exposition Universelle Agriculture Industrie Beaux
Arts
Silver medal W.T. Copeland, Alderman of London 1855

1862 LONDON
International Exhibition
Bronze medal Alf. Copeland, Juror Class XXXIV
Bronze medal Copeland, Class XXXIV
Bronze medal W.T. Copeland, Class XXXV

1867 PARIS
Exposition Universelle de MDCCCLXVII à Paris
Gold medal W.T. Copeland & Fils Recompenses

1879 SYDNEY
International Exhibition
Bronze medal W.T. Copeland & Sons First Award etc.

1889 PARIS
Exposition Universelle
Gilded bronze medal Copeland & Sons

1958 BRUSSELLS
Exposition Universelle et Internationale Bruxelles 1958
Diplôme d'Honneur W.T. Copeland & Sons Ltd
Bronze medal R. Copeland Juror Class Ceramics & Glass

The Firm also exhibited at other International Fairs including:

1853 DUBLIN
Great Industrial Exhibition, at which Alfred Copeland
was a juror which denied an award to the firm

1871 LONDON
First Annual International Exhibition

1872 LONDON
Second Annual International Exhibition

1873 LONDON
Third Annual International Exhibition

1873 VIENNA
Weltausstellung 1873 Wien

1925 WEMBLEY
British Empire Exhibition

Appendix XIX
Some of the artists working for Copelands

Robert Abrahams 1870s–1890s

Felix Xavier Abrahams 1890s

F.W. Adams 1895–1914

Samuel Alcock 1882–early 1900s figures

John Arrowsmith 1881–c1931 birds and flowers

William Ball c1870–1895 gilder and 'jeweller'

Lucien Besche c1881–1891 figures, cherubs

William Birbeck 1861–c1895 landscapes

Charles B. Brough 1881–1903 birds, shells

F. Furnivall early 1900s landscapes

Harry Hammersley 1889–c1931 flowers

Tom Hassall ?–1944 flowers

Charles Ferdinand Hurten 1859–1897 flowers

H.C.Lea 1880–c1900 fish, flowers

Daniel Lucas Jnr. c1862–?1879 landscapes

Frederick Micklewright c1920–c1939 fish, landscapes

Arthur Perry c1885–c1889; c1895–c1928 landscapes, fish, birds, flowers

Thomas Sadler 1893–1909 flowers, roses

Charles Weaver 1869–1887 birds

James Worrall 1902–1919 flowers, roses

William Yale 1869–c1892 landscapes, animals

Bibliography

BOOKS ABOUT SPODE

Bedford, J. (1969) *Old Spode China*

Cannon, T.G. (undated) *Old Spode – A collector's notes on his collection.* London: T. Werner Laurie (c1924)

Copeland, R. (1980, 1990) *Spode's Willow Pattern and other designs after the Chinese.* London: Studio Vista

Copeland, R. (1994) *Spode.* Shire Album No 309

Copeland, R. and Townsend, A. (1983) *Spode-Copeland 1733–983. Potters to the Royal Family since 1806.* Stoke-on-Trent: City of Stoke-On-Trent Museum and Art Gallery

Drakard, D. and Holdway, P. (1983) *Spode Printed Ware.* London: Longman

Hayden, A. (1925) *Spode and His Successors.* London: Cassell

Sussman, L. (1979) *Spode-Copeland Transfer-printed patterns found at 20 Hudson's Bay Company Sites.* Hull, Quebec: Canadian Government Publishing Centre, Canadian Historic Sites Series No 22

Whiter, L. (1970) *Spode: a history of the family, factory and wares, 1733–1833.* London: Barrie & Jenkins, Re-published 1990

Wilkinson, V. (1989) *The Copeland China Collection at Trelissick, Cornwall.* R.Spencer Copeland

Wilkinson, V. (1994) *Copeland.* Shire Album No 306

Williams, S.B. (1949) *Antique Blue and White Spode.* London: Batsford. An earlier edition was published in 1943 with less information and fewer illustrations

COMPANY PUBLICATIONS

Copeland's non-crazing tablewares (1897)

Copeland's (Late Spode) China. Established 1770. (1902)

The Hand of the Potter. Commemorating the Bi-centenary of the birth of Josiah Spode. (1933)

The Story of Spode. (1950) Written by G. Bernard Hughes

Tradition Spode-Copeland (1960)

The Spode Story 1770–1970 (1970)

Spode – Never out of fashion (1975)

EXHIBITION CATALOGUES

Spode-Copeland 1765–1965. Steingut and Porzellan. Catalogue to an exhibition displayed in Frankfurt, Cologne, Hanover and Hamburg, and in Florence. 1965–7

Spode-Copeland 1765–1965. Engelsk porcelain og fajaance. Catalogue to an exhibition held in Oslo and Copenhagen 1966

200 Years of Spode. Catalogue to the exhibition held in the Royal Academy of Arts, London, to celebrate the Bi-centenary of the founding of the firm. 1970

Historic China. Catalogue of an exhibition of Spode and Copeland wares specially commissioned throughout two hundred years. Held in Goldsmiths' Hall, London. 1970

Spode-Copeland 1733–1983. Potters to the Royal Family since 1806. A book to accompany the exhibition held in the City of Stoke-on-Trent Museum to mark the 250th anniversary of the birth of Josiah Spode I. 1983

ARTICLES WHICH RELATE TO SPODE
published since 1960

Anon. (1979) *The Copeland-Spode Loving Cups and Vases 1900–1977.* Journal of the Commemorative Collectors Society. No 11, Summer 1979

Arch, N. (1976) *Spode Ceramics in the National Army Museum.* Annual Report of the National Army Museum 1975–76, pp 16–21

Collard, E. (1971) *Spode's Bi-centenary Year 1970.* The Australasian Antique Collector. Vol 3, No 10. Jan–June 1971

Collard, E. (1971) *The Crockery Trade.* Canadian Antiques Collector. Vol 6, No 8. Nov–Dec 1971. pp 39–42

Copeland, R. (1967) *Josiah Spode and the Chinese Trade.* Canadian Antiques Collector. Vol 2, No 12. December 1967

Copeland, R. (1976) *Feat of Clay.* In Britain. Vol 31, No 6, June 1976. London: British Tourist Authority

Copeland, R. (1976) *Ceramic View of Byron Country.* Country Life. Vol CLX, No 4140 November 4 1976, pp 1296–7

Copeland, R. (1977) *Josiah Spode and the China Trade.* English Ceramic Circle. Transactions Vol 10, Part 2, pp 99–108

Copeland, R. (1978) *Spode – The hub of Stoke-on-Trent.* Industrial Development Officer. Vol 4, No 5. May/June 1978

Copeland, R. (1978) *Josiah Spode and the Origins of the Willow Pattern.* Antique Collector. London: December 1978

Copeland, R. (1980) *Spode and the China Trade.* American Ceramic Circle. Bulletin No 2, pp 97–112. 1980

Copeland, R. (1983) *Spode's Chinese Landscapes.* Antique Collector. London: September 1983

Copeland, R. (1984) *Pursuing the Potter's Tribute. The Spode Wellington Service.* Country Life. Vol CLXXV No 4528 May 31 1984. pp 1560–1

Copeland, R. (1984) *Painted Landscapes of the Spode Factory.* English Ceramic Circle. Transactions Vol 12 Part 1, pp 29–37

Copeland, R. (1986) *Parian Porcelain Statuary: Sculpture for the Many.* American

Ceramic Circle. Bulletin No 5, pp 66–88

Copeland, R. (1987) *Satisfying a Market Need: Josiah's Stone China*. Ars Ceramica No 4, pp 14–16. Wedgwood Society of New York

Copeland, R. (1989) *Spode's Creamware and Pearlware*. English Ceramic Circle. Transactions Vol 13 Part 3, pp 175–181

Copeland, R. (1992) *Closer to the Bone: the Development of Bone China*. Journal of the Northern Ceramic Society, Vol 9 pp 1–24

Copeland, R. (1993) *Copeland and the Hudson's Bay Company 1836–1872*. English Ceramic Circle. Transactions Vol 15, Part 1, pp 111–121

Drakard, D. (1984) *Politics on Pottery: Napoleonic Cartoons on Spode Ware*. Country Life. December 6 1984. pp 1782–4

Drakard, D. (1986) *Heroes, Trophies and Teacups: Nelson Commemorative Spode Ware*. Country Life. December 6 1986. pp 582–4

Fontaines, J.K. des. (1969) *Underglaze Blue-printed Earthenware with Particular Reference to Spode*. English Ceramic Circle. Transactions Vol 7, Part 2, p 120 et seq

Godden, G.A. (1970) *Two Hundred years of Spode*. The Antique Dealer and Collectors Guide. London. August 1970

Godden, G.A. (1975) *Where to begin with Spode*. Art & Antiques Weekly. Vol 20, No 8. September 13, 1975. London

Hamilton, J.F.A. (1982) *Ceramics Destined for York Factory: An Examination of Hudson's Bay Company Archival Sources*. Material History Bulletin No 16, pp 47–68. Ottawa: National Museums of Canada

Hughes, G.B. (1967) *Spode Blue and White Ware*. Country Life. Vol CXLII No 3683. October 5 1967

Hughes, T. (1967) *Fadeless Flowers of the Potter Spode-Copeland at Stoke-on-Trent*. Country Life. Vol CXLI No 3667. June 15 1967, Collectors Number

Hughes, T. (1969) *The Spode way to dress a desk*. Country Life Annual 1969. pp 44–49

Jackson, L. (1989) *Non-Native Ceramics in South Western Alaska c1820–1920: A Key to Chronology*. Los Angeles: Department of Anthropology, University of California

Johnston, A.J. (1985) *Dating Spode*. The Magazine Antiques. Vol CXXVII No 6. June 1965. pp 1368–1373

Markin, T. (1992) *Robert Hamilton and William Arrowsmith of Stoke-upon-Trent*. Journal of the Northern Ceramic Society, Vol 9 p80 (Figure 1)

Markin, T. (1994) *Procurement of Raw Materials by the Spode-Wolfe Partnerships*. Journal of the Northern Ceramic Society, Vol 11 pp 1–18

Pulver, R. (1987) *Spode's Blue Italian Pattern*. Antique Collecting; the Journal of the Antique Collectors' Club. Vol 22, No 4. September 1987. pp 30–33

Roden, P.F.C. (1995) *The Life and Times of Josiah Spode (1733–1797)*. Unpublished draft research. Also personal correspondence

Scott, D. (1980) *Spode: Fine Earthenware*. Antique Collector. Vol 51, No 6 June 1980. London: National Magazine Company

Sussman, L. (1990) *Copeland at Glacier House*. Spode Society Review

Sussman, L. (1979) *The Ceramics of Lower Fort Garry: Operations 1–31*. History and Archaeology/Histoirie et Archaeology, No 24. Ottawa

The Review and the Recorder of the Spode Society

Publications of the Northern Ceramic Society

Publications of the Friends of Blue Journal of the Commemorative Collectors Society

GENERAL BOOKS

Atterbury, P.ed. (1989) *The Parian Phenomenon – A Survey of Victorian Porcelian, Statuary & Busts*. London: R.Dennis

Barker, D. (1985) *Parian Ware*. Shire Album No 142

Bergesen, V. (1989) *Majolica: British, Continental and American Wares 1851–1915*. London: Barrie & Jenkins

Berthoud, M. (1981) *H & R Daniel 1822–1846*. Micawber

Berthoud, M. (1982) *An Anthology of British Cups*. Micawber

Berthoud, M. (1990) *A Compendium of British Cups: revised and enlarged*

Collard, E. (1967, 1984) *Nineteenth Century Pottery and Porcelain in Canada*. Kingston & Montreal: McGill-Queen's University Press

Copeland, R. (1972) *A Short History of Pottery Raw Materials and the Cheddleton Flint Mill*

Copeland, R. (1982) *Blue and White Transfer-printed Pottery*. Shire Album No 97

Copeland, R. (1995) *Wedgewood Ware*. Shire Album No 321

Coysh, A.W. & Henrywood, R.K. (1982) *Dictionary of Blue and White Printed Pottery 1780–1880* Volume II

Fay-Halle, A. & Mundt, B. (1983) *Nineteenth-Century European Porcelain*

Godden, G.A. (1961) *Victorian Porcelain*

Godden, G.A. (1978) *Godden's Guide to English Porcelain*

Godden, G.A. ed. (1983) *Staffordshire Porcelain*

Godden, G.A. (1988) *Encyclopedia of British Porcelain Manufacturers*

Karmason, M.G. & Stacke, J.B. (1989) *Majolica: A Complete History and Illustrated Survey*. New York: H.N. Abrams Inc

Lewis, G. (1985) *A Collector's History of English Pottery*

Lockett, T.A. (1979) *Collecting Victorian Tiles*

Miller, P. & Berthoud, M. (1985) *An Anthology of British Teapots*. Micawber

Shinn, C. & D. (1971) *Illustrated Guide to Victorian Parian China*

Spours, J. (1988) *Art Deco Tableware: British Domestic Ceramics 1925–1939*. London: Ward Lock

Cushion, J.P. (1974) *Handbook of Pottery and Porcelain Marks*

Godden, G.A. (1964) *Encyclopedia of British Pottery and Porcelian Marks*

Index